Augsburg College
George Sverdrup Library
Minneapolis, MN 55454

Politics Through a Looking-Glass

**Recent Titles in
Contributions in Political Science**
Series Editor: Bernard K. Johnpoll

Ethnic Groups and U.S. Foreign Policy
Mohammed E. Ahrari, editor

Referendum Voting: Social Status and Policy Preferences
Harlan Hahn and Sheldon Kamieniecki

Ordered Liberty and the Constitutional Framework: The Political Thought of Friedrich A. Hayek
Barbara M. Rowland

Policy Evaluation for Local Government
Terry Busson and Philip Coulter, editors

New Tides in the Pacific: Pacific Basin Cooperation and the Big Four (Japan, PRC, USA, USSR)
Roy Kim and Hilary Conroy, editors

Campaigns in the News: Mass Media and Congressional Elections
Jan Pons Vermeer, editor

Cultural Policy and Socialist France
David Wachtel

Liberalization and Redemocratization in Latin America
George A. Lopez and Michael Stohl, editors

Terrible Beyond Endurance? The Foreign Policy of State Terrorism
Michael Stohl and George A. Lopez, editors

Adjusting the Balance: Federal Policy and Victim Services
Steven Rathgeb Smith and Susan Freinkel

U.S. Policy on Jerusalem
Yossi Feintuch

The Ethics of Public Service: Resolving Moral Dilemmas in Public Organizations
Kathryn G. Denhardt

Politics Through a Looking-Glass

Understanding Political Cultures Through a Structuralist Interpretation of Narratives

ELOISE A. BUKER

Contributions in Political Science, Number 184

GREENWOOD PRESS
New York • Westport, Connecticut • London

Library of Congress Cataloging-in-Publication Data

Buker, Eloise A.
  Politics through a looking-glass.

  (Contributions in political science,
ISSN 0147-1066 ; no. 184)
  Bibliography: p.
  Includes index.
  1. Political culture. 2. Hermeneutics.
3. Functionalism (Social sciences). 4. Tales—
Structural analysis. 5. Political culture—
United States—Case studies. I. Title. II. Series.
JA75.7.B85 1987   306'.2   87-8671
ISBN 0-313-25662-4 (lib. bdg. : alk. paper)

British Library Cataloguing in Publication Data is available.

Copyright © 1987 by Eloise A. Buker

All rights reserved. No portion of this book may be
reproduced, by any process or technique, without the
express written consent of the publisher.

Library of Congress Catalog Card Number: 87-8671
ISBN: 0-313-25662-4
ISSN: 0147-1066

First published in 1987

Greenwood Press, Inc.
88 Post Road West, Westport, Connecticut 06881

Printed in the United States of America

The paper used in this book complies with the
Permanent Paper Standard issued by the National
Information Standards Organization (Z39.48-1984).

10 9 8 7 6 5 4 3 2 1

To Robert S. Cahill

Contents

Acknowledgements	ix
Preface	xi

1. Stories and Politics: 1
   In the Looking-Glass House
   - Stories: Windows on Society   2
   - Fictional Truth: Narrative Form and Science   8
   - Politics and Language   23

2. Examining Reflections: 28
   Structuralism and Hermeneutics
   - The Reader and the Story: Action and Symbol   29
   - Hermeneutics: Truth, Science and Interpretation   41

3. Down the Rabbit Hole: 52
   Listening to Stories
   - Two American Cultures: Essex and Kumu Aina   52
   - Collecting Stories   64

4. Essex's Political Community: 67
   Bonds and Boundaries
   - Building a Model of Community   68
   - Community Bonds and Boundaries   84
   - Politics and the Master Plot   87

5. Community Bonds and Boundaries: 98
   Kumu Aina
   - Kumu Aina Leadership   98
   - Leadership and Humility   115
   - Community Cosmology: Bonds and Boundaries   118

6. Transforming Institutions: 128
   Participation in Essex
   - Private Property and Public Responsibility   129
   - Public Status and Private Funds   138
   - Social Change and Political Institutions   143

Contents

7. Kumu Aina:
   Challenges to Social Institutions 148
      Institutional Demands and Community Commitments 148
      Politics Transforms Institutions 158
      Kumu Aina and the Politics of 166
         Confronting Institutions

8. Essex:
   Creating Unity and Freedom 172
      Independence and Community 173
      Public Life and Independence 190

9. Kumu Aina: 196
   Barriers Unite Citizens
      Trouble, Friendship and Politics 196
      Freedom and Community 208

10. Politics in Reflection 222
       Liberalism in Essex and the Polis in Kumu Aina 223
       Essex and Kumu Aina: New Directions in Politics 229

Notes 233

Bibliography 241

Index 249

Acknowledgements

The Political Science Department at the University of Hawaii not only provided me with a community but with teachers who made this work possible. I am especially grateful to Michael S. Shapiro, who taught me the power of language and freedom; Manfred Henningsen, who encouraged me to find the spirit of the symbols; Deane Neubauer, whose powers of political imagination opened new horizons for my own intellectual journey; and Henry Kariel, who has shown me the genuine power of reflection. Alice Dewey, from the Department of Anthropology, gave me intellectual guidance and a sense of cultural understanding, as well as respect for the variety in the human spirit.

My mother and father both encouraged me to find my own story and to live it fully.

The East-West Center in Honolulu, Hawaii, provided me financial support for the year-long field study for this project as well as much encouragement.

The political leaders I interviewed gave me the benefit of their wisdom, and as teachers, they gave me insight into politics and community building. I wish to thank the communities of Essex and Kumu Aina for accepting me into their midst and giving me a home, and I especially want to thank the women and men who shared their stories with me.

This book would not have been possible without the continued support and wisdom of Robert Cahill, who understands Hawaii and Ohio but, even more important understands the power of language. His editing suggestions were most helpful to me, and I continually learn from him and the stories he tells.

Preface

"Tell me a story," is a cry heard in all times and places, from people of all ages, from a young child to an adults sophisticated social analyst, and it is no stranger to my own lips. As a youngster, I begged stories from every adult within earshot; as a sometimes television addict, I plea with my willing screen to yield the tale; and as a social scientist, I elicit stories from political leaders, from history, from legal briefs, and even from political theory. Why? What is the connection between storytelling and politics?

This book answers this question by exploring how stories, both imaginative narratives and historical narratives, offer ways of understanding social and political life. In it, I develop a model for interpreting narratives that builds upon structural analysis and philosophical hermeneutics, and then apply it to the interpretation of narratives from leaders in two different political cultures: a rural working-class community in Hawaii and a suburban upper-middle-class community in Ohio. My purpose is to demonstrate the model and to reveal the political wisdom these leaders offer through their stories. The stories themselves are presented, along with my analysis of them. Before collecting these narratives, I lived in both communities for extended periods of time, engaging in field studies similar to those conducted by anthropologists.

The book argues that stories are windows through which we can catch a glimpse of a culture and gain insight into a community's experiences, values, struggles and conflicts. But to glean these insights in a systematic, scientific way requires a careful examination of the connection between stories and politics. This examination develops out of the literature that studies the connection between language and politics. Taking Plato and Aristotle as founding theorists, it argues that in language societies create systems that organize and apprehend the world and through this language system citizens speak with each other about the nature of their society, the cosmos, what they find good and just in it, and what they find in it that is ill and unjust.

Communication, achieved through language and speech, is the foundation for a political community. Hence, it is one of the most fundamental political activities in which we can engage and, therefore, has attracted the attention of a range of contemporary scholars, from deconstructionists to feminists.

Building on this connection between language and politics, I argue that storytelling and politics share an even more intimate relationship because, through stories, citizens share their ideas about life and these stories constitute models of how society works, what roles societies offers, how conflicts arise, and how they get resolved. In addition, storytelling, unlike sophisticated language analysis, is available to ordinary citizens. Anyone can tell a story and anyone can listen to a story. It is a mechanism by which Presidents talk to citizens and citizens talk back to Presidents, legislatures, courts, and countless other authorities. My own political purpose in this analysis is to help to empower all of us to tell our stories and to listen more carefully to the stories of others, so that we can learn from them and from each other.

The first chapter examines the connection between storytelling and politics by looking at how stories reveal the politics of a society. In this examination, I argue that stories, even fictional ones, provide us ways of apprehending the truth about societies. Exploring Plato's arguments for throwing the poets out of the Republic, I argue that narratives do not imitate social reality but, rather, give citizens a guide for understanding their world and acting in it, very much like a constitution serves as a guide for understanding and action in a legal sense. I explore the ways in which narratives educate us by entertaining us, and I examine the ways in which stories embody our traditions while arguing for transforming them.

In the second chapter, I develop a structural analysis for interpreting narratives that builds upon structural anthropology, particularly the work of Claude Levi-Strauss; semiotics, especially the work of Roland Barthes; and deconstruction, focusing chiefly on the work of Michel Foucault. While I argue for the scientific value of this analysis, I place it in the tradition of philosophical hermeneutics, relying heavily on the work of Paul Ricoeur and Hans-Georg Gadamer. In doing this, I argue that our interpretations of narratives depend on our cultural and historical contexts, and that, because they do so, they are relevant to the problems that confront us in our own immediate political communities. Not only do stories tell us about the world of the storyteller, but our interpretations tell us about our own worlds, providing us with valuable tools for reflecting on our political circumstances.

Chapter Three describes the conditions under which I collected the narratives and briefly sketches the two communities from which I gathered the stories, in order to provide a context for their analysis. The Ohio community, culturally a predominantly Euro-American town, sees itself as "typically American," and its leaders were happy to share their stories because they were in the process of renewing their own sense of their historical roots and exploring more deeply what their community represents. The community in Hawaii, while composed of citizens from Asian, Pacific Island, and Euro-American cultures, sees itself as influenced primarily by the native Hawaiian culture, understanding itself not as being "typically American" but as having its own special island heritage. In this heritage, furthermore, storytelling has a privileged position. Even people who have lived a short time in Hawaii soon learn that it is important to take time to share experiences by telling stories. People in Hawaii call this "talk story." It refers to a conversation in which friends or acquaintances sit on the beach, or in homes or offices or stores, and share their thoughts by giving personal accounts of their experiences in story form. "Talk story" calls not only for storytelling but also for careful listening, the better to understand the ideas and feelings that storytellers present. In multi-ethnic Hawaii, where no single ethnic group has a majority, "talk story" plays an important role in enabling people of different backgrounds and traditions to understand one another and to build a workable, pleasurable, political community.

To focus the narrative analysis on politics, I have arranged the analysis around three perennial political questions: (1) How can persons create genuine communities? (2) How can those communities maintain institutions which pass on a tradition while still responding to the constant need to alter and change those institutions in response to new circumstances? (3) How can political communities maintain a just order and freedom for their citizens?

Chapters Four and Five respond to the first of these questions as they apply in the Ohio and Hawaii communities, respectively. The second question supplies the context for Chapter Six, which deals with the Ohio community, and Chapter Seven, which focuses on the Hawaii case. Following a similar plan, Chapters Eight and Nine respond to the third question as applied to the two communities.

Chapter Ten explains the way in which these narratives constitute political theories, which are themselves nested in long-standing traditions in political theory. The Ohio stories articulate the political theory of liberalism, while the Hawaii narratives have much in common with the political theory of classical Greece. Both, however, offer interesting challenges to the traditions they represent, and these challenges hold promise for revealing more clearly the American political experience and for moving the American community itself closer to a just society.

Because, in this book, I wish to connect language, politics, and storytelling, it seems appropriate to turn to Lewis Carroll, who himself liked to tell stories both to children and to adults in order to explain the power of language in their everyday lives and to show how imagination can lead to greater understanding.

> You can just see a little peep of the passage in Looking-glass House, if you leave the door of our drawing-room wide open: and it's very like our passage as far as you can see, only you know it may be quite different on beyond.
>
> Lewis Carroll
> Through the Looking-Glass

Politics Through a Looking-Glass

1
Stories and Politics:
In the Looking-Glass House

> And here I wish I could tell you half the things Alice used to say, beginning with her favourite phrase "Let's pretend." She had had quite a long argument with her sister only the day before--all because Alice had begun with "Let's pretend we're kings and queens;" and her sister, who liked being very exact, had argued that they couldn't, because there were only two of them, and Alice had been reduced at last to say "Well, <u>you</u> can be one of them, then, and <u>I'll</u> be all the rest."
>
> Lewis Carroll
Through the Looking-Glass

Creating stories delights us, because they open up our imagination by allowing us "to pretend." But, is there more to this delight than mere fantasy? In this story, Lewis Carroll suggests that childhood fantasy games construct a world out of tradition and imagination by showing that Alice and her sister must negotiate to decide what parts of their tradition to adopt into the fantasy and what parts to change. Alice's sister argues that grammar demands that kings and queens (plural forms) requires four persons, which cannot be done since they, Alice and her sister, are only two. Alice evokes a different portion of tradition and suggests that, as a self-defining person, one can play many parts, echoing Shakespeare's observation that we all play many parts on the world stage. From this perspective, an imaginative game like Alice's can help people explore different ideas and free them to consider new options. A playful game of "let's pretend" can open up new possibilities for action that earlier worldviews obscured. This is part of how stories delight us; they rely upon old patterns and traditions but give them new twists. In this sense, stories constitute an important part of political life, for they not only allow us to celebrate our great events, but they also allow us to explore new ways of living together.

But stories both <u>de</u>light us and <u>en</u>lighten us, and since the delight is obvious, I shall explore how stories enlighten us. First I discuss how stories clarify social phenomena in daily life. Stories are windows into society. Because stories are such integral parts of daily conversation their key role may go unnoticed even by social scientists and historians. In addition, modern American culture gives the storyteller an ambiguous role; stories are considered vital to our cultural and intellectual development and yet, insofar as storytelling is considered a leisure activity, stories have lost legitimacy as sources for serious social knowledge. To explore the connection between stories and social knowledge, I discuss three questions: How do stories work? What is a story? How do citizens and social scientists use stories? Next, I show how fiction apprehends truth. To explore the connection between storytelling, social truth, and politics, I examine Plato's reasons for exiling storytellers from his Republic. Doing so illuminates the powerful role storytelling plays in shaping political values. Finally, because story is so much a part of language, I discuss how language itself shapes social and political processes, by examining the connection between power and discourse. My hope is that, by more clearly understanding the connection between storytelling and society, readers themselves can interpret the stories they encounter and in some measure add to their understanding of the societies in which those stories are told.

STORIES: WINDOWS ON SOCIETY

What Do Stories Tell?

Stories, whether created by children, citizens, or poets at play, invoke imaginative ideas that can provide windows through which to view our lives. In doing this, stories explain abstract ideas, illustrate points, and describe events, roles and actions. Appearing in one guise or another in all our conversations, stories stay with us. Often, what we most vividly remember from our conversations and bring with us to still other conversations are the stories we have been told. Stories make neat packages, small units of experience, which not only illustrate complex abstract ideas and feelings but also entertain those who hear them. Government officials and even U.S. Presidents make speeches in which stories serve to highlight their political points. Ministers and priests use stories to make theological points and journalists use stories to make news--or, perhaps, they use news to make stories. Neighbors share stories over the back fence. What is it about stories that enable them to enrich so many different situations? Why do stories do so much work?

Scholars have been aware of the importance of stories to their work. Historians glean knowledge about a historical period by reading its literature; anthropologists discover the cosmological perspectives of other cultures by studying their myths; political scientists assign novels to their students as part of their attempt to explain American politics. In doing these things, intellectuals demonstrate their belief that stories serve not only as vehicles of communication among people but also as means of articulating cultural historical values that enable readers to apprehend the storyteller's perspective. Using stories to gain a greater understanding of a specific culture or historical period, they let us know that the story can serve as an excellent resource for those who wish to understand societies. But how is it that the story represents the values or worldviews of the storyteller?

First, the story can speak about values by demonstrating them at work in the characters' lives. The demonstration entices the reader to leave behind his or her own world and enter into a new one, like Alice stepping through the looking-glass. The frame of the story helps the listener to accept, at least provisionally, a new perspective. Framed by the plot, the beginning and end of the story, the story entails a time commitment between the storyteller and the listener. Thus, we consider it impolite to interrupt a friend's story. This time "set aside" permits the story to develop a microcosmic world that storyteller and listener enter together. The deep breath one takes before embarking on a story--sometimes accompanied by a stage setting comment on the order of "I hope you like this one," indicates the speaker's readiness and marks the beginning of this "other" world in the midst of a conversation.

Second, the story's form brings together characters, setting, and action. In this way it constitutes a complete world: people, places, actions. The power of the storyteller comes in part through the expectation of an uninterrupted time in which to tell the story. Thus enabled, the storyteller can construct the story's microcosmic world and entice the listener into enjoying its features. Hence, the story as a whole becomes an experience for the listener, an experience shaped by the storyteller. The microcosmic reality that the story creates in discourse, along with the time allocated for its creation, gives the story a powerful role in conversation. It sets up an extended "lecture" within even a casual conversation. It gives the storyteller time and space, and therefore power, to create the possibility of communication between two different value systems or worldviews. Hence, the story especially facilitates conversation across groups who do not share similar values and assumptions, whose worldviews differ, because it provides the necessary time to communicate a complex set of assumptions about societies.

An analysis of this worldview not only enables citizens within the society to work more effectively, it enables social scientists and others who take a stance "outside" that society to enrich their understanding of it. In cross-cultural communication, stories powerfully connect persons who do not share basic assumptions. The story allows the speaker time, which in some sense resembles a "time-out," in which to portray the details of place, character, and action that describe the philosophical basis of a culture. This allows the listener to become familiar with the fundamental premises of a new cultural context as well as the immediate tasks at hand. So, it is not then surprising that anthropologists were among the first to discover stories and myths as resources for cultural understanding. However, it is important to distinguish story as one _form_ of discourse among others, to examine both the content of narratives and their form, because the power of stories to shape political structures lies both in their form and in their content. This leads to an important question: How is narrative, story, different from other types of speech? What is a story?

What Is a Story?

While conversation, discourse, or writing contain many genre, four basic forms of composition that exist are (1) argumentation, which develops a thesis with evidence in order to establish the truth of a position; (2) exposition, which clarifies, classifies, and so analyzes phenomena; (3) description, which attempts to reproduce for the reader the essential details of a phenomenon; and (4) narration, which gives an account of an action, an event. While this fourfold classification of composition comes from William Flint Thrall and Addison Hibbard's _A Handbook_ to Literature,[1] I have expanded their definitions of each form in order to include social science discourse as well as literary discourse.

Having distinguished narration from other composition forms, it is important next to indicate the characteristics of narration itself. What is it? In using the terms narrative or story, I refer to a purposeful composed speech, either written or oral, that has four characteristics. (1) It contains a plot, an action: a beginning, middle, and end. This focuses the story on specific events and creates a common expectation between the storyteller and the audience, which gives the storyteller the authority to command the audience's attention until the story's end. So, the plot organizes the story around an action and organizes the time relationship between the storyteller and the audience. (2) The narrative develops characters. The story progresses through unfolding actions in the lives of particular characters, who enact the plot. The storyteller introduces these characters in such a way as to induce empathy for them. (3) The narrative is set in a particular space and time, separate from the storytellers. This means that it does not claim to be a general observation about human nature but a focus on a particular experience and particular characters. (4) The narrative gives the audience an experience that develops both the logos, the understanding of patterns in social life, and the mythos, the vision of cosmological connections among nature, society, and Supreme Being or given reality in such a way that they can respond intellectually, aesthetically, and emotionally.

In this definition, I have not emphasized the distinction between "true" stories and "fictional" stories. While this distinction has its uses, it is out of place here because it emphasizes how stories reproduce or report events. For example, literary critics explore an author's biography to determine what aspects of the novel, play, or poem may refer to "actual" events. By shifting the emphasis to the story itself and the world it lays out, I wish to focus on the values the story communicates, rather than on its correlation with events external to it. Hence, the distinction between history (stories referring to actual lived events) and fantasy (stories creating events) is not the issue here. By telling a story, the speaker constructs an event, whatever its relation to circumstances beyond itself. No storyteller tells everything that actually happened. To do so would entail more time than the event itself took, for things occur simultaneously but language is linear, enabling a speaker to say only one thing at a time. In addition, one does not want to know everything that took place but rather the significant things. Because deciding what is significant requires the storyteller to impose values upon events, the storyteller, even in referring to an actual event, must construct or shape a story out of the welter of materials it presents. Storytelling involves making something, and it depends upon a particular worldview for its construction. To construct any story--history or fantasy--necessitates value choices. It is the values that stories articulate that provide the focus of this book.

By looking at the story as a form of communication rather than as either a symbolic account of a lived event (a history) or as a wholly artistic construction (a fantasy), I focus on what the story reveals about social and political relationships within the world it constructs. Each story presents a microcosmic society inviting social reflection. It is this aspect of the story that enables the listener to enter into the worldview of the storyteller and come to an understanding of that worldview: the values of the storyteller and the storyteller's society.

How Do Social Scientists Use Stories?

Anthropologists have done some pioneering work in studying the connections between narratives and societies. Anthropologists, such as Joseph Campbell, study many societies in order to discover "myths to live by."[2] Campbell's scholarly work, such as The Hero with A Thousand Faces[3], studies myth from the perspective articulated by Mircea Eliade: "Our study will deal primarily with those societies in which myth is--or was until very recently--'living,' in the sense that it supplies models for human behavior and, by that very fact, gives meaning and value to life."[4] For many social scientists, this approach applies to all societies, because even without recognizing it societies are served by myths (special founding stories) that guide collective action and articulate collective values.

Claude Levi-Strauss, working out of a post-positivist scientific model, explains how studying myth (narratives) can help set aside Western prejudices that make it difficult to understand so-called primitive societies:

> The real question is not whether the

> touch of a woodpecker's beak does in fact cure toothache. It is rather whether there is a point of view from which a woodpecker's beak and a man's tooth can be seen as "going together" (the use of this congruity for therapeutic purposes being only one of its possible uses), and whether some initial order can be introduced into the universe by means of these groupings.[5]

Levi-Strauss enters the realm of other cultures by suspending the Western scientific tradition. From this perspective, he develops a theory of myth that guides his four-volume work on the science of mythology. Here, he comes to the conclusion that science itself constitutes a myth. In doing so, his intention is not to discredit science but to credit it differently:

> As the myths themselves are based on secondary codes (the primary codes being those that provide the substance of language), the present work is put forward as a tentative draft of a tertiary code, which is intended to ensure the reciprocal translatability of several myths. This is why it would not be wrong to consider this book itself as a myth: it is, as it were, the myth of mythology.[6]

He comes to the conclusion that social science itself is mythic because it forms a worldview and proceeds to build a story to tell others of its insights, its vision.

Psychologists also turn to stories. Led by Sigmund Freud's dream analysis, psychoanalysts enter into their patients' dream narratives to uncover their significance and the repressed experiences they present. Bruno Bettelheim, following in this intellectual tradition, argues that fairy tales provide contexts in which children can work out their negative feelings toward persons in their lives. He considers these tales of such importance that he organizes his book around a detailed interpretation of central fairy tales to show how children use these narratives. For example, "Little Red Riding Hood" works through negative feelings about a grandmother by showing the grandmother transformed into a wolf. When Grandma is unpleasant her behavior can be explained by projecting this wolf image upon her. Reconciling negative and positive perceptions of the grandmother in the context of this narrative legitimates negative feelings. The story permits the expression of this negativity without directly challenging or forfeiting affection for the child's grandmother or mother.[7]

Feminists emphasize the various roles played by stories from consciousness raising to biblical scholarship.[8] Not only is storytelling a method of analysis,[9] but it is seen as a way of practicing politics. Carol Christ considers storytelling a revolutionary act for feminists. Throughout feminist scholarship, there is a call for women to tell their stories. Adrienne Rich's <u>Dream of A Common Language</u>--one that is not man made[10] calls for a new voice to express these stories. Feminist poets like Anne Sexton offer new versions of old stories like Cinderella, retelling them and explaining that the rags-to-riches story has a magic that invokes not only an impossible fantasy but also false, disabling expectations about marriage that leave out "diapers," "dust" and "middle-aged spreads."[11] Sexton's new stories prepare women to participate differently in modern society.

While modern political scientists have, perhaps, been slower to incorporate story into their analysis, political science certainly has not ignored the politics of storytelling. Early Greek political thought gave such a primary role to storytelling, particularly in the form of myth and drama, that Plato worried that it might prevail over philosophy as a source of knowledge. Eric Voegelin explains that this historical period represents a transfer of power from the symbolic representations of the tragic playwrights to Platonic dialogues and, hence, to discursive philosophical forms.[12] This represents a shift from <u>mythos</u> (symbolic narrative explanations about the connections of humans to the cosmos) to <u>logos</u> (systematic explanations about the connections among abstract propositions, expressed in general laws). The Platonic dialogues represent a middle ground between storytelling (<u>mythos</u>) and systematic inquiry into the laws that govern the order of things (<u>logos</u>).

FICTIONAL TRUTH: NARRATIVE FORM AND SCIENCE

While many people may believe that stories come from the muses, artists know that it takes work to produce them. The story as a product develops in a historical cultural context and reflects that context no less than other artifacts do: architecture, painting, machinery, and ordinary implements of daily living. Hence, it is not inappropriate to consider narratives as cultural artifacts, the products of a people.

But, in a more important way, all stories, even fictions, apprehend the truth. Because the narrative form involves characters, actions, and a historical setting, it especially lends itself to social analysis. Characters establish roles and connect those roles to action. The plot establishes a model of actions and their results. When Macbeth wishes to become king he kills the reigning king, which brings him guilt and ultimately his demise. The linear order of storytelling--one thing follows another--makes it an excellent avenue for examining action. The setting, the time, and place of the tale ground the story in a concrete case, but also present is the implication that the story has things to say that go beyond its concrete details. It says something general about human nature and the spirit of a people, but it makes no deterministic statements about the laws of human nature. It suggests patterns in a range of human possibilities. This frees the listener to consider the story as one possible pattern among many rather than seeing the story as a didactic law. For example, Macbeth's tragic end suggests that murder can lead to tragedy for the murderer, even if he obtains a kingship in the bargain.

But it is difficult for modern Americans to accept these patterns in stories as true insights. While historical narrative occupies a respectable place in modern America's quest for true understandings, fiction has occupied a more ambiguous position. Universities have departments of literature and educated persons consider it necessary to know literature. Nevertheless, the study of literature must constantly justify itself by explaining that it is necessary for cultural enrichment and that the aesthetic experience heightens the quality of life. Scientists and even historians rarely find themselves engaging in such defensive language. Literature teachers enjoy no such immunity. Americans accept this marginalization of fiction and storytelling. Fiction occupies a less prestigious place. High school English teachers explain to their students, parents and other teachers that reading fiction helps people to become better writers. So it is legitimate in its role as a tool for learning linguistic grammatical skills rather than as a means for understanding social patterns.[13]

This difficulty may have begun with the early Greek rivalry between poets and philosophers. Claiming that poets produced pleasure rather than knowledge, Plato banished the poets--fantasy makers--from his Republic. Before we fully restore storytellers to our republic, it may be prudent to consider Plato's objections and the modern versions of them. Plato's charge through the person of Socrates is a dramatic one, "And if you admit the sweetened muse in lyrics or epics, pleasure and pain will jointly be kings in your city instead of law and that argument which in each instance is best in the opinion of the community."[14] But, even he invites a counter argument:

> All the same, let it be said that, if poetry directed to pleasure and imitation have any argument to give showing that they should be in a city with good laws, we should be delighted to receive them back from exile, since we are aware that we ourselves are charmed by them.[15]

My case for Homer and other storytellers has four points. First, I shall argue that narratives are not __imitations__ of action but rather __imaginative__ constructs of the principles of human action. They do not make false phantoms that dazzle us but rather images that reveal action to us. Second, I shall argue that the narrative form does not __entertain__ its readers but rather __educates__ them. Fictional narratives teach about society. Third, I shall argue that, in narrative, __time__ and __transcendence__ intersect; the narrative offers a vehicle through which the reader may remove the self from a particular time and gain a transcendent view of a situation. This enables the reader to go beyond himself or herself and intimately encounter another. Because the story evolves through particular characters, it focuses on individuals; because these characters are abstractions, they represent persons and actions designed to reveal the human condition. In this sense, the narrative links time (a particular circumstance and set of characters) with transcendent issues (universal patterns in human experience.) Fourth, I shall argue that the narrative form blends __traditional__ structures with structural __transformation__. The story relies on a tradition with characteristic patterns of action, yet offers a new twist to those patterns. So the narrative relies on cultural expectations while offering a commentary on contradictions in the cultural patterns.[16] Because the narrative form itself articulates contradictions, rather than merely speaking about them as discursive forms do, it is particularly useful in understanding the contemporary political tension between tradition and revolution. Narratives can confront this issue not only in content but in form as well--not only in what is said but in how it is said.[17]

Imitation or Imagination?

Plato's charge is that the storyteller is a clever liar, a creator of phantoms: "The maker of the phantom, the imitator, we say, understands nothing of what is but rather of what looks like it is."[18] Modern Americans make a similar charge when they argue that fiction does not tell us about real, concrete societies but rather provides entertaining cultural manifestations that should be appreciated from an aesthetic perspective rather than studied from a sociological or political perspective. An indication of how rooted this notion of "phantom" is in modern America is the practice of calling someone a liar by saying, "That person is making up stories." Politeness and prudence may prevent Americans from directly charging the poet with lying. Even so, Americans characteristically find it difficult to take fiction seriously as a resource for political knowledge. The liberal university lauds literature but often insists that fiction belongs only in literature courses, not in social science courses. In so doing, while it treats literature as pleasurable fantasy and, in that role, commends it to students, it simultaneously denies it any status as philosophical commentary on social experience.

The problem begins in the connection between fiction and truth. Plato explains that the poet is third removed from the truth, because the poet makes an imitation of a particular object that itself is a representation of a universal essence. A ruling king represents the ideal of a king, while a play about a king presents an image of a particular king and, hence, is third removed from the ideal or essence of kingness. The modern American comes to the same conclusion by a different route, by arguing that because a fictional narrative about a king does not refer to a particular king and accurately duplicate the events of his life, it is merely fiction. Hence, it does not tell us about real kings. Both positions come from the assumption that narratives are symbolic reproductions of phenomena. Since the reproduction is symbolic, by definition it is inferior to the original; Plato even worries that the painting of a sofa will lead the foolish to think that the painter is a carpenter.[19] Likewise, the king on the stage may be mistaken by the foolish for a real king. Not many, if indeed any, such mistakes actually occur. People do not try to sit on pictures of sofas nor do they try to petition kings on stage for political rights. Though this may be Plato's humorous way of pointing out the limitation of his own argument, both Plato's argument and its modern equivalent evaluate fiction as a <u>production</u> of an imagined phenomenon. In doing this, they emphasize the creative character of fiction as against the imitative character of nonfiction. Hence, Plato and moderns confer higher status upon historical narratives that symbolically <u>reproduce</u> events thought to be <u>actual</u> and relegate fiction to a lower status because it is not grounded in "the truth."

The poet symbolizes an imagined event, a possible event, while the historian and social scientist ground themselves by using self-conscious methods to construct accurate <u>imitations</u> of events. Such methods hold them accountable for the accuracy of their representations, and because their statements refer to events, they are checked against the events themselves (as manifested, to be sure, in other accounts of them), against the "facts"--observations already certified to correspond with the world. For Plato and the modern perspective, literary works freely "speculate" about the human condition; but the more the speculation, the more the imagination, the greater the distance between the work, the fiction, and the truth.

There is nothing out of the ordinary about the belief that fictional images do not refer or point out particular real events. This understanding, however, depends upon both a referential language theory and a radical empirical epistemology. Operating within such an understanding, social scientists check hypothesized phenomena against the observable world and then use words to refer to these "observed" events. Along with many of their compatriots in the field of history, they create symbolic duplications of real world events--word replicas--rather than perspectives on these events. The entire enterprise depends upon a theory of language that construes words as neutral tools that point out, refer to, objects.

To understand a different view of social science and history requires a shift involving two primary theoretical components. The first is the incorporation of a semiotic theory of language, as opposed to a referential language theory; and the second is an understanding of speech and written texts as <u>productive</u> images.[20] A semiotic understanding of communication argues that words do more than point out objects; they <u>constitute</u> objects. This view of communication produces a quite different understanding of fiction.[21] A language system offers a context which gives words meaning by the connections that exist among them. Within this system of connections meanings emerge, and by virtue of this system words not only point to things but also locate them in relationship to other words/concepts. This language system creates an "order of things."[22] Semiotics argues that all words do this because they acquire meaning as a feature of their associations in the language system as a whole. These associations render judgments and map relationships. Hence, a word does not merely point out some object but also simultaneously suggests a number of ways in which that object is connected to other objects or ideas.

For example, if a citizen says that Ferdinand Marcos (former president of the Philippines) was a tyrant, the word <u>tyrant</u> not only points to Marcos but also indicates his political actions and renders a judgement about his ethical commitments. It does this by linking <u>Marcos</u> to <u>tyrant</u> which is the opposite of <u>benevolent</u> <u>dictator</u> (quite different from <u>president</u>) and which also contains the understanding that "tyrants" rule in a cruel and authoritarian manner rather than in a just, constitutional manner. These implications are embedded in the web of relationships within the language system. The word <u>tyrant</u>, simply because it <u>is</u> a word in a system of words connected within a language, does more than merely point to someone. It locates that person in an order of things and assigns status to the person thus located. Because <u>tyrant</u> assigns status, it has political implications. Any word used to refer to Marcos would locate him within a language system and, hence, assign status to him. Some would have positive implications and others negative ones. Some differences in terms, of course, would make only small status differences as far as locating him in the political order of things. Suppose, for example, one referred to him as a <u>husband.</u> This would not make a large difference, although it might enhance his status somewhat because people often feel more positively toward a "family man." The point is that by speaking about someone or something, the speaker locates that person or thing within a system of meaning; and that has political implications, because it not only points out someone or something but also assigns it to a place in the political order. Hence, to speak is to engage in a political action.

To connect this semiotic view of language to the

role of fiction, Paul Ricoeur makes a distinction between "image" and "copy." He argues that fiction is not the <u>reproduction</u> of events but, rather, the <u>production</u> of events. The reader uses fiction to see the world anew, as one uses a metaphor to see new connections between things. Although one realizes that the metaphor is not an actual description of the world, it is still useful.[23] For example, one does not really think it rains cats and dogs. But the metaphor is a device to reveal something about the world. In the same way, fiction as an extended metaphor reveals something about the world by naming things in the world and creating a system of meanings that assign status to persons and things within it.

Ricoeur sees the speaker as actively shaping images and metaphors. He uses the case of fiction to demonstrate how this takes place. Beginning with the premise that metaphors and fictions locate things within a symbolic order of things, he takes this revelation one step further when he urges his reader to note that, "Under the shock of fiction, reality becomes problematic."[24] Fiction makes the actual world problematic, and this is the way in which it apprehends truth and plays its political role in social understanding.

To make this point, Ricoeur observes that the word <u>fiction</u> comes from <u>facere</u>, which means to make or re-make.[25] By emphasizing that the fiction writer makes something--an image of the truth--one can see that all writers use words to make things and a fictional work creates an image of reality that can reveal the truth.[26] This perspective brings about a different conclusion about fiction's relevance to our understanding of social and political life than that to which we are led by the referential language theory.

The implication of this argument is that the fiction writer is not further removed from reality but simply more in touch with his or her own particular connection to reality and with the ways that connection can give the reader a particular view of the world. The social scientist, who also shapes reality through images, models, and metaphors, may be less aware of the role images play in the production of his or her work. Part of the power of both the poet and the scientist lies in the power of the metaphor[27]--the form of their messages. Imagination is an essential element for both the scientist and the writer. Since no word copies a lived experience but only creates an image of it, both social scientists and fiction writers produce imaginative interpretations of reality rather than imitations or copies of it. All written works, whether fiction or nonfiction, embody the imaginations of their authors and, hence, are productive images. They are produced by an author from his or her perspective, and they produce for the reader a view of the world. They are creative works.

Entertainment or Education?

Arguing that even fictions produce truth does not establish that the production of this truth is useful in building societies. Such truth might be no more than amusing trivia. Plato challenges storytellers by asking if their stories help citizens make better laws. Modern America seems to expect little of substance from stories. Even as they ascribe didactic purposes to children's stories, modern Americans easily dismiss adult equivalents by calling them "just stories," hardly a flattering label. The modern American liberal intellectual tradition separates the humanities from the social sciences, literature from political science. Generally speaking, liberal culture puts fiction in the same category as entertainment and leisure time. In this perspective, the primary role of fiction is to divert us in those scattered moments when the press of "reality" is suspended. It is not to educate us to more fully understand that "reality" and certainly not to suggest grounds upon which we might work toward changing the world. In fact, the creation of an entertainment industry with its accompanying film, television, and record technology explicitly claims entertainment, not education, as its goal.

This presents a problem for fiction, because in the work ethic of American culture entertainment, for all its centrality in our lives, has residual status. It is what is left over after the real business of life attracts our attention; it is a frill, not a necessity. The liberal state shapes a world in which both popular culture and to an extent art itself complies with this mandate, endlessly producing material for leisure-time consumption, as Walter Benjamin and other scholars in the Frankfurt school have explained in their telling accounts of the "culture industry."[28] Ultimately, liberal ideology leaves to art the political function of narcotizing its clientele, providing entertainment, distraction, symbolically constructed "recreational" drugs. In such a world, it becomes virtually impossible to see literary work as an important source for understanding the nature either of human beings or societies.

Examining this distinction between education and entertainment opens up the question: What makes a story entertaining? Is it entertaining because it has no connection to the "real" world? Or, instead, is it entertaining because it reassures us that all is well with the world, and so does not challenge our world or invite is to view our lives critically? If the second of the two models of "entertainment" is the more accurate, and I believe it is, then the distinction that needs to be observed here is not between amoral and moral narratives. Instead, it is between narratives that merely entertain, and therefore chiefly echo the present moral order, and those that challenge the reader to examine it, to reflect on its ethical and political premises and contradictions, and even to evaluate their own roles within it. Narratives that entertain leave the reader ready to relax, lie back, and nod off to sleep. Narratives that genuinely educate leave the reader reflecting on the world and ready to take up action within it. This goes back to the point Ricoeur makes in explaining that fiction produces meaning by a "shock of difference." Politically, fiction challenges the order of things as it is laid out in the reader's society. Narratives, by inducing a shocking new vision of the world, challenge the reader to see its political reality with a more critical eye. This challenge invites the reader to act in order to bring the political world more in line with the image of the good and just order that the author illuminates through the story. While such aesthetic insights might not be revolutionary, they can lead to new understandings of the human condition that have serious implications for political change. Without considering the political ramifications of his thesis, Ricoeur argues that literary art augments the reader's reality.[29] Herbert Marcuse, more clearly political in his focus, argues that the literary artist communicates by providing a frame of reference, the story, that makes the reader a stranger in his or her political lived-in world.[30] Thus estranged, the reader becomes open to new possibilities for political action. In this way, the story itself is a structured experience that reflects on the human condition and on politics. It invites the reader to consider problems of injustice within his or her society and to move society closer to the image of justice that the story reveals.

Beyond the substantively new horizons a specific narrative can offer, the narrative form itself is especially well suited to political education, because it organically unites [31] three vital elements in the formulation of serious political thought or theory: identity, action, and experience, which in its own particular manner encompasses the relationship between objectivity and subjectivity and between time and transcendence.

In reading or writing a fictional narrative, one, first of all, becomes poignantly conscious of the construction of identities: characters. While the social construction of identity is vital for understanding politics,[32] the formulation of <u>fictional</u> characters supplies an opportunity for <u>political</u> thought that goes beyond a simple exploration of identity. In the fictional narrative, the character's identity is a nexus between a particular person, whose existence is only within the narrative, and the representation of a universal identity type. For example, the audience experiences Hamlet as an individual whose fate concerns them but, at the same time, Hamlet is a study of the type of person who, in contemporary America, represents a man unable to act. Different historical periods emphasize different aspects of Hamlet's character, but the point remains that the character supplies a nexus between a particular person and a more generic type that is somehow within the ordinary experience of the audience.

Second, the narrative unfolds through an action. The plot is an action that has a beginning, middle, and end. In a sense, the story is an elaborate logical argument in the form of "if this is the case, then that outcome may evolve."[33] The plot brings human types together with an action and its outcome: the story's conclusion, "the end." Both Plato and Aristotle argue that all action seeks the good and the most comprehensive good is the political good. Because the narrative form draws attention both to the action and its outcome, it is useful as a means of understanding politics.[34]

Third, the narrative form offers an experience into which the reader or listener may enter empathetically. But to understand the nature of this experience, one must take account of two issues: an epistemological issue, of objectivity and subjectivity; and a metaphysical issue, of time and transcendence. Objectivity (distance) and subjectivity (intimate involvement) shape the reader's experience of fiction. The story claims to be outside of the reader's immediate culture or political community; so the reader can adopt the role of the disengaged objective observer. At the same time, fiction requires the reader to identify intimately with the characters and empathetically share their world. In this sense, fiction unites objective and subjective orientations.

In its objective dimension, the story constitutes a separate reality. No action within the story will directly affect the reader. Hamlet's fate will affect the life of no U.S. citizen. Thus, the reader can suspend critical judgement and for the moment "pretend" that these events are "real." This protected "let's pretend" game enables the reader to explore perspectives that may be difficult to apply in his or her immediate political life. The distance makes it easier. Because Lear exists in a separate reality, the reader can more readily apprehend his suffering than the suffering of such persons as Ronald Reagan or Jesse Jackson. The reader's own immediate political concerns do not inhibit his or her ability to hear the concerns of opponents, those who play the "other" in their own lives. Suspecting that Reagan or Jackson may tell their tales of woe for "political" ends, the reader may take these tales with some reservation. Things are different with Lear. The reader trusts him in a different way. Of course, Shakespeare inspires trust in still another way, for he has no turf to protect in our realm, no budget to worry about, and no particular party to satisfy. In any case, because the story is a safe place to explore opposing perspectives, it is possible for the reader to take up the most fundamental issues of the human condition without fear of manipulation or deception. All the story is there; the end of Lear is fixed, and its outcome does not harm us in a direct political fashion. Since outcomes are not directly at stake, the audience can "playfully," openly, listen. This is the objective character of narrative.

But the narrative invites a subjective posture as well. It does so because it offers characters with whom the reader identifies. The reader can develop subject-to-subject connections with the characters: The characters <u>matter</u> to the reader. Their fate is of consequence; the reader is involved with them. This subjective dimension, the empathy that the fiction generates, can bring a new consciousness to those who enter into it. Hence, the narrative offers the simultaneous experience of distance or objectivity, and closeness or subjectivity. Because a narrative unites characterization and action, and offers the reader an experience of objectivity and subjectivity, it is more than "just" an entertaining story. It is political commentary and, as such, an occasion for political thought. If the writer is an artist, interested in the truth of the human condition, and if the reader is open to reflective thought, the narrative provides an educational experience that challenges the reader to reexamine his or her political realm, measuring it against the tale's moral vision. In the context of this reexamination, the reader may well come to new political understandings and commitments, which themselves lead to political action.

Time and Transcendence?

Reinforcing this objective-subjective dimension of the reader's experience, the story gives readers the opportunity to set aside egoistic concerns and ideological commitments to consider more basic issues regarding the meaning of life itself. While a fictional work takes place in a particular time and place, it does not refer to life "here and now." It may not even refer to any place or time that humans have ever known. Still, if the reader considers the story seriously, then the story seems to have relevance for all times and all places, because it deals with the basic issues of humanity. Perhaps it never was, and yet it is. Giving readers an experience of some other time and place while suggesting that what is said in the story may be relevant to their own political community, the story invites them to reflect on the tensions they experience between themselves and the various "others" with whom they find themselves linked in the world "outside."

Transformation and Tradition

On the premise that fictional narratives do indeed provide instruction, Plato worried that the instruction they provided might invite action based on emotion instead of reflection and reason. From his perspective, the narrative form, far from merely diverting its audience for a moment's entertainment, was so powerful that it overshadowed other forms of discourse, such as philosophy, and so could lead its audience into unreflective, even destructive action. Plato's concern is that narrative may be simply <u>too</u> powerful:

> And as for sex, and spiritedness, too, and for all the desires, pains, and

> pleasures in the soul that we say follow all
> our action, poetic imitation produces
> similar results in us. For it fosters and
> waters them when they ought to be dried up,
> and sets them up as rulers in us when they
> ought to be ruled so that we may become
> better and happier instead of worse and more
> wretched.[35]

Plato worries that the passionate plea of the poet can mobilize the citizen in ways that do not foster public virtue but that destabilize society. In the modern world, liberals and Marxists similarly worry about the mobilizing effects of fiction. Liberals worry that fiction may inspire violent crimes; Marxists worry that fiction may inspire bourgeoise consumption patterns. Whatever differences might otherwise distinguish these three perspectives, they share the assumption that fiction has political power.

At the same time, both liberals and Marxists find positive educational value in fictional narratives, although each sees different political ends as being served by them. Twentieth-century political thought emphasizes the tension between tradition (the laws, norms, and institutions that maintain it) and revolution. Liberals tend to embrace the former, Marxists the latter. In the context of these two polar ideologies, fiction is an especially apt form for understanding politics. Its structure fuses two horizons, the culture in which it arises and an alternative order of things, the culture it anticipates. Most liberals give their warmest welcome to stories that at once enshrine the central premises of their tradition and sound the alarm at the prospect of threatening alternatives to it. For example, George Orwell's <u>Animal Farm</u> plays this role nicely by demonstrating the difficulties inherent in a communist society along with the threat to cherished elements of the liberal tradition. Meanwhile, Marxists' commitment to "socialist realism," as a criterion against which to measure the political acceptability of fiction, witnesses both to their respect for fiction's power and their embrace of fiction's ability to undo traditional sentiments and, hence, prepare for revolutionary changes.

While both liberals and Marxists judge fiction on the basis of its ability to serve their political ends, neither fully examines how fiction exercises power. To explore this issue, it is necessary to examine the form of fiction. In order for fiction to work, it must be believable. The reader must accept that persons like these can exist. To create this believability, fiction echoes patterns characteristic of a particular tradition.[36] To make the story plausible, it must in some manner mimic familiar patterns within the reader's experience.[37] To some degree, it must represent arguments, actions, characters, and perspectives already present in the reader's culture. Even fairy tales do this, and hence, parents can use them to socialize their children, to teach them a cultural tradition. They can do so because such tales, for all their fantastic and esoteric paraphernalia, in fact, echo primary relationships, values, and tensions in the culture.

However, this point goes beyond a functional explanation of narrative as a socializing agent. Because narrative cannot rely upon a real world event for legitimacy, it acquires its legitimacy by echoing patterns in the reader's social and political life. This is especially important for modern Western cultures that use an empirical paradigm as the basis of scientific knowledge. Because fiction makes neither the scientific claim nor the historical claim that it describes actual events in the world, it relies upon a verisimilitude: a sense of truthfulness, a sense of representation of events that could occur in the "real" world. It dare not be totally fantastic; it must echo patterns existing in the "real" world. If fiction goes too far in its invention of a new world vision, it will be either idiotic, the writer speaking only to himself or herself, or it will be mad, lacking sense to inhabitants of any society. While fiction walks the line between imagination and madness,[38] it must retain its conservative ground if it is to have enough verisimilitude actually to be fiction and not merely babble.

Thus fiction dare not invent too much. This explains the aphorism "truth is stranger than fiction," because the reader can accept a greater degree of the unexpected in factual representations, anchored by empirical evidence, than in fictional narratives. For fiction to retain its verisimilitude, it must come as less than a complete surprise to the reader. So, it carefully manages its surprises. Its connections with the world are meticulously preserved in its mimetic qualities. Hence fiction, however inventive, necessarily embraces tradition. Yet, the form of fiction also involves transformations. The narrative unfolds through an action that is a transformation: something happens. Things are not the same at the end as at the beginning. Because the plot unfolds through some transformation, the storyteller offers a model of change. Hence, fiction relies on tradition for its verisimilitude and on transformation for its plot development, and together they give the story its political power, in which tradition and transformation are combined. But, its most important political power is its ability to proclaim the truth. Literary critics like Ezra Pound see novelists and poets as modern prophets who, like the child in "The Emperor's New Clothes," proclaim the truth amidst ideological forces bent upon suppressing it.

Fiction has played just this role in America's history. For example, critics credit Uncle Tom's Cabin with stimulating the Civil War.[39] There is a story, possibly apocryphal, about how Lincoln claimed that this novel launched the Civil War. While this story is difficult to substantiate, and even if substantiated would not prove a causal connection, it shows the power ascribed to a novel. That particular novel clearly both facilitated and shaped the development of an American consciousness, which was critical of slavery and vehemently argued for its abolition from America's political life. But, it is important to note that even the apparently radical critical argument in Uncle Tom's Cabin asserts a conservative American orientation. The abolition argument was based squarely on religious grounds. So while Uncle Tom contained a revolutionary force that argued for the eradication of slavery, it did so by affirming the traditional values of the family, the institution of marriage, and other Christian-based positions.

The "poet's license" issued by modern citizens is issued on the condition that art be wary of its powers. Not trusting that wariness to the artists, modern societies warn their citizens not to trust art too much. However, as long as art keeps within its bounds and awakens in citizens the ability to laugh at society's foibles and cry at its tragedies, it can speak to us about truths that we dare not examine under other lights. Hence, it plays an important role in society. The modern republic needs fictions to apprehend these truths. It is important for contemporary social critics to see clearly the role that fiction plays. Fictions, therefore, should take their rightful place alongside historical narratives and social scientific accounts of society as means for apprehending social and political truth. The symbolic realities that these diverse discourses construct and display have in common the power to hold up a mirror before us and, thereby, more fully expose us to ourselves.

POLITICS AND LANGUAGE

Speech Constitutes Order

While Americans often consider politics a "dirty business," even if it is an unavoidable facet of social life, they also have a long tradition of valuing political participation, and within this latter perspective, politics acquires a more positive definition.

In exploring storytelling's political role, I define politics as the process by which citizens build a community, the process by which they assume an identity and act, as <u>a people</u>. This means that politics takes on a broader range of action than simply those of government, which represents only one mechanism by which a people assumes a collective "official" identity and invests it with the powers to act <u>for</u> them. A political analysis of storytelling invites reflection on how citizens create a language and body of thought that governs the habits of everyday life; it is an analysis of how the public political realm is ruled <u>by</u> the people. Such an analysis focuses on power not as a mechanism of <u>control</u> but rather as the <u>energy</u> that enables citizens to act collectively to shape their lives, their neighbors' lives, and ultimately the life of the nation. In this context, storytelling is understood as an act that generates symbolic power and, thus, shapes consciousness and helps give form to citizen's actions.

Modern political and social theory along with modern American political culture emphasizes the power of <u>tool</u>-making, material production and the mechanisms that control it, rather than <u>symbol</u>-making. However, as scholars and others have encountered the limits of material explanations for human behavior, they have turned with renewed interest to an examination of the role symbols play in shaping human action. Philosophy itself has taken a linguistic turn[40]; semiotics, media analysis, and a general appreciation of the powers of speech has renewed the classical Greek interest in rhetoric. A leader in this linguistic turn, Michel Foucault, while acknowledging that people build society both by making tools and making symbols, has focused his own work on the power of language. Foucault represents an emerging interest in the social power of language, a perspective that has not gone unnoticed by political science.[41]

This symbolic focus begins in the West with Aristotle, who explains that symbols differentiate humans and enable them to be political, because it is through language that humans distinguish the just from the unjust:

> Now, that man is more of a political animal than bees or any other gregarious animals is evident. Nature, as we often say, makes nothing in vain, and man is the only animal whom she has endowed with the gift of speech. . . the power of speech is intended to set forth the expedient and inexpedient, and therefore likewise the just and the unjust. And it is a characteristic of man that he alone has any sense of good and evil, of just and unjust, and the like, and the association of living beings who have this sense makes a family and a state.[42]

He further argues that the purpose of all human action is to obtain the good. Because politics represents the most inclusive and indivisible good, the good for the whole community, it has the greatest potential for good and, therefore, is the kind of activity most essential to the good life itself:

> Every state is a community of some kind, and every community is established with a view to some good; for mankind always act in order to obtain that which they think good. But, if all communities aim at some good, the state or political community, which is the highest of all, and which embraces all the rest, aims at good in a greater degree than any other, and at the highest good.[43]

Modern political analysts, less given than Aristotle to constructing arguments from premises of intent, argue that language nevertheless plays this role whether or not the speaker or anyone else acknowledges the political significance of speech.[44] Language and speech articulate our understandings of our situation, bringing us to _terms_ with existence. Such terms enable a community to name things and, by naming them, to see them more clearly and evaluate them politically. In language, we make explicit judgments and articulate evaluations: hopes, desires, decisions, and even laws. One example illustrates the power of speech. To call an adult Black man boy withdraws power from him. Speech does more than refer to objects; it locates them in a language system that provides an order of things. To identify people as children connects them with immaturity and withdraws the full powers normally accorded to participating adults. For the same reason, college students would prefer not to be called boys and girls. Language has power and, therefore, speech has political meaning because it allocates power and authority by assigning persons and objects to positions within a system. To become identified with children is to have one's status diminished, just as being labeled an adult enhances status. Thus, to speak is to engage in a political act that distributes power and authority within the community. Naming things constitutes claims about the proper order of things and their relative locations within the system.

Stories Constitute Action

In order to understand fully the powerful role language plays in shaping the habits that make up everyday life, it is necessary to differentiate the referential theory of communication from the semiotic theory of communication. The referential theory explains that words serve as neutral tools that point or refer to things. Language provides speakers with unambiguous definitions of terms; speakers then employ them in speech in order to symbolize their ideas and thus represent the reality to which they "refer." Meaning occurs to the degree that words are precisely defined and speakers and listeners acquire skill in using them precisely as defined. Unclear definitions and undisciplined speech produce confusion and frustrate communication.

In contrast, semiotics argues that communication takes place because listeners and speakers share a language that creates meaning by generating a system of similarities and differences. One knows black as the opposite of white and child as the opposite of adult. Meanings depend on this system, in which words acquire significance through their relationship to other words. Communication takes place between speakers and listeners because they share a language system. Semiotics, however, differentiates between speech and language. The language system depends upon the community for its static quality; it changes very slowly over time and the community sustains its rules and grammar. Individual speech acts, in contrast, function as the dynamic element in communication.

Such acts gradually alter the language system. For example, in the first half of the twentieth century most citizens used the word <u>Negro</u> to designate relatively dark-skinned Americans of African descent. The cultural critique of the sixties effectively substituted the term <u>Black Americans</u>, which signaled a new status for such persons within the American culture. This example represents a deliberate attempt on the part of citizens to introduce a new symbol and, hence, a new set of relationships between <u>Black</u> and <u>White</u> Americans. In doing so it implicitly argued that America is both black and white; it is not a nation of <u>Whites</u> with a few <u>Negroes</u> in it. Hence, the introduction of a term constitutes a new set of relationships. In a less conscious way, slow shifts in meanings occur continuously within the language system. Like words, stories themselves not only preserve, affirm, and pass on cultural traditions but also introduce complex new ideas and new ways of speaking and thinking about society.

Because stories serve both conservative and transformative functions, they are excellent windows through which the careful viewer can gain an understanding of society. The stories a society enjoys telling reveal its worldview. These stories, whether fictional or historical, reflect and articulate social consciousness and offer their readers social truth. For those interested in understanding a society, this means that both fiction and history offer ways in which to comprehend social values and philosophical perspectives. Similar to other types of social and political studies, storytelling analysis requires careful observation. In this case what needs to be observed is the political act of storytelling itself. Like other observational methods, the interpretation of stories requires a technique of analysis specific to the ways in which stories function in societies and articulate social reality. The method used in this text, described in the next chapter, develops out of a semiotic language theory.

Although Lewis Carroll, the author of <u>Through the Looking-Glass</u>, predates Ferdinand Saussure, the founder of semiotic language theory, Carroll's awareness of the power of language certainly anticipated contemporary concerns with language, and in the following passage he comments quite extensively on how language works. Carroll explains that the "sentence," no doubt including words and phrases, comes before other forms of judgments, "verdicts." Sentences and words have power. To be sure, official decision makers wield power, but they do so in a context of options and constraints already shaped by language and speech. In the story, Alice is on trial. The Queen explains that the sentence (the words and phrases) come before the "verdict"—the judgement:

> "Let the jury consider their verdict," the King said, for about the twentieth time that day.
> "No, No!" said the Queen. "Sentence first--verdict afterwards."
> "Stuff and nonsense!" said Alice loudly. "The idea of having the sentence first!"
> "Hold your tongue!" said the Queen, turning purple.
>
> Lewis Carroll
> *Alice in Wonderland*

2
Examining Reflections:
Structuralism and Hermeneutics

> She puzzled over this for some time, but at last a bright thought struck her. "Why, it's a Looking-glass book, of course! And, if I hold it up to a glass, the words will all go the right way again."
> This was the poem that Alice read.
>
> JABBERWOCKY
>
> 'Twas brillig, and the slithy toves
> Did gyre and gimble in the wabe:
> All mimsy were the borogoves,
> And the mome raths outgrabe.
>
> Lewis Carroll
> <u>Through the Looking-Glass</u>

Alice attempts to decode the poem by using a looking-glass, but even though this makes the words "go the right way," the meaning is still unclear. With the help of critic Martin Gardner, modern readers can more easily decode the poem. Glossing the terms, Gardner explains that <u>brillig</u>, for example, comes from the word broil and alludes to the late afternoon when it is time to broil dinner.[1] What Carrolls suggests is that understanding involves two steps. First, Alice deciphers the words at a rudimentary level, a mechanical operation that establishes the order of the words; second, she struggles for their meaning by creating links between the words and her everyday life activities. The full decoding process requires both the rudimentary ordering of the words, done with the mirror, and the creative search for meaning. The meaning must make sense within the context of the poem, and it must make sense <u>to</u> <u>the</u> <u>reader</u>. This second step in meaning creates a shared context between the reader and the poem.

In Chapter One, I argued that stories are a primary ingredient in political communication and, as such, foster social and political reflection, which can serve as a basis for social action. In this chapter, I will show how to use stories as an effective tool for political analysis. This chapter offers a mechanism, similar to Alice's mirror, for interpreting stories. The interpretive strategy facilitates making connections between the reader's social circumstances and the story's message so that the story will speak to the reader's concerns while maintaining commitments to scientific objectivity. Structuralism plays the mirror role in this project by providing a mechanism for finding an order or pattern among the stories, and hermeneutics, often called interpretive theory, furnishes a framework for linking stories to the issues of a particular social political context and, thereby, enlisting them as guides for human action in particular political communities.

To interpret the social-political dimensions of a narrative, I have developed a structuralist approach, influenced by such structuralists as Claude Levi-Strauss and deconstructionists like Michel Foucault. This structuralist approach enables a reader to apprehend the political patterns articulated in the deep structure of narratives. Such an approach brings rigor to the work of organizing a story's perspective. However, story interpretation, like other modes of social analysis, requires both rigor and imagination, both science and art. The artistic component of the enterprise develops out of hermeneutics, which helps readers understand the link between the story and their own social political situations. Hermeneutics serves as the philosophical basis for the analysis, engendering a shared dialogue between the storyteller and story readers. At its best, this dialogue aspires to a conversation that bridges both historical and cultural boundaries, opening up texts from other times and other cultures so that, even as they reveal these other worlds, they enable readers to better understand their own historical and cultural context and, perhaps, to find in that understanding new ways of seeing society that free them for creative political action.

THE READER AND THE STORY: ACTION AND SYMBOL

Social scientists, historians, literary critics, and others who seek to understand society through story analysis face a complex task in searching for meaning, for reliable interpretations. The meaning sought must link the storyteller's social experiences with those of the social analyst. In addition, it must bear the weight of scientific criteria. Social analysts ask:

How can an interpretation be sufficiently reliable to yield accurate social knowledge? How can it satisfy the epistemological demands of social science? These questions spring to the lips not only of the social scientist but also of the literary critic, who insists on a reliable interpretation that will stand up under the rigorous demands for truth made by twentieth-century citizens with commitments to reason and empirical evidence. A political perspective demands an interpretation that does not merely reproduce the concrete ideology of a particular time or locality but builds a common understanding that speaks to universal aspects of human experience, or at least establishes links between people of different times, such as between Carroll's nineteenth century and our own twentieth century, or between people of different cultures, such as England and the United States.

However, while social analysts study other times and places to gather knowledge, they also direct their attention toward knowledge that will help to define and solve the problems of their own society. This practical aspect of social analysis plays an important part in making an analysis meaningful; it is meaningful to particular people in confronting and solving the problems of their daily lives. Such analysis focuses less on the acquisition of abstract knowledge about the universal characteristics of existence than on the discovery of particular knowledge about specific peoples' situations for purposes of improving them.[2]

I shall first describe the structuralist method which I developed and then place it within the interpretive or hermeneutical tradition to construct a rigorous and imaginative interpretive strategy. My purpose is to describe this process so that those who wish to interpret stories as means to understanding societies can use it for their purposes, whether they be academic in character or more directly aimed at both understanding and shaping some particular political situation.

Structuralist Analysis: What Is it?

Since structuralism itself takes many different forms in contemporary social theory,[3] I shall begin with a brief sketch of those aspects that bear most directly on this project.

Structuralism's early manifestations drew from positivism and attempted to find rigorous methods of analysis that would enable all interpreters to find the same meaning in a text. Claude Levi-Strauss, one of the foremost architects of this approach, argued in his early work that _the_ interpretation emerged from the text itself.[4] Levi-Strauss's later work and other later manifestations of structuralism, including its second cousins now referred to as post-structuralism or deconstruction, make less grandiose claims, looking toward _an_ interpretation and focusing attention on exposing the power relationships within a text.[5] This latter approach forms the basis for the structuralist interpretive strategy I develop here. By calling it a strategy, I wish to differentiate it from empirical methods that proceed from a different epistemological basis. By referring to it as interpretive, I wish to remind the reader that this strategy develops out of humanist philosophy rather than the empirical analytical philosophy that shaped much of structuralism.

Because narratives contain so much detail and invite such a wide range of interpretations, a rigorously reliable analysis requires a strategy that enables readers both to enter into the story (leaving behind their own perspectives) and to emerge from the story with a systematic analysis of it. Structuralism together with hermeneutics provides such a strategy. Since the strategy I develop is informed by both structuralism and hermeneutics, I refer to it as a _structuralist interpretation._

A structuralist interpretation proposes to interpret a narrative to understand its deep structure as revealed in the form and content of its themes. The plot, by repeating these themes throughout its development, articulates this deep structure. To explain this feature of the plot, Levi-Strauss uses the image of a symphony score. He explains that the story delivers its message in the linear progression of the plot that, like music, expresses themes and variations on those themes as it moves forward to its conclusion. Its beat moves it along (horizontally represented on the score). Simultaneously, the conductor's score (read vertically) indicates the themes that various instruments pick up and repeat throughout the musical piece. As themes repeat, the music tells its story at two levels: the progression of the piece from beginning to end, which the conductor follows by reading across the musical score, and the repetition of themes and counter themes, which the conductor apprehends by reading the score vertically to see their repetition by the various instruments. Levi-Strauss suggests reading narratives in the same way: "horizontally" (in a linear mode) and "vertically." To follow the plot development, he reads them horizontally. At this level a given story represents a series of chronological statements about action. Reading stories vertically involves searching for the themes (called mythemes by Levi-Strauss) that the story repeats, over and over, as it moves toward a conclusion. In this way, he reduces the story to a few central propositions, which he then arranges like a conductor's score by placing them horizontally in terms of their plot development and vertically in terms of the set of actions, themes, they repeat.[6] By dividing a narrative into small components of action, each the equivalent of a sentence, he arranges the story like a conductor's score. Reading across, he follows the linear progression of the plot. Reading vertically, he discovers the several classes of actions (which he calls bundles of actions) that the story repeats in its telling. This exposes the social patterns the story articulates and enables a "reading" of the story as a whole in terms of its social messages. Its strength is that, like the conductor's score, it takes account of the work as a whole.

In analyzing the patterns that these themes reveal in the two cultures examined in this book, I have constructed a matrix that looks very similar to the conductor's score. It can be read across to follow the chronological plot development and down to see how the various stories repeat the mythemes. This matrix is placed at the end of each chapter in which stories are presented. In arriving at this pattern, I began with each narrative and constructed a score similar to the one that Levi-Strauss describes in his analysis of Oedipus.[7]

Part of the purpose of this analytical work is to discover the contradictions that narratives articulate. Levi-Strauss explains that myths articulate contradictions within cultures that other forms of discourse cannot address. For contemporary Americans, stories serve this purpose, since the sacred myth does not occupy a privileged position in modernity. The logical demands of argumentation and the unreflective commitment to detail, which description requires, make it difficult for these forms of articulation to discuss contradiction. On the other hand, narrative with its opposition between protagonist and antagonist is an ideal structure for displaying tensions and contradictions. Structural analysis, as Levi-Strauss understands it, aspires to uncover the contradictions in a culture as they are expressed in its stories.

Structuralist Interpretation: How It Works

Following the logic of this structuralist approach, I have developed four dimensions for analyzing narratives.[8] These call for an analysis of the oppositions central to each narrative, the metaphors that help to illuminate the varied texture of the story, the transformations the story presents as the action unfolds, and the contradictions that the narrative expresses.

Another way of thinking about this close analysis of the story's text is that it facilitates careful listening to the narrative, which will generate a systematic interpretation of it. It aspires to enable the reader to listen to both the story's linear plot progression and to the themes repeated within the story, the deep structure, that constitute a worldview or model of society. By applying these four dimensions to any narrative, a structural analysis yields a systematic interpretation of the social messages that the story carries. This analysis can be performed on one narrative or several, in which case the analyst can discover patterns within several stories that illuminate a culture. Its application works to interpret high culture, such as literary works like Moby Dick, or popular culture, such as television dramas.[9] The method involves constructing a simplified version of the linear order of the plot and then comparing several stories in order to find a pattern among them. Finding common bundles of relationships enables the reader to read several stories at once or to construct a more abstract master story that reveals the plot pattern within a group of stories. For example, in this book I use two groups of stories representing two different cultures: a middle-class culture in the Midwest and a working-class culture in Hawaii.

Once the master plot is presented, the book moves to a close analysis of each narrative, focusing on the four dimensions I have mentioned--oppositions, metaphors, transformations, contradictions--each of which involves a different kind of consideration of the narrative under study.[10]

Oppositions

The first step examines the story to discover its primary oppositions. Narrative structure itself presents an opposition between the protagonist (the story's primary figure) and the antagonist (the force or character that opposes the primary figure). One way to learn about a culture is by becoming familiar with the oppositions traditionally laid out by that culture. Color presents a simple example. In the American culture, black represents death and sorrow while white represents joy and life. Widows wear black; brides wear white. Black and white symbolically articulate opposites. The colloquial phrase "varying shades of gray" alludes to the mixtures of these two colors arranged on a spectrum between joy and sorrow. In contrast, for traditional Chinese, white signals death while red represents joy. Mourners wear white; brides wear red. At a more complex level, to understand American post-World War II spy novels requires the assumption that democracy and communism represent opposites. Similarly, to follow early Western romances requires the reader to accept the idea that within the context of "the times," cowboys represent the brave and good and Indians the wily and evil. To understand a culture, one becomes familiar with its worldview and the oppositions that it takes for granted. A story's structure reveals and echoes oppositions.

Since the plot takes place through the conflict between the protagonist and antagonist, the reader confronts the central issue in the plot by considering the opposition between these two characters or forces. By considering how other characters or forces within the narrative connect to these two central figures, the reader achieves a holistic analysis of the narrative, which views it as a web of relationships tied together by the primary conflict that brings the plot to its resolution. Hence, an analysis of opposition is the first step in the structuralist interpretation.

By searching for the oppositions in the narrative the reader identifies some of the primary categories in the storyteller's worldview. These categories constitute a set of identities that hold some importance from the storyteller's perspective. Because these identities are complex--Hamlet is a prince, a young boy, a Dane, a future ruler, an honorable person, a man--the reader selects among them in order to construct an interpretation. The same applies in interpreting historical figures: Abraham Lincoln, along with other things, is a president, a Republican, an attorney, a man, and a person from a family of moderate economic means. The story offers a list of possible identities and from this list the reader selects those that appear most relevant to his or her situation.[11] By attending to opposite identities, the reader sees these identities in relationship to the structure of the entire story.

Because a plot, most simply, represents a conflict between two forces, the discovery of oppositions offers an excellent place to begin narrative analysis. This is not totally unlike the social scientist's search for "key variables" except that, in the case of narrative analysis, the storyteller (subject of the analysis) generates the categories and the reader (social analyst) attends to those found most meaningful. This means that the analyst chooses among the various identities that the character presents. A political analysis might seek out rulers/ruled, powerful/powerless, just/unjust, leaders/followers, women/men, communism/capitalism, or any other set of oppositions that look at the structure of power. What is important is that the analyst develop the categories through a careful consideration of both the narrative itself and its categories and the analyst's own cultural situation.

Metaphors

Once a key set of oppositions has been selected and carefully considered in terms of what the narrative reveals about that opposition, the reader can turn to the language within the narrative, to see what it reveals about the opposition. Metaphors are centrally important linguistic elements composed by drawing on the tension between similarity and difference.[12] A simple metaphor, "she turned into a mad dog," illustrates this point. One who understands the metaphor in its most common sense does not think that she acquired two long furry ears and four paws. This would simply be a category mistake because it would place her into the category dog which is not the usual meaning. By developing an analogy the reader understands that she became like a dog who has rabies and acts in an atypical and threatening manner. Thereby, the reader understands that she is both like a "mad dog"--dangerous, unpredictable, and vicious--and unlike a mad dog in that she does not have rabies and has not acquired the physical characteristics of a dog. Colin Turbayne makes the point that analogies work in a similar way, by cross-sorting frames of meaning that produce explanations.[13] In this sense, metaphors bring together two fields of discourse to make a point.

Michel Foucault shows how metaphors that link two fields of discourse can be used for social analysis. In Madness and Civilization he explains that a shift in the social meaning of madness takes place when the discourse shifts from a religious category ("possessed by demons") to a medical category ("mentally ill"). Such a shift not only produces new understandings of a phenomenon but also introduces new authorities for confronting that phenomenon (moving from "priests" to "doctors") and new mechanisms for control (shifting from "prayer" to "drugs" as means of effective human intervention).[14] Both Turbayne and Foucault advocate an analysis of metaphor in order to see the world that language creates. Turbayne explains that this is the difference between "using metaphors" and "being used by them": "The victim of metaphor accepts one way of sorting or bundling or allocating the facts as the only way to sort, bundle, or allocate them."[15] In analyzing metaphors in a narrative, the reader reverses this process. As an outsider to the tale's worldview, the reader, by paying careful attention to its metaphors, can enter into the way in which the storyteller sorts and bundles social factors. Not only does this enable the reader to understand the storyteller's worldview, it also uncovers alternatives to his or her own worldview. Foucault provides his readers with this type of opportunity through historical analyses, introducing them to another time frame and opening an alternative worldview to them.

Analyzing metaphors invites a reader to look not only at what the storyteller says but how it is said and, hence, to listen more completely to the story. It also encourages the reader to find patterns in the metaphors of various related tales, the better to expand and develop the overall interpretation of the story. Because metaphors appear infrequently in stories, they have dramatic impact. Because they highlight points and bring together fields of discourse, they represent an important aspect of the narrative's message.

Transformations

The analysis of metaphor and opposition focuses on the static qualities of the narrative. In contrast, by examining what _changes_ take place within the narrative, the reader acquires a dynamic model of the story's society. An essential component in the politics of a culture is how it incorporates change into its political institutions and social practices. Narratives organize themselves with reference to an action--a chain of events that present a problem and resolve it. In this regard narratives present a series of events whose meaning depends upon an implied cause-effect argument. Seymour Chatman explains this by distinguishing between two types of narrative propositions: (1) "stasis" propositions, which explain actions; and (2) "process" propositions, which move the action forward. The linear order of these statements forms the argument. The storyteller can subtly alter the narrative (keeping the plot similar) simply by changing the order of these propositions. The point that Chatman makes is that when the forward motion of the story requires an explanation in order for the reader to follow it, to believe and accept it, the storyteller supplies a stasis proposition.[16] A reader can learn about what types of processes require explanation by carefully observing the linear order of stasis and process propositions. Because cause-effect and agency play central roles in the politics of an event, the reader can also use this distinction to understand the social model that the story subtly presents. Story A and Story B present different social explanations even though the order of events (actions) are the same (first the resignation and then the revolt).

Story A: The President resigned.
          The people had little food or freedom.
          The people revolted.

Story B: The people had little food or freedom
          The President resigned.
          The people revolted.

Story C: The President resigned.
          The people revolted.
          The people had little food or freedom.

This example illustrates that different orderings of the stasis proposition (The people had little food or freedom) produces different social arguments. In Story A, the lack of food and freedom leads to revolt. In Story B, the President's resignation serves as the impetus for revolt, and in Story C, the resignation and revolt lead to the lack of food and freedom. These are subtle differences but a careful interpretation can reveal the complexities suggested by a particular linear order. The choice of sentence order plays an important part in shaping the political model the story presents. The mode of analysis proposed in this chapter incorporates the model presented in the linear structure by including transformations as part of its framework.

     Two questions draw out the transformations that a narrative presents and, thereby, focus on its dynamic dimension: (1) What <u>values</u> do characters seek in their transformations? (2) Who or what serve as <u>agents</u> of transformation? For example, Cinderella's transformation from servant girl to princess presents a dynamic model that suggests women's access to power and happiness is to be found in marrying a prince and that a good strategy to that end is to gather the proper wardrobe to attract his attention. Her fairy-godmother and her own good, obedient, nature (in addition to her physical beauty) are the factors responsible for her transformation. In this sense, the story models social change and offers a set of values: being beautiful and obedient and living happily ever after in a marriage. Whether the reader wishes to make a feminist critique of the model or assert it as a desirable life plan, attention to transformations illuminates the dynamic message the story tells.

     Because social explanation speaks of social change, a focus on transformation enables the reader to examine social structure. For political analysis, this is a central issue, since politics involves looking at power and at the processes by which power and authority shift from one group to another. It is perhaps an especially important issue for modern twentieth-century societies that have experienced such rapid transformations. By asking what transformations central characters seek, the analyst can discover what they value. By looking at the tensions between the protagonist and the antagonist, the analyst can see what values conflict with one another. By examining the plot, the analyst can discover what types of characters serve as agents of social change in the political model that the story presents.

Contradictions

According to structural anthropologists myths (sacred narratives) mediate cultural tensions or contradictions that cannot be resolved within the context of the culture. Other forms of discourse, such as essays or discursive speech, do not represent them realistically, because such forms of address are directed toward logical conclusions. A narrative has more freedom because of its ambiguity. It can represent arguments that go beyond a logical linear structure. It can represent emotions and show both sides of a contradiction in an even-handed manner. Hamlet, for example, is a man torn between trying to determine whether justice requires him to challenge the King or instead to submit to his authority. Because the narrative form does not require the orderly and definitive conclusion of the essay, it is especially useful for representing contradictions. Edmund Leach explains how narratives mediate contradictions in his analysis of the Solomon story, in which tribal members are admonished both not to marry outsiders and not to marry kinfolk. In many such tribes, this entails an impossible requirement since all members of the tribe may well be kin. Leach argues that by a structural analysis of this narrative, a reader can obtain a deeper understanding of Israelite culture.[17] The exogamy/endogamy conflict intensifies in a society where rule depends on lineage. The story mediates the contradiction by providing a way to discuss it publicly, even though it cannot be finally resolved. It provides consolation to those who must face this type of no-win situation while preserving the legitimacy of the conflicting rules.

By reading a narrative that is popular with a particular culture and by carefully noting its contradictions, a reader can discover the tensions within the culture. Because social transformations arise out of these tensions or contradictions, understanding them is helpful to understanding the social challenges and potential changes with which the culture struggles. Stories help readers locate key problems or contradictions within a culture, because these same stories help the culture to deal with those problems. Contradictions have particular interest for political analysis because they represent the locus of problems and tendencies toward political transformation. Because contemporary citizens, perhaps especially Americans, often hesitate to present their deepest problems lest they seem "unpatriotic" or worse yet "unsuccessful," it is particularly helpful in American social analysis to turn to contradictions as a means of clarifying contemporary tensions.

To discover the contradictions that a particular narrative articulates requires the reader to take account of the entire story. By starting with oppositions in the first section of the analysis, the reader can connect the analysis of contradictions to the analysis of oppositions by asking what type of contradictions arise from particular oppositions. For example, in <u>Uncle Tom's Cabin</u>, the opposition between Tom and his owners comes out of a contradiction between slavery and Christian values and between political views about freedom and economic views about property in the form of slaves. This is manifested in the characters of Tom and the slave owners, for in the tale, Tom finds himself in the hands of progressively more cruel slave owners.

Four Structuralist Dimensions

In summary, the structuralist interpretation employed in this study involves four components. The reader first locates oppositions within the narrative and focuses the analysis by articulating the ways in which these characters or forces represent opposites. Second, the reader observes the metaphors that the narrative employs to discover what fields of discourse the narrative unites and how the story represents the oppositions. Third, the reader analyzes linear and vertical aspects of the plot to discover the central transformations that the narrative models. Fourth, the reader looks for the contradictions that the story articulates and that arise out of the oppositions that the story establishes. In this final step, it is important to remember that contradictions are not necessarily resolved but only set to rest for a moment, at the conclusion of the narrative. The story sets forth the problem, but not necessarily its solution.

These four analytical components inform each other. While it is best to proceed through them in the order presented, the analysis also can proceed in such a way that the reader can use the entire framework to embellish its components. For example, it may be that in seeking transformations the reader will become aware of additional metaphors. The plot analysis and the articulation of transformations and their agents helps to locate oppositions; statements about precise types of oppositions facilitate plot analysis; an analysis of metaphors involves the reader in closely observing not only what is said but in how it is said. The fourth step takes a more distant view of the narrative and makes explicit the contradictions that the narrative articulates. Here, the reader considers the oppositions, the metaphors that link fields of discourse within the narrative, and the transformations that constitute the transformative models the plot presents. Because all facets of the analysis view the narrative as a unified artistic expression, they respect the organic aesthetic features of the story. Because each facet invites the reader carefully to <u>observe</u> the story and its components within an analytical framework, a structuralist interpretation enables the reader to speak with confidence, with awareness of the epistemological commitments that make up the scientific strategy employed, about the narrative and its social-political message.

HERMENEUTICS: TRUTH, SCIENCE AND INTERPRETATION

The creative part of the analysis is by no means magical. Hermeneutics provides a clear explanation of how an interpretation can be creative in a way that encourages the subjective experience of the analyst to play a role in the objective enterprise. This role calls for more than inspiration, for the analysis both requires and encourages reflection on the immediate political community that the analyst inhabits. In this sense, hermeneutics insists that the analysis have a practical political purpose.[18]

To explain this process, I place the structuralist strategy into the tradition of philosophical hermeneutics. Philosophical hermeneutics studies humanity by studying its messages and language. For the social sciences, philosophical hermeneutics is the study of society by looking at the ways in which a society uses symbols and language to gain self-understanding. This includes its sense of what it means to be a person and how social life is connected to a cosmological order of things. While the term comes from Hermes, the messenger of the gods, the first practitioners of hermeneutics were biblical scholars who had a passionate desire to decipher messages that they felt were of supreme cosmological importance. They sought to decipher these messages because they were certain that, if they could do so accurately, they could use them as guides for their lives. But, they were not so certain about what the messages said. Faced with a vast range of interpretations, these early biblical scholars searched for a method that would explain how the inspired words of God could reasonably acquire so many different meanings. They decided that, in interpreting the Bible, it is necessary for all readers to see what it says to them in their historical circumstances. Such an act of interpretation requires careful reading and thought, so that the Bible's true message can be understood in a particular circumstance, which differs from biblical times. In proposing such a project, of course, these biblical scholars assumed that the Bible is written with such breadth of vision that it does, in fact, speak to everyone in every situation, if only it is properly understood.

Beyond its role in biblical interpretation, hermeneutics has offered a solution to a problem that social scientists have struggled with throughout the twentieth century. Looking for a solid vantage point from which to study society, modern social scientists have begun to turn toward hermeneutics. They have been moved to do so in the context of the acknowledged failure of positivism to provide a satisfactory basis for social understanding. Positivism in the social sciences searched for universal laws that determine human behavior and, hence, could be used to predict it. To find these laws they required a "value-free" method that would give them a "neutral" position from which to observe society. To their methodology, they assigned the role of disciplining inquiry so that their personal and cultural contexts would not influence their observations. Positivists also sought a language that would serve as a neutral tool, which would simply refer to observable phenomena in the world "out there." However, it soon became apparent that a value-free methodology could not be developed. It also became apparent to many that neither could a neutral language for describing social phenomena be found. Although some hoped that mathematics might provide the answer, even here the extramathematical language required in social scientific analysis, which was not neutral but culturally specific, destroyed the neutrality of the mathematical language. It became clear that scientists had to use particular languages with currency in particular cultures, if they were to speak about social phenomena, so that cultural bias was inescapable. In fact, even the most determined effort to escape it seemed to eliminate an important aspect of social reality, for much of what happened in society happened in the context of language. In addition, social actors themselves gave meanings to their own actions that were not entirely separable from action but instead were constitutive of it. It became necessary to conclude that social action occurs not only in the world "out there" but also in the world within each person's consciousness and that these two worlds are intimately tied together by language.

Because language and culture played such an important part in the critique of positivism, it was natural for workers in these fields to search for an alternative view of science and the apprehension of truth. The debate between subjectivity and objectivity signaled the wane of the positivists' hold on the social sciences. Ethnomethodology and phenomenology argue that what counts for the social understanding of an action is the actor's interpretation of the event. Thus to understand why Jake lifts his arm and moves it back and forth, requires knowing whether he intends to wave to someone or if he intends to shake a fly off his arm. However, this solution merely shifts the focus from the "world out there," the outside observer of action, to the "world in here," the actor. It shifts the purposes of social research from the positivists' goal of finding universal laws on the basis of which to predict behavior to searching for an understanding of action that focuses exclusively on the self-understanding of the actors. While this is fine if Jake is honest or if his self-understanding is sound--he knows what he is actually doing. However, it has distinct limits of its own.

Clifford Geertz, an American anthropologist, introduced a different approach, drawing upon European continental philosophy. He argued that anthropology did not so much describe culture as build bridges between cultures; it explained one culture to another.[19] In his perspective, a common understanding rather than a set of universal laws motivated inquiry, and this common understanding could be found by searching for similarities and differences among societies. This meant that by studying another culture the anthropologist could gain more concrete knowledge of his or her own culture. Hence, understanding required learning simultaneously about the self and the other: "Bent over his own chips, stones, and common plants, the anthropologist broods, too, upon the true and insignificant, glimpsing in it, or so he thinks, fleetingly and insecurely, the disturbing, changeful image of himself."[20]

Levi-Strauss, whose earlier works demonstrate the influence of positivism and its search for the one right answer, moves toward a similar perspective in his later works:

> For if the final aim of anthropology is to contribute to a better knowledge of objectified thought and its mechanisms, it is in the last resort immaterial whether in this book the thought processes of the South American Indians take shape through the medium of my thought, or whether mine take place through the medium of theirs. What matters is that the human mind, regardless of the identity of those who happen to be giving it expression, should display an

increasingly intelligible structure as a result of the doubly reflexive forward movement of two thought processes acting one upon the other, either of which can in turn provide the spark or tinder whose conjunction will shed light on both.[21]

While building bridges between cultures is a noble enterprise, the question is: How can it be done? Is it possible to build bridges and still retain commitments to scientific objectivity or must science be compromised in order to gain intercultural community? Philosophical hermeneutics argues that authentic truth requires an awareness of one's own historical and cultural context, which turns out to mean that the acquisition of knowledge about another culture changes the person who undertakes it. Indeed, such change marks the genuine truth seeker. Committing themselves to both scientific objectivity and authentic understanding, Paul Ricoeur and Hans-Georg Gadamer explain how it is possible both to build community across different cultures and to be governed by rigorous requirements for truth.

Their approach takes two unusual turns. First, it argues for focusing on language as the medium in which community and order is made, maintained, and changed. Ricoeur, for example, tells us that language rules us. In <u>The Rule of Metaphor</u>, he presents a sophisticated argument about how language shapes the lives of people from their everyday practices to written law. Second, this approach invites us to see social analysis as play. Because language is also the medium through which social analysis takes place, it is important that language itself be free, or more precisely, that speakers find in language not only discipline and focus (limitation) but also creativity and freedom (a means of transcending limitations). The best way to understand this point of view is to consider that meanings, shared understandings, emerge in the to-and-fro process of communication between two persons or two cultures. In the case of readers and writers, the reader tries out different interpretations against the language system that he or she shares with the writer to see which one fits. This language system is a circuit of communication. Good communication requires both reader and writer to share a common language system if the circuit is to be complete.[22] For example, English teachers insist that their students learn some Elizabethan English before claiming that Shakespeare has nothing to say to them. Readers need to work at acquiring or appropriating the language system of the writer in order to understand what they read. Because the circuit of communication can involve many different persons representing diverse perspectives, a variety of interpretations can arise. This does not mean that communication never takes place. It does mean that the ambiguity within language both presents a problem for precise communication and facilitates creativity. A narrative that relies on a complex system of meanings involves an additional layer of ambiguity, which is both its strength, in that more is said, and its weakness, in that it becomes more difficult to fix the meaning of what is said into a single model. Even so, none of this means that a narrative or an ambiguous phrase is equally open to any and all interpretations.

Paul Ricoeur explains that the "surplus of meaning"[23] which narratives carry makes it possible for a story to have different meanings in various contexts. Yet, the range of admissible interpretation is also fixed and closed because interpretations must be tested against the story itself. If a reading is to qualify as an authentic interpretation, the reader must find commonalities between his or her world and the story's world. Like Geertz's cultural anthropology, the reader then bridges two cultures, the reader's and the narrative's. The dialogue can take place between persons from two different cultures, in the ordinary sense of the term, or between the culture of scientific analysis and the culture of everyday life. For Levi-Strauss, it occurs at both levels.[24]

Hans-Georg Gadamer explains how this kind of dialogue affects community formation. In Truth and Method, he argues that language lays the foundation for tradition and culture and, thus, occupies the central place in the social construction of knowledge. In this context, he develops an image of communication that describes how meaning takes place. He uses the metaphor of play to describe language and learning:

> The player himself knows that play is only play and exists in a world which is determined by the seriousness of purposes. But he does not know this in such a way that, as a player, he actually intends this relation to seriousness. Play fulfils its purpose only if the player loses himself in his play. It is not that relation to seriousness which directs us away from play,

> but only seriousness in playing makes the play wholly play. One who doesn't take the game seriously is a spoilsport. The mode of being of play does not allow the player to behave towards play as if it were an object. The player knows very well what play is, and that what he is doing is 'only a game'; but he does not know what exactly he 'knows' in knowing that.[25]

What Gadamer demonstrates in this passage is that play or expanded consciousness requires both a commitment to the rules of the game (knowing the game very well and taking it seriously) and a creative impulse, which does not know what is to take place next and which delights in action and response, the to-and-fro that transcends rules. All of this moves toward delight in an interplay of forces that is motivated by the satisfactions of play itself, of staying with it. A social analyst might well speak of this as "staying in the community." Gadamer makes this point to conclude his discussion of play: "In each case what is intended is the to-and-fro movement which is not tied to any goal which would bring it to an end."[26]

To apply this to a storyteller and reader, one might imagine a dialogue in which storyteller and reader find a common ground for understanding. In the case of a reader, where dialogue cannot take place, the reader tests an interpretation against the whole text to find this common ground. Both storyteller and reader submit to some rules and structures that guide the process. The reader then undertakes to use those rules to discover the particular structures that engage the storyteller in the story. Narrative form itself provides such a common ground for understanding. While stories may differ, all cultures appear to have stories, and all cultures apparently have ways of listening carefully and interpreting the stories they tell.

Playful Analysis

The playfulness that Gadamer finds in intellectual pursuits and that Levi-Strauss alludes to in his quest for the human mind has both an open and a closed dimension. Play requires some structure and rules. Even child's play, which may be the most open, has in it a rule system that careful observers can articulate. Anthropologists extract the rules of a culture for their audiences. The question for narrative analysis is: Can one combine rigorous rule analysis with the open imaginative playfulness that an aesthetic narrative experience elicits? Can the rigors of scientific observation blend with the creative energy of humanistic inquiry?

Paul Ricoeur provides an answer to this question by proposing a marriage between structuralism and hermeneutics.[27] His response to the problem of conflicting interpretations is to argue that structuralism supplies empirical scientific values (distance, methodological procedure, and objectivity) while philosophical hermeneutics supplies humanist values (reflection, ethical concern with life decisions, and connections between the analyst and the subjects of study, or subjectivity). He explains that structuralism seeks knowledge of others, of persons outside the analyst's community, while hermeneutics seeks knowledge of the self and one's own tradition. The former requires distant vision; the latter close vision. The former expands horizons; the latter interprets a transmitted tradition, which necessitates intimate knowledge of a particular position on the horizon. Hence, the two modes of inquiry complement each other. He explains:

> The structuralist explanation bears (1) on an unconscious system which (2) is constituted by differences and oppositions (by signifying variations) (3) independently of the observer. The interpretation of a transmitted sense consists in (1) the conscious recovery of (2) an overdetermined symbolic substratum by (3) an interpreter who places himself in the same semantic field as the one he is understanding and thus enters the "hermeneutic circle."[28]

While this sketches the connections between structuralism and interpretation, it does not explicitly describe its epistemological basis. A key aspect of this knowledge enterprise is the relationship between the researcher and the researched subject. Empiricism argues for distance; humanism argues for empathy and intimacy. Ricoeur explains that the interpretation of a story requires both and, therefore, entails a tension between them. Thus, he does not choose between subjectivity and objectivity but instead calls for an integration of these two modes of inquiry. While the American culture tends to view narrative interpretation as a quest for the truth <u>behind</u> the story, Ricoeur offers a different view, which represents an important shift in how to apprehend the truth of a story:

> What must be understood in a story is not first the one who speaks behind the text, but that which is spoken about, the <u>subject matter of the text</u>, that is, the sort of world that the work lays out in front of the text. . . . Thus, there is no question of denying the subjective character of understanding in which explanation is completed. It is always someone who hears, makes his own, appropriates the meaning.[29]

Ricoeur explains that the relationship between the reader and the storyteller is not that the reader, or analyst, uncovers a hidden meaning "behind" the text but rather that the reader constructs a meaning "in front" of the text. Meaning is not something buried by a clever writer and discovered by a wily critic. Rather, the reader constructs meaning in terms of his or her own cultural-historical context. The story speaks <u>to</u> someone (the reader, the analyst) who plays a vital role in the communication process. This does not mean, however, that the reader makes the text say whatever he or she wishes. An authentic interpretation, the truth, requires that the reader see the text as both open and closed. Taking account of Ricoeur's observation and the hermeneutic interest in the messages of texts leads to three steps in the development of a structural interpretation: (1) pre-understanding, (2) explanation, (3) understanding.

Pre-Understanding

The pre-understanding from an interpretive perspective, is the historical and cultural context that the analyst or reader brings to the text. No analyst comes to a text with a tabula rasa, a blank slate. Instead, he or she brings the experiences of a particular culture along with its values and technologies. For example, an Elizabethan English reader approaches a text from a point of view quite different from that of a twentieth-century American. A post-Mao Chinese views a text differently from the way a Russian Stalinist views it, and each of these differs from the point of view of an American feminist. Each of these perspectives interprets a story differently. The interpretive approach values these differences, believing that the fact that the reader brings his or her own cultural historical perspective to the interpretation of a text makes it possible for the text <u>to speak</u> to the problems that confront a particular society. Jurgen Habermas moves toward this perspective when he argues that all knowledge comes out of particular interests and, therefore, is necessarily value-laden.[30] Gadamer's philosophical approach gives such "interests" or values a positive role in inquiry, by explaining that precisely such cultural commitments make it possible for research to address practical social problems.[31] A primary component of an interpretation of a story or a social action is the language in which it is expressed. Gadamer argues that language establishes a worldview that embraces traditional values and established ways of being; language constitutes reality. Hence, the selection of a language in which to formulate an interpretation constitutes a "bias." It is a bias in the sense that it slants the interpretation toward one culture and gives its values priority: "For language is not only an object in our hands, it is the reservoir of tradition and the medium in and through which we exist and perceive our world."[32] Of course, when Gadamer speaks about bias in this way, he is reversing our normal understanding of the word. Ordinarily, we think of it as carrying a pejorative force. But Gadamer argues that a bias is in fact a perspective, and that perspective is essential to understanding. Hence, the existence of bias or perspective is not a problem but an essential part of the solution to the problem of truth. It enables an interpretation to <u>speak</u> to a people, to address their values and problems. What an interpretation finally reveals is not only the subject under study but the analyst's own perspective, which itself becomes more clear as awareness increases of the values that shape his or her pre-understanding.

Explanation

The second step in the process is a search for an explanation that makes sense out of the story or text. In the narrative analysis proposed in this book, the analyst makes use of the structuralist strategy in order to explain the story. Structuralism offers a device that analysts can use to distance themselves from their pre-understandings, so that they can genuinely confront an alternative perspective or culture. This genuine confrontation means reading the story carefully and taking seriously the images and ideas the story presents. It requires the analyst to set aside his or her own perspective to follow a different point of view. Thus, it relies upon the scientific skills of distance and helps the analyst acquire an objective mode of inquiry. However, at the same time, the analyst, motivated by issues from his or her pre-understanding, endeavors to use that "foreign" culture or "foreign" perspective to discover fresh solutions to the problems his or her society confronts. Thus the pre-understanding and explanation form a dialectic, or a to-and-fro, in which the analyst moves forward on two trajectories. He or she learns more about the other by focusing on the other's perspective and more about the self in light of that "foreign" perspective. This process clarifies the social context that the researcher inhabits as well as the "foreign" culture or perspective that is the immediate occasion for inquiry.

Understanding

The third step is to come to an understanding or an interpretation of the story or text. Having confronted the foreign culture or perspective, the analyst utilizes the tension between his or her pre-understanding and the explanation to construct a synthesis of these two perspectives. Incorporating elements from both perspectives, he or she attempts to find a resolution to problems of interpretation. By doing so, the analyst appropriates the foreign culture or perspective and makes it his or her own. Because of this appropriation, analysts can experience changes in themselves. Such a criterion distinguishes this approach from empirical approaches that seek new knowledge of "subject matter" but neither anticipate nor welcome a new self-understanding in the experience of the researcher.

Through analyzing stories, then, readers expect to broaden their horizons. They expect to experience some change in their own social political perspectives in the light of those stories. In each case, the interpretation is the product of this new perspective and, hence, the interpretation serves to bridge those who share the reader's perspective with the story's perspective. The interpretation helps the reader to understand the story or appropriate it into his or her own social political experience. This means that the final goal of interpretation is to enable the story to speak to a people, of which the analyst is a representative. The interpretation is designed for a people in a particular cultural-historical context, the analyst's context. It aspires to bridge the analyst's context with that of the storyteller to make

the communication complete. If, as is the case with
the stories in this book, the analyst focuses on
politics, the story will speak to those who have an
interest in power and how power shapes public activity
and in the ongoing problems involved in creating
communities, especially in modern America.

3
Down the Rabbit Hole:
Listening to Stories

> In another moment down went Alice after it, never once considering how in the world she was to get out again.
> The rabbit-hole went straight on like a tunnel for some way, and then dipped suddenly down, so suddenly that Alice had not a moment to think about stopping herself before she found herself falling down what seemed to be a very deep well.
>
> Lewis Carroll
Alice in Wonderland

Understanding a political culture resembles Alice's journey. It requires becoming submerged in a new political reality; it begins with a leap very much like Alice's leap down the rabbit hole. The journey of these tales leads to two places: Essex, a Midwestern suburb, and Kumu Aina, a rural community in Hawaii.

First, I shall briefly sketch these communities to show in what ways they represent two different cultures. While they reveal many cultural differences, I shall emphasize four aspects of their cultural diversity: (1) identity and ethnicity, (2) historical institutions and traditions, (3) economic class, and (4) geographic location and resources. Then, I shall describe the context in which the community leaders told me their stories.

TWO AMERICAN CULTURES: ESSEX AND KUMU AINA

The name of a community indicates something of its character, its identity. Even though I have changed the names of the communities, I have retained in the fictionalized names some of the cultural features of the original. The name Essex connects this town with its English heritage. Some of its citizens have even conducted a pilgrimage to visit Essex, England. While this articulates a wistful look to a British tradition, the town simultaneously points proudly to its American frontier spirit. In speaking of the town, leaders retell the tale of settling the area, clearing the land, and developing a modern "civilization." For that matter, the pilgrimage to earlier British roots also serves as a reminder of how far they have come and re-enacts their pioneer spirit of adventure. The Anglo-Saxon heritage shapes the town's local culture, which blends the British heritage with the American spirit, but the blending of cultures does not stop there. Essex citizens like to see themselves as members of a multiethnic community, often reminding outsiders that there is a large Jewish population and that even a few Blacks reside in the community. They claim fondly that their community is open to all ethnic groups, even though the representation of ethnic minorities is quite small in comparison with surrounding communities. Leaders point to the representation of Protestant, Jewish, and Roman Catholic clergy in public celebrations as evidence of their cultural diversity. Tolerance for different religions and ethnic groups is a publicly articulated value, although it most often manifests itself as respect between the large Jewish minority and the White Anglo-Saxon Protestant majority. In Essex, these two groups, while representing different religious and cultural heritages, for the most part represent a single upper-middle-class culture, which may well facilitate the genuine understanding and respect that does exist. Essex has a reputation in the surrounding communities as a homogenized, distinctly upper-middle-class town.

In Hawaii, place names are often Hawaiian and indicate geographic configurations. This suggests a special relationship between natural phenomena and the daily lives of citizens. To emphasize the importance of land in the Hawaiian tradition, I chose the name Kumu Aina for this community. In the Hawaiian language, kumu means teacher and aina "land or earth"; hence, the name suggests that the land teaches. Kumu Aina citizens, especially those connected to the native Hawaiian tradition, explain that the land is an elder who teaches about life. They see land as a vital spirit that gives life and deserves recognition and respect. It is not a resource for, but a source of, life. Although the Hawaiian culture plays a major role in this community, Kumu Aina's culture is also shaped by Asian, Euro-American, Black American, Samoan, and other Pacific Island traditions. The stories presented in this book come from contemporary Kumu Aina, which represents a blend of all of these traditions, even though it takes its name and a good part of its identity from the native Hawaiian tradition. To remind the reader that I am not speaking about the native Hawaiian culture itself but rather the culture of Kumu Aina, I have not used the Hawaiian diacritical marks in the name Kumu Aina. Kumu Aina represents a community that blends a diverse cultural composition with a superimposed American political culture in which English is the primary language. However, Hawaiian words and the Hawaiian dialect of English (often called pidgin English in Hawaii) play prominent roles in oral communication.

Identity and Ethnicity

In comparison to Kumu Aina, Essex has a homogeneous ethnic population. Citizens are predominately Euro-Americans and even though Essex citizens like to emphasize the multiethnic (melting pot) quality of the town; diversity is described primarily in religious terms--Protestants, Jews, and Catholics--rather than in terms of ethnic categories. While some citizens remind outsiders that there are Blacks living in Essex, none make the claim that Black culture in any way shapes town politics. In contrast, the cultural diversity of Kumu Aina is global in scope, involving a blend of Asians, Euro-Americans, and Pacific Islanders. Some 48 percent of its citizens consider themselves Hawaiian or part Hawaiian; 16 percent identify themselves as Caucasian (Euro-American, largely of British or Portuguese ancestry); 12 percent consider themselves Filipino, and 8 percent claim Japanese ethnicity. Other groups represented include 2 percent Samoans, 1 percent each Korean and Chinese; and 12 percent of the population's constituents identify themselves by a mix of ethnicities.

Historical Institutions and Traditions

Essex's Historical Society begins the political history of Essex with its founding in 1908, which took place when the surrounding metropolitan area tried to incorporate the area. Citizens "fought" this and established an independent municipality. They then formed an Essex Improvement Association to induce "desirable" people to buy property and reside in the area. Citizens place a high value on independence and property. In this sense they represent the American liberal political tradition, which emphasizes self-rule and casts local government primarily in the role of providing law and order to maintain the security of private property. Another central value is education. Today, Essex advertises its excellent school system as a means of attracting new residents. The Essex Historical Society underscores the centrality of education by explaining that the little red school house erected in 1875 on Main Street was the first public structure erected in the community, even before it was incorporated as a municipality in 1908.

Today, the City Hall, built in 1952, provides office space for the mayor, police, auditor, and city council. The mayor, who is chosen in a nonpartisan election, receives a salary. His administrative duties include giving careful attention to police work, and he even monitors police calls to keep a finger on the city's pulse. City council members, who serve in an advisory capacity, receive only a token salary. Each year they vote to donate their salaries to the city. Citizens point with pride to the fact that city elections are free of partisan politics.

Essex's east side borders on an "inner city" community composed of working-class Blacks. Fundamental differences between this affluent White community and its less affluent Black neighbors is immediately apparent. The neighboring Black community has homes and apartment complexes which have very small green areas outside of them and the street, sidewalk, and living areas are composed of a continuous landscape of concrete. The crowded conditions and accompanying social stress are easily seen by the iron bars and boarded over windows which protect the street lined merchants from preditors. Many buildings lack good repair and their appearance suggests the frustration of their occupants. On the other hand, many Essex homes are incarnations of <u>Better Homes and Gardens</u> and the large old trees that line city streets provide a cool green summer cover.

For Essex citizens, nature appears in abundance in the form of planted trees and ample yards with colorful summer gardens. The town could easily serve as a set for the usual television version of the "typical" American family, a version that nearly always locates the "typical" in the special forms and styles of the White upper-middle-class. In fact, the citizens of Essex understand their community in precisely these terms, delighting in describing it as an incarnation of the spirit of America.

Two factors that the citizens of Essex see as hallmarks of success are hard work and education. They see themselves as hard-working people and inculcate the value of hard work in their children. Education, in turn, is both a source of necessary knowledge and skills and an arena in which the value of work can be realized early in the lives of their children. The town has three elementary schools, which divide the town into three geographical areas, each with a slightly different level of affluence. There is one intermediate school and one high school. Essex citizens claim that their educational system is one of the nation's best. Fully 85 percent of its high school graduates go on to college and the town itself also hosts a small Protestant liberal arts college, founded in 1875, the same year in which the little red schoolhouse was built.

Appearances are important in Essex. The town closely regulates private home care and maintenance in order to "keep up appearances,"[1] and an Association for Essex Civic Development monitors the physical appearance of the town, bringing pressure to bear on citizens and officials in the interest of strict norm enforcement. Residency in the town in some respects resembles membership in a country club. It also has economic currency in the surrounding community, providing residents with a "good address." Hence, control over appearances serves not only aesthetic, but also economic values.

The Essex Celebrations Association annually sponsors six events for the entire community. The Fourth of July celebration articulates the political culture of the community. It begins with an Independence Day Parade, designed to demonstrate "Americanism." The afternoon celebration consists of games of various kinds, and the evening climaxes the day with speeches followed by a fireworks display.

Traditionally, the grand finale is a flaming celestial replica of the red, white, and blue flag. The Essex Celebrations Association also sponsors an Easter Egg Hunt, a Flag Day Observance, a Christmas Tree, a Holiday Decorating Contest, and a Newcomer's Party. These rituals serve as occasions for the town to articulate its cultural spirit. Religious organizations provide another center for community activity. Four Protestant churches represent three denominations. Two synagogues organize Jewish religious activity. Community celebrations are ecumenical, including leadership by Protestants, Jews, and Catholics.

The tree-lined streets, the orchestrated community celebrations, and the country-club setting articulate the importance of "order." As the citizens of Essex see it, "order" represents the proper setting for the pursuit of freedom and happiness. The town has standards that its civil and religious institutions define and enforce; but, within the orderly world thus created and maintained, they celebrate freedom and independence. Private family life provides the ideal location for the full experience of freedom, and the citizens boast that this municipality offers an excellent environment for raising a family.

Kumu Aina citizens trace the history of their community back to ancient Hawaii. Heiaus (temples) remain in Kumu Aina and mark the presence of this ancient tradition. Although the heiaus are not necessarily identified with public markers, local citizens know where they are and respect their presence. They set the tone for the Hawaiian songs that one hears while walking along the beach or in the streets in the evening. A second and more recent layer of architectural marks on the land are the remnants of plantations. The sugar plantation founded in 1879 by a Euro-American man, who married a native Hawaiian woman, brought many citizens to Kumu Aina. The founder had access to the kinship ties of a large Hawaiian family as well as his own kinship ties, and he had knowledge of both Western market practices and the Anglo-American legal system. While the plantation helped to develop the community, it also created problems. Plantation life provided uncreative drudging work and its use of water reduced water access for other farmers, who had been tending the land Hawaiian-style for generations before the plantation's arrival. The plantation, maximally satisfying its own cultivation needs, diverted water away from the taro farmers. Taro is the root used to make poi, a staple in the Hawaiian diet. Small farmers suffered. The plantation owners drilled their own wells and so freed themselves from any control, as well as from any payment, for water use. Not surprisingly, this produced tension between the White plantation owners and the Hawaiian farmers.

When the plantation closed in 1947, the developer who bought the land began to attract citizens who were looking for either a rural life or an inexpensive home. These early development years meant many hardships for citizens. Kumu Aina High School students collecting oral histories describe the period as a time that made for "roughened hands and broken backs."[2] While, in some respects, this might be compared to the frontier spirit admired by the Essex citizens, it is a frontier that acknowledges itself as forged amid the tensions of two cultural demands: Euro-American culture with its Anglican-based law and American ties, and the Hawaiian tradition with its own culture, including its own legal tradition. This represents a pattern in the displacement of the indigenous native Hawaiians, which differs from the displacement of American Indians on the U.S. mainland. In Kumu Aina, native Hawaiians were not militarily displaced but forced off their own land by alien groups of Euro-Americans bent on developing a system of industrial agriculture in Hawaii, which tended to monopolize water and land, making it impossible for native Hawaiians to continue their own agricultural system. The traditional system of subsistence agriculture had made Hawaii a rich food source, able to provide for the nutritional needs of its people. With plantations and other Euro-American land-use practices this self-sufficiency disappeared and the lives and values of native Hawaiians were correspondingly threatened, or worse.

Three social institutions transfer the traditions of this community to its citizens. The first is the formal educational system. Education in Hawaii is controlled by a centralized state system. In Kumu Aina, there are four elementary schools, two intermediate schools, and two high schools. Two cultural centers, supported primarily by grants and donations, teach Hawaiian language, arts, sciences, and music, offering specifically Hawaiian cultural education to citizens. A number of private hula schools provide additional education in the Hawaiian cultural heritage and its religious traditions. The public school, some counseling centers, and some religious schools offer additional education in the Hawaiian culture as a means of addressing their students' interests and needs.

Religion provides a second institution for passing on traditions to children and newcomers. Sixteen churches serve as religious and educational centers. Two Roman Catholic churches are well attended and the Jehovah Witnesses provide a similarly pronounced presence. Public community meetings often open and close with prayers. Many Hawaiians maintain practices from their religious-cultural tradition, and spirituality in general is highly regarded within the community as a mark of virtue and a genuine source of strength and power. Hawaiian spirituality is characterized by a worldview that integrates culture and nature. Citizens tend to think of themselves as working with, rather than attempting to control, nature. Religious experience plays a role in public life and Catholic charismatic spirituality, along with other mystical religious movements, finds a receptive audience. Spirituality also plays an important role in daily events. For example, one evening a young woman had a problem. Her group had planned a large political rally at a community center, but she discovered, hours before the event, that the persons controlling the center, who were native Hawaiians, had decided against giving permission for the use of the facility. The young woman did not know what to do and hastily called a few of the organizers together to figure out a solution. All were inexperienced, discouraged, and ready to give up the project. An elderly woman, who is one of the primary native Hawaiian leaders in Kumu Aina, appeared quite unexpectedly at the hastily called meeting, saying that "something told her" that her assistance was needed. A woman in her sixties, she was nearly six feet tall with long dark hair tied up on top of her head so that it seemed almost like a crown. Her flowing floor-length dress, the customary muu-muu, gave a regal quality to her presence. But more than this, her manifest sense of the importance of the group's political purposes and of the needs of each group member brought immediate relief and hope to the group. She had come to mediate the problem, and she did so while respecting the needs of the organization and without discrediting the center that had cancelled the event. Her explanation about what had prompted her to come into their midst and perform that role demonstrates the centrality of spiritual discourse in Kumu Aina.

The family is a third institution that communicates cultural traditions. Kinship ties are universally important elements in identity construction, but the kinship network of Kumu Aina goes beyond "blood" to encompass friends and "adopted kin." Through kinship ties a network of extended families forms a basic component of the community, each such family acknowledging such responsibilities as sharing food, resources, childcare, and emotional support.

A "Satellite City Hall" of the Honolulu city government has offices in the area and provides services. In some ways this satellite, run by Kumu Aina citizens, provides a buffer against the encroachments of Honolulu's bureaucratic life style. An Interagency Council combines the social services of government and churches to provide a united community front for seeking funds from government and church agencies located in downtown Honolulu. Such coordination allows for a cooperative approach to problem solving. In formal government terms, however, Kumu Aina, unlike Essex, is not a separate municipality. Formally, it is simply one part of the City and County of Honolulu, a single jurisdiction covering the entire island of Oahu. However, both the residents of Kumu Aina and the general population of the island think of it as a separate area. Surrounded by farm lands, mountains, and the sea it presents the image of a distinct and separate place, an image quite opposite to that of Essex, which enjoys a separate government system but which is closely surrounded on all four sides by a large metropolis. Essex's government is separate, even if the town itself is geographically contained by another city with its own government. Kumu Aina is geographically separate from the urban center of Honolulu but is formally subject to its government. What these two communities share is a reputation for being genuine communities with their own special life styles, cultural practices. Both have the reputation of being tightly knit communities where citizens feel strong bonds with one another.

Economic Class

Essex citizens take pride in describing themselves as upper-middle-class. The town is financially independent and receives its revenue from small business and inheritance taxes, which supply funds amply enough to maintain a town country club that includes a large swimming pool, recreation area, tennis courts, and meeting rooms. Essex is "exclusive," and only its residents can use these country club facilities. In their self-understood upper-middle-class status, upper emphasizes their desire to represent themselves as hard workers who have succeeded financially (better than most), while middle suggests that, even so, they are part of mainstream America and proud of it. Theirs is a "balanced" and good life, in the "middle," where it should be.

Since it is not a separate municipality, Kumu Aina must depend on "outside" government sources--the City and County of Honolulu--for revenue and social services. Many citizens in Kumu Aina have a hard time financially; they are predominately working-class citizens with a median income of about $12,500, one of the lowest on Oahu. The highest median income for an area of comparable population size on the island is $26,000.[3] Among residents of the island, Kumu Aina has the reputation of being an economically depressed area. It invokes images of poverty and "welfare" in the minds of "outsiders" and is even seen as a dangerous place with a high concentration of violence, even though other areas have higher crime rates. Many Kumu Aina residents prefer to keep their community separate from the tourist trade and its accompanying life style, hoping to maintain Kumu Aina's rural and more traditional "local," or Hawaiian, life style. In fact, they are not anxious to have "outsiders," either people from Honolulu or tourists, coming into the area to spend time. Many residents resent the negative reputation accorded Kumu Aina by surrounding areas. They do not consider the community "dangerous" but describe it as "tough" or "strong." The politics this creates is one of protest against the urban areas's efforts to impose its own model on the local community. Residents feel that Kumu Aina has its own "special culture," which differs from the dominant culture of Honolulu, and they feel safer there than in Waikiki, the major tourist area on the island. There is ample evidence to confirm the correctness of their impressions.

Since Kumu Aina has a park with tennis courts, a meeting hall, and a swimming beach, it offers recreational services similar to those of Essex. However, unlike those in Essex, these are formally open to anyone, even though "outsiders" are expected to defer to community standards of conduct. This is due in part to the fact that Kumu Aina is not a separate government municipality, but even if it were, state law requires that the beaches be open to all. Kumu Aina's negative reputation with many "outsiders," however, tends to inhibit them from visiting in the area and in some respects constructs a barrier similar to that which secures Essex against what it understands as alien encroachment by its own "outsiders." Both communities have a strong sense of themselves as separate cohesive units, each held together by a strong core of similar values

Geography and Resources

Essex enjoys the sharply differentiated seasons characteristic of the Midwest. Situated on 2.4 square miles of flat land, it is totally surrounded by an urban metropolis. Citizens describe their population as 4,800 families, which underscores their pride in Essex as a place for families. Its total population is 14,250. Travel to other areas of the U.S. is easy. Highways, railroads, bus routes, and airlines radiate abundantly in all directions. Few empty lots are yet to be occupied by homes and there is no possibility of territorial expansion, so the population is expected to remain fairly constant. Essex is a place of residence not work. There are few businesses, and most residents hold white-collar jobs in the surrounding metropolitan area.

The residents of Kumu Aina live on an island separated by some 3,000 miles of ocean from the mainland United States. It is expensive for citizens to visit other states and by no means a casual weekend activity, as it frequently is for their counterparts in Essex. For most members of this community, even interisland travel within the state of Hawaii is forbiddingly expensive. The climate is constant throughout the year: the coldest month averaging 72 degrees and the warmest 80. The refreshing trade winds maintain what on the mainland would be regarded as a pleasant summer all year long. The geography is spectacular with an expansive ocean lining one side and resident's homes locating themselves in two valleys that stretch from the sea to the mountains that frame the area on the other side. The mountains rise abruptly from the valley floors, and from nearly every point in Kumu Aina one can catch sight of their sharp purple-hued peaks. In their higher reaches, the valleys between the mountains are covered with lush tropical undergrowth while the lower elevations, which experience less rainfall, are substantially less rich in natural vegetation but provide rich land for irrigated agriculture.

Kumu Aina citizens have important food sources within their own area. Forty percent of its 38,000 acres is zoned for agriculture and another 40 percent for conservation. The year-round growing season makes backyard gardens a continuous source for food, and increasingly citizens are utilizing this option. There is also a significant group of full-time farmers in the community, deriving all or most of their sustenance directly from agriculture. While a number of the 28,000 residents live on farmland, much of the land contains steep mountains and is uninhabitable. Most residents, as in Essex, live on small lots. In Kumu Aina, however, the homes are surrounded not by a metropolis but rather by farmland and spectacular natural features--the sea and mountains. Citizens maintain an intimate relationship with the natural elements that surround them. They speak especially about their relationship to the ocean. For example, when they talk about fishing they are apt to explain that the ocean is their refrigerator. Hence, they admonish people to be wary of taking out more than they need at one time lest the fish spoil. Fishing is a means of supporting life, and for them fish should be used as a source of food, not abused by being made an object of sport. For many Kumu Aina citizens this relationship to nature is an ethical issue. It requires a citizen to establish the proper relationship to the ocean and to the life forms it holds. Neither the ocean nor the fish are to be understood as objects, things to be exploited, but are beings that deserve and demand respect.

Summary of Cultural Differences

Measured against these four dimensions Kumu Aina and Essex clearly represent contrasting cultures. First, Kumu Aina's cultural heritage draws heavily on the native Hawaiian tradition, while combining an ethnic diversity that spans Europe, Asia, and the Pacific Islands. Essex draws from a European heritage and its ethnic composition is radically less heterogeneous. Essex likes to see itself as embodying a pioneer spirit that civilized and cultivated the land. Kumu Aina sees itself as a community that stands in almost a kinship relationship to the land and sea. Second, the heritage of Essex draws on its British roots, and its institutions support a Euro-American culture with an emphasis on the community's independence and self-reliance, even as it embodies the "typical" American community. Kumu Aina sees itself as a Hawaiian community that draws on a multiethnic heritage, emphasizing Pacific Island and Asian traditions. Its institutions regard friendship highly and its network of interdependent, interfamilial, interpersonal relationships makes this community especially strong. Third, Kumu Aina is a working-class community, struggling to survive economically, while Essex is an upper-middle-class community, whose members are economically comfortable. Fourth, Kumu Aina is a rural community, geographically separate from the United States, while Essex is a suburban community, located in the center of the United States, in the Midwest.

COLLECTING STORIES

This project's purpose was to learn about the political culture of these two different communities by listening carefully to the stories each community enjoys. But, how can one select particular stories from the vast array of stories that have currency in the community?[4] To find narratives that would directly address the political culture of these two communities, I collected the stories of community leaders. In order to discover who served as leaders within this community, I asked some one-hundred citizens in each community for a list of both male and female leaders. From this list, I selected the ten women and ten men most frequently mentioned and asked these community leaders to grant me an interview.[5] By selecting leaders, I was able to talk with people who had a good working model of the community's political culture. I asked them to tell me stories, either fictional ones or actual historical ones, that for them illustrated good community relationships. From these leaders, I obtained the stories that form the data base for this analysis.[6] From the in-depth taped interviews, I took the longest stories for the analysis.[7] Since Kumu Aina was a less familiar culture to me, I returned to each person interviewed in order to discuss my analysis of their narratives and to make adjustments where needed.

Since, in both Essex and Kumu Aina, community leaders are proud of their community and think that it has something distinct to offer other communities, I was able to approach my interviewees as teachers. Though their stories, they taught me about the politics of everyday life within their community. But, these stories also contain insights into American politics in general, because each of these communities is trying to establish and maintain a good and just political life in the over-arching context of the American political tradition and its institutional structures.

Both communities think highly of stories. In Essex, the historical society collects oral histories from citizens and, through these narratives, tells Essex citizens about their own history and their own values. In Kumu Aina, citizens like to sit around and "talk story," sharing personal experiences that reveal insights into life. Because story plays a important role in the lives of citizens in both of these communities, it made sense to these leaders that I wished to understand the political knowledge that their communities had to offer by gathering stories illustrating good community relationships.

While I have changed names in the stories to mask the identities of narrators, I have accurately represented their ethnicity and sex. The following chapters contain the stories and my analysis of them, which applies the structuralist interpretation described in previous chapters in order to discover the worldviews that the narratives articulate and the political knowledge to which they give witness.

I have placed the stories into six groups, so as to show how each of the two communities addresses each of three fundamental political questions. First, how does the community construct its identity; how does it establish bonds among its members and boundaries between its members and those "outside" the community? Second, how do citizens confront and change the political institutions that shape their lives? Third, how does the community maintain a balance between giving its members freedom and maintaining its own integrity and unity?

4
Essex's Political Community:
Bonds and Boundaries

> "Curiouser and curiouser!" cried Alice (she was so much surprised, that for the moment she quite forgot how to speak good English). "Now I'm opening out like the largest telescope that ever was!"
>
> Lewis Carroll
> Alice in Wonderland

Once down the rabbit hole, Alice discovers two realities. In one, she grows to nine feet tall. Suddenly, she shrinks to two feet and finds herself swimming in a salty pool of tears created only moments before by the eyes in her nine foot high body. Reflecting on her newly acquired tininess, she realizes that the large animal, which at first she imagines to be a walrus, is in fact a mouse. Like Alice, by taking different perspectives, we can gain a richer understanding of the social worlds we inhabit; and, more important, exploring a new social realm sharpens our awareness of our own perspective. Fundamental to understanding politics is a keen appreciation of alternative perspectives.

A basic component of any political perspective is how people come to acquire a collective sense of themselves as a people, how they acquire an identity as a group and what that identity represents to them. The question of who "we" are is the most fundamental political question, because not only does it define the community or political unit, it also allocates qualities and goals to that community. These qualities and goals make up its political philosophy, which shapes its ethical commitments and ultimately its policies.

To form a community people must consciously bring their lives together so that they can live and act as one: a nation, a tribe, a city, a village, a group, or collectivity of any kind. Community in this sense differs from an aggregate of people who may be living in one area or under a single government. A community is a group of persons who genuinely consider themselves a unit, a people. Living in the same town under one government does not necessarily create this unity. This chapter explores how Essex citizens understand themselves as a community. Two questions give this inquiry focus: What binds them together? What boundaries separate them from others?

Seven Essex narratives speak to these two questions. These narratives could be described as stories about "rites of passage" to citizenship, because they show persons moving from an exclusive preoccupation with their "private" family lives to active "public" participation as community members--citizens. To show this pattern, the narrative that articulates the master plot of all the others comes first, followed by a structural analysis that reveals its central oppositions, metaphors, transformations, and contradictions. Reading the story to understand the opposition between community members (insiders) and nonmembers (outsiders), the analytical framework addresses the general question about community formation. Following each of the first three stories is a structural analysis showing how the narratives constitute community bonds and boundaries. Next, come four abridged stories with a structural analysis of the seven stories taken together to show what binds Essex citizens together and what separates them from others. A table at the end of the chapter charts the plots of the seven narratives.

For Essex citizens, community encompasses three dimensions: cultural, governmental, and social. Its cultural heritage is American[1] and Essex takes pride in being "typically" American. A sign on the road, marking the municipal boundary, welcomes drivers into the "All American City." Yet, in order to be typical, it must assert its own independence in terms both of its government and its community identity. Essex is a separate municipality with its own government structure, even though it is surrounded by a large metropolis; this gives it independence. More important it is the foundation for the special commitment that Essex citizens have to each other. This commitment makes them a community. It is the bonds that form this commitment that the following narratives reveal.

BUILDING A MODEL OF COMMUNITY

Becoming a Minister

In this first story, Tom Peters, who grew up in the town but moved away, returns to serve as the minister

Essex: Bonds and Boundaries

of one of Essex's major churches. His journey follows a rite of passage from young adulthood to full Essex citizenship. His story articulates the pattern of the other Essex stories and illuminates the master plot for all the Essex narratives. In particular, it defines the Essex community by describing both the boundaries that make Essex a separate, independent political community and the bonds that tie its citizens together. In this master story, Tom begins to shape his adult life by seeking a "public" position, a career that will give him full community membership. He grew up in Essex, studied for the ministry in Essex, went away to gain career experience, and returned as a minister some fifteen years after his ordination. This is Tom's story.

>   Dr. Drew--the president of Trinity College and a member of this church, who lived over on Montview--called me into his office during the year I was in graduate school and offered me a job as a traveling auditor for the church.
>   I said, "Well, Dr. Drew, I am not in business administration. I have had no courses in accounting. I am in pure math and I want to teach math."
>   He said, "Oh, Tom you know the difference between red and black. You know how to add and subtract. We will teach you the rest. Don't worry about it. The church needs you."
>   I said, "Well that is very flattering." He knew how to get to me. "I will tell you what. Give me one week to think it over." We had one child at the time. It was right after Fred's birth. And so I knew I needed to get a job.
>   I went home and talked it over with Sue, my wife. As we talked something seemed to say--"Look, if the church really needs you..."
>   I asked him, "How far can a layman go in the work of the church?"
>   He said, "Pastors are funny people. They like to talk to other pastors, and you will always be an auditor. But we guarantee that if you keep your nose clean, you will have a job all the days of your life. But you won't make much money."
>   At that time, I was ambitious and that

thought got to me. If I was going to get anywhere in the church, I would have to be a minister. I thought, "Why don't I become a minister first, and then I will be able to get somewhere and maybe get Dr. Drew's job one day and become president of the college." I was ambitious and wanted to be more than just an auditor.

I said to Sue, "Do you think that you would mind being a minister's wife, for awhile until I get the experience, and then I will be able to move up the administrative ladder?"

She said, "Well, I married you for better or worse, and we could do worse. It is up to you. I will support you no matter what you want to do. You have to make the decision."

This has always been her attitude in any major thing that comes along. She solves all the minor problems but in any major thing, she says, "I will support you, no matter what."

The pressure was on me, and so that is the point at which I decided to go into the seminary. I went back to see Dr. Drew the next Monday, and I said, "Dr. Drew, I have made up my mind. We are flattered that the church needs us, and so we have made up our minds, or I have made up my mind to go to the seminary."

He sat back in his chair, laughed, and said, "That is a horse of a different color. He was real pleased that I made that decision and encouraged me. He got a minister, Reverend Walker, to become the auditor. He probably wasn't making it in the ministry.

So I went to the seminary and four years later went to Logan, Ohio, until 1966. They gave me this Essex job when I left there.

But part of the story is that three years after I had been in Logan, which is the amount of time that they like to have young men gain experience, I had a call from the office headquarters to become Regional Eastern Director of Missions. I would have had to move to Atlanta and travel half the year.

The answer to that challenge was

clear. I had found my niche. I loved
parish ministry. This is where I belonged.
The ambition that encouraged me to go to the
seminary had now changed, and I did not want
administration. I wanted to be a parish
pastor. I told Dr. Drew that because I knew
he was responsible for the call. I just
told him I wasn't interested anymore in
becoming somebody. I wanted just to be a
parish pastor and was no longer
ambitious--in that way.

Oppositions

To see how Tom constructs his definition of the
political community requires careful attention to how
he draws a boundary between the community and his
private life, and between community members and those
outside it. Opening his narrative, Tom introduces Dr.
Drew by locating him in both his public community
life, as a college president, and his private life,
his family residence on Montview Avenue. He uses his
occupation to locate him in the public political
sphere and his address to locate him in the private
family sphere. This is a pattern in other Essex
narratives. Drew's church membership indicates an
intermediate area; the church is connected to the
college, where he works, but furnishes a place where
he and his family can worship and establish social
relationships.

At the opening of the story Tom, the protagonist,
explains that because of his son's birth he now needs
to find a job which will give him and his family a
public place--a public role. He is not unaware of the
implications this decision has for his family, so he
asks his wife if she would mind playing the role of
minister's wife. His private family life, now
including a child, necessitates a public life. The
two roles have more than a purely economic
connection. The family provides him with emotional
support, which he straight-forwardly acknowledges, and
he provides them with public status. Although he
explains that he needs to get a job because he has a
child to care for, he does not get a job but instead
enrolls in a three-year seminary program. What is
important, then, is not simply economic necessity but
a public role or career. It gives him and his family
a public place to occupy, an occupation. It secures
for him and his family political status in the
community and, hence, political power.

By establishing a public role, he simultaneously

works out his status within the family--the reciprocal responsibilities governing his relationship with his wife. Mindful that his professional selection will determine not only his own public identity but that of his family as well, he consults with his wife. This both secures support for his activity and helps to establish decision-making rules in the family, hence its political order, including his rung on the familial ladder. While they discussed the issue, "something seemed to say--'Look, if the church really needs you'." Did this signal God's call to him, or his wife's agreement, or both? Declaring her willingness to play "the minister's wife," she gives him support and the authority to make decisions for the family. This family decision suggests a kind of republic in which he gains the right to represent her. She gives consent to his rule. But, it also resembles the constitutional model that Aristotle suggests for the family, in which the man is assigned permanent ruling power.[2] Tom refines Aristotle's distinction by indicating that he makes the major decisions (quite possibly "public" decisions), because it is his role that defines their public position, while she makes the minor, private decisions, which bear only on narrow family concerns, not on larger community concerns.[3] Nevertheless, it is the minister's political perspective.

His report to Dr. Drew illustrates the initial ambiguity in the internal dynamics of the family's decision making. He says, "I have made up my mind. We are flattered that the church needs us." His alternative use of I and we signals that he represents the family, which means he has the right to speak about a we as well as to speak of his own individual interests. In this rite of passage to citizenship, he creates a boundary between his family life and public life that involves gaining his wife's support while also acquiring a means of supporting her. Hence, he simultaneously gains a status for himself in the public social order and within his family. In this division of roles, he becomes the economic center while his wife becomes the emotional center, which includes granting him the right to represent the family in public. This order established, he finds that the next major challenge, deciding whether to move "up" or to stay in the church ministry, presents no problem. He mentions no consultation with his wife on this question, not necessarily because it did not occur but because the family authority structure now renders this issue unimportant.

This second challenge creates another boundary

between his family and his ties to the external public community. He rejects the directorship because it requires forfeiting a locally centered parish ministry and becoming a traveling administrator instead. His commitment is to a local community and its network of relationships. This creates a boundary between the local community (town) and the larger order of which it is a part. These two boundaries, family and the larger order, define community for him. Tom's definition of community assigns particular activities to all three spheres (see Figure 1).

Figure 1

Private Family	Community	Outside the Community
husband/wife talk		
he decides	he represents family	Traveling auditor Eastern Region Director
wife's emotional support	his economic support for family	Church supports him

Metaphor

Because metaphors create links between general fields of discourse, an examination of Tom's metaphors illuminates his understanding of community. In speaking about the public realm, Tom uses metaphors that link space to movement. Dr. Drew calls him into his office, but Tom also indicates the location of Dr. Drew's home. While movement between home and office seem natural, Tom rejects wider travel and economic participation in the Eastern Division. He rejects the auditor's position because it does not offer sufficient travel up the "ladder" (it won't allow him to "get anywhere") and rejects the second position because it offers too much "travel," even though it means travel "up" the ladder of success. He finds his "niche," which enables him to make a commitment to a local community. The ladder metaphor itself creates a hierarchical image of social order. This image of climbing "up" subtly argues that by hard work, climbing, an improved social and political position can be gained.

In a society that emphasizes the idea of equality among citizens, it may be somewhat surprising to see such an emphasis on the hierarchical image that a ladder presents. A metaphorical solution to the apparent tension between ambition and equality comes about through a shift in the image of movement. Instead of "climbing up a ladder" Tom finds that "things were moving along." "Travel," even though associated with some kind of power and ambition, suggests excessive movement in his perspective, while "moving along" (lateral movement) signifies his satisfaction that his life is on track. Perhaps, as he had set out to do, he had "got somewhere" by embracing his role as church pastor. He resolves the tension of endless ladder climbing by finding a comfortable "niche." An explanation for his rejection of further advancement is that it would pull his private family life too far from his public work, decreasing his ability to participate fully in each. Hence, his solution balances his role in the family and the community.

Transformations

The narrator's initial response to Dr. Drew's offer shows his own desire for authority and power. He rejects the auditor's position because it lacks status and pay, even though it promises security and he needs to find an occupation because of a major transformation in his life, the birth of his first child. The seminary, an educational institution, transforms him from a "pure math" student into a minister. His work in the Logan parish brings forth a second transformation. Now, he no longer seeks to become "somebody." This role of minister lies midway between those of the excessively ambitious administrator and the subordinate auditor, who must "keep his nose clean," like a child in order to hold his job. On the surface, the phrase "just to be a parish pastor" carries a hint of defeat, but the narrator explains that this choice represents a new type of ambition. "I wanted just to be a parish pastor and no longer was ambitious--in that way." Becoming a father, getting an education, and working at his first assignment as parish minister are occasions for the major transformations in his story and together bring him into the public world with a clear sense of his own ability to make social contributions, having "found" his "niche." Unlike the Reverend Walker who wasn't "making it in the ministry," Tom Peters finds both success and satisfaction.

Contradictions

The narrator articulates a contradiction between norms that argue, on the one hand, that he should advance up the ladder of success and, on the other, that he should care for his family and for the members of his parish. Dr. Drew occupies the apex of the church's hierarchical structure. However, the center of church work is by definition "ministering." While climbing to the top of the ladder signifies accomplishment, everyone cannot occupy the top. In this culture, ambition for the top provides motivation but at some point it becomes disfunctional for the community, insofar as it intensifies competition and creates disharmonies at the expense of needed community services. The narrator deals with the fact that he is not at the top of the "ladder" by transforming his ambition. While this eases the contradiction, it does not eradicate it. The culture values ambition for top positions and yet its structure requires that the lower, and by far more plentiful, positions be occupied by able people. This narrator obtains satisfaction in a lower position by discovering a new way of being ambitious--moving "along" rather than "up."

The political contradiction the story articulates is the tension between competition in climbing the ladder, a major mechanism for recruiting persons for positions of community responsibility, and community solidarity, which asks citizens to occupy, in some satisfactory and self-satisfying way, each and all of the various positions on which the community depends. Only then will they be able to refrain from devoting themselves to pushing their fellow citizens out of their "niches" in the competitive attempt to climb up the ladder, undoing the cooperation upon which genuine community depends.

Baseball or Mortar Shells

Many scholars of American culture find in baseball the articulation of America's political spirit.[4] Pride in "our" team dramatizes the spirit of Middle America from the Ohio State Buckeyes to the Little Leaguers. These contemporary "warriors" defend a community's honor. Woody Hayes, the long-lasting former football coach at Ohio State University, wrote a book whose title represents a fundamental premise in Ohio's culture: You Win with People.[5] Winning is a mark of success. By honoring its winners, the community rewards excellence, and by having the excellence determined in a way that resembles a competitive game, the community preserves its neutrality. No <u>one</u> makes heroes; they earn their victories in the context of an "impartial" mechanism--the rules of the game--that decides the victor. So this story is not only about sports; it also explains how the community rewards excellence while preserving an egalitarian democratic ethos.

Through its Recreation Department the Essex government sponsors Little League games played on public school grounds. Such events serve as both celebrations of community solidarity and arenas in which individual talents are put on display. Here, too, ambition with its accompanying competitive orientation and satisfaction with its accompanying cooperative attitude play key roles in shaping the Essex community. In this narrative, a Little League coach, Ben Miller, confronted by an unhappy parent, finds himself attempting to resolve the tension produced by the emphasis placed on "winning."

> One Saturday, I was a few minutes late to practice. One Daddy got there early. He was upset because his son's team had lost two or three games, so he told the kids to be there a little early. I didn't know it. They were to have a little practice beforehand, and it was about twenty minutes before the nine o'clock game. There was a Dad out there. He had eight of the early shows out in the outfield and was hitting balls at them. He was hitting the ball about one hundred and fifty to two hundred feet out to them. There is maybe one boy per team that might be able to catch a ball hit like that--six boys in the whole league. He has got his whole team out there--hitting what looks like a mortar rounds dropping in on those little boys out there. This hard ball flying in--boom.
>
> I said, "We will take over. We will take over. One of these kids is really going to get hurt." I showed him how we do it. "Usually, I will walk out twenty yards and flip the ball underhanded in the air and make sure that they are all spread apart so no one gets hit. I throw the ball in front of a boy so he will come forward, and it

might hit his glove and fall off. If the ball is thrown over their head, they might run into it."

He said, "Well, why can't they catch?"

And, I said, "Well, they are only six or seven. They, we are just learning to do this together." It was frustrating for him because he can catch. "You know you are thirty-eight years old. You ought to be able to catch."

Oppositions

At one level, this opposition between the coach (protagonist) and father (antagonist) represents a conflict between the public and private realms. The father's claim to authority over the team comes about through a private family tie. Fathers teach their sons to play ball, so it seems reasonable to extend this authority to the team. On the other hand, the coach has authority over the team because it is a public activity and the city hired him to perform this task. It is his professional occupation and he has special training in physical education. The father challenges this authority by calling a practice. More importantly, he challenges the private/public distinction when he tries to extend his private authority to the public Little League team. The coach reasserts this same distinction by taking over the practice immediately upon his arrival. He then draws on his public authority as a professional coach to assume the prerogative of teaching the father how to teach baseball to young boys. As teacher, he explains why little boys can't catch and grown men can. However, by identifying with the boys ("They, we are just learning to do this together."), he signals his own subordination to the father (who already knows how to catch) while justifying his position as a professional teacher. In this way, he is able to undercut the father's authority on the field without discrediting him altogether. As a town citizen, the father employs the coach. This arrangement gives the coach authority over the team but acknowledges some distant or "supportive" authority for the father, not unlike the authority accorded the minister's consenting wife in the previous narrative. To be sure, the governed are governed, but only in the context of consent already given. Public bureaucrats in their occupations take over the responsibilities of directly governing community life and the division between public and private is put to use in resolving the conflict between these two kinds of persons.

Metaphors

The image of baseballs dropping like mortar rounds on seven-year-old children dramatizes the threat inherent in overzealous ambition and competition. This military language alludes to the sportsman as a warrior in defense of the community, but in this case, the coach argues that young warriors at this stage in their training should not be expected to risk life and limb. The connection between the warrior and the citizen has a long tradition in the West, and to a degree, the clearest claims to citizenship have been accorded the man who is willing to defend his country in battle.[6] Still, warriors have to be trained, and these particular young "warriors" must learn the game before they can be expected to play "for keeps." The father's competitive zeal encourages him to rush things and, to that extent, to threaten the viability of the collective enterprise. He would have the boys climb the ladder when they are still learning to walk.

Transformations

To balance competition with cooperation the coach places winning and losing in the background and focuses on the game as a learning experience. Along with this, he adjusts the rules to fit the boys' abilities. He doesn't hit the ball into the field; he pitches it. The conditions of "practice" differ from those of a "real" game, and even a "real" game, in Little League terms, is a radical departure from the conditions of more grown-up competition. The boys are students. This sets the stage so that what the father originally assesses as a defeat can now be understood as a victory. It is a learning experience. This transformation resembles the minister's reevaluation of his own goals, which turns the loss of "ambition" into a gain, a victory of sorts. Both the minister's story and the baseball story speak of rites of passage into adulthood. The minister is ready for entry because he has become a father; the Little Leaguers are not ready, and the father's intervention brings an adult norm prematurely into the environment. From a political perspective, however, it is more than merely a rite of passage to citizenship, because it asserts the proper public/private authority patterns and helps citizens to adjust to the allocation of authority within the community, which argues that all citizens are equal and yet some govern others. Both narratives offer symbolic reassurance[7] to so-called losers, but even more significantly, they justify and honor those who find themselves on the lower rungs of the ladder. In this sense, they work toward maintaining a sense of equality among citizens and reassert a democratic order of things that constantly confronts a hierarchy of power in the day-to-day activities of public life. Both narratives allocate responsibility and values between the private and public spheres. In the first narrative, the church provided an intermediate ground for working out this distinction. In the second narrative, the baseball game provides the same kind of intermediate ground. In the minister's narrative, his church role becomes his public place just as, in the second narrative, the coach's public activity is defined by his role as an educator.

Contradiction

Transforming a defeat into a learning experience helps in part to alleviate the contradiction between individual competition for status, on the one hand, and community cooperation, on the other. Since the City Council sponsors a number of teams that compete against each other in a single program, there will be as many losers in Essex as there will be winners. Because the games carry real status in the community, losses produce real pain. But, if players experience too much pain, they will withdraw and the program will fail. At the same time the structure of the game itself requires an intense desire to win. One solution is to focus on the prospect of winning the next game, but this solution is not very effective for a team whose primary experience is losing. Under these conditions, the more apt strategy is to turn the game into a learning experience, thereby not only minimizing the pain of particular losses but also redeeming the prospect of hope for future victories.

The tension between the father and the coach demonstrates the difficulty of reconciling a cooperative community spirit with rigorous competition. By bringing the father into the game, this narrative not only integrates the private family agenda (status) with the public agenda (education) but helps turn the family into a private retreat where the boy can get consolation from his father, who now will say "You are learning to catch" rather than "Why can't you catch?" While the coach asserts his public authority, he accords a distant supportive (consenting) authority to the private realm. The son supports his team by continuing to play and the father gives emotional support to the boy. The coach redefines the rules of the game for the father, thereby minimizing the father's status anxiety and allowing him to find satisfaction in giving his son a valuable learning experience rather than experiencing frustration in his son's defeat. This legitimates the game as a learning activity, so that it no longer represents a mock war with balls falling from the sky like mortar rounds, but instead is a classroom in which the coach plays the role of teacher, controlling the game so that it maximizes learning and minimizes casualties. The story serves as an antiheroic narrative that consoles the "losers," and the politics of this consolation permits competition to continue while controlling the damage it can do.

The Story of Joe

The next narrator more directly confronts the ethical and economic issues in the tension between competition and cooperation. He summarizes a Neal Simon play, which for him describes Essex life. Joe, the protagonist, represents a typical Essex businessman whose failure to observe some typical business practices creates trouble. The narrator is an executive, an educator, and a person who takes his Protestant religious commitments quite seriously.

> Joe Falkenberg was a very successful businessman, a typical Essex citizen. He had a somewhat flamboyant wife, which was less typical--very much the country club set, with jewelry and so on. He had two sons and a daughter. The one boy was a hippie and the daughter was afraid she wasn't going to get married although she was only sixteen years old. She was into it with everybody and often said, "I don't want to be an old maid." The third child was somewhat spoiled.
> A fellow came to Joe's house and said, "Joe, it has come to me that you are giving an awful lot of money to the church--entirely too much. Why don't you keep a little for old Joe?"
> Joe said, "You know, it is the funniest thing. The more I give to the church, the more I earn."
> The guy says, "Well, you know that is

not right, Joe." He put his arm around him.

The first act ends with Joe and this guy walking over to the door. Joe looks out. The guy looks out, and he says, "Gosh, what is all that light? It is ten o'clock at night."

Joe says, "that looks like a fire."

The guy replies, "Boy that is a fire--a tremendous fire."

Joe says, "It's down by the river."

"Why it looks like it is going up like a box"

Joe says, "There is only one business down there-- my box company."

It was completely gone. Finally, as the lights are beginning to lower to close the first act, this guy says, "Well Joe, you can rebuild. Don't worry about it. The insurance will cover it."

Joe says, "I never believed in insurance. The Lord will take care of me." The curtain drops.

When the curtain rises, Joe is in rags--complete ribbons. It turns out his house has burned down, too. His wife comes in with soot all over her face. The two boys are filthy dirty. The girl is trying to daintily step around the burned house. Nothing is left.

This friend has come and puts his arm around Joe and says, "Now Joe, the Lord didn't really help you out. He is not a friend of yours."

Near the end of the play, the hippie son who has been drinking loses his eyesight.

It almost made me teary eyed. Joe is talking to the Lord and says, "Now look, you know that I take whatever you give me. And that is okay, but I'm angry with you. I'm angry as I can be about this kid losing his sight, but I am never going to turn you down."

About this time, one realizes that this is the story of Job.

Oppositions

The opposition between poverty and wealth appears dramatically in the contrast between the first and second acts. Although Joe is a "typical" Essex "businessman," his wife has an excessive interest in wealth as displayed in her jewelry and obsessive country-club life style. In contrast their hippie son has an excessive interest in poverty, while the other son is "spoiled," reproducing his mother's narrow focus on material comforts. In some respects the daughter mirrors the father's simple and excessive trust, not trusting in God's but in her boyfriends' care, which she tries to gain through sexual excesses. Joe gives away too much money away; she gives away too much affection.

However, according to his friend, Joe's generosity is not wholly without calculation. When queried, he justifies his gifts as investments. "The more I give to the church, the more I earn." The story opens with a separation between his business and his home, but closes with a dramatic picture of their connectedness; both burn to the ground. The story offers an explanation in his "friend's" admonition--Joe failed to properly separate business practices from private family practices. Thinking the community was a family, he gave away too much to the church and neglected to protect his business and his home. However, these excesses also appeared in the private realm, where he gave his wife and son too much in the way of material goods. Perhaps, even this generosity affected his hippie son, who may have had so much money that he failed to recognize its value. The daughter's sexual excesses also blur the private/public distinction, for she makes her sexuality a public phenomenon. Joe's mixing of business with religion leads him to extend too much trust to public life. He doesn't even have fire insurance. Even his "friend,"[8] is surprised.

His excessive trust and disregard for material wealth makes it impossible for Joe to protect his family, even though his relationship with God consoles him. At one level, the tale warns about violating public norms by excessive attachment either to the material realm, jewelry, or the nonmaterial realm, religious faith, and by excessive generosity with earthly resources. While Joe entered into an intimate relationship with God, even conversing with God, the story makes no mention of any interaction with his family. We have only his exchange with the mysterious visitor. Both his public and family life suffer from the same excess--too little regard for money. The struggle between good and evil takes place as a struggle between submission to God, blindly trusting in the future, and submission to business norms, insuring the future against problems. The former assumes that God will take care of problems, the latter that one ought to take care of one's own future. Joe's failure to separate the public world of business and the private world of relationships with family members and with God produces disaster for him and for his family.

Metaphors

Joe's story mixes business language with religious language. His trust in God is presented as an "investment." He explains that he never "believed" in insurance. This lack of faith in the institution of insurance proves economically disastrous, though it may be religiously profitable. Joe is not foolish because he is religious but he is foolish because he applies the principles of religion and family life to the public realm. His son has to lose his eyesight before Joe realizes that his trust in God should be spiritual (placing it in the private realm) rather than material, which concerns the public order.

Transformations

Events force Joe to confront the inadequacy of his model of how the Lord will take care of him. What begins as a contract model, in which Joe invests in the Lord and the Lord pays off, becomes a genuine commitment: "I am never going to turn you down." This transformation resembles the minister's because Joe, who has fallen to the bottom of the ladder, gets a new understanding of "ambition." Like the baseball father, he has a learning experience. Joe shows his faithfulness and learns not to expect the Lord to make or keep him wealthy. Like the baseball father, he learns to keep private matters private (between God and himself) and public matters public (he will accept the rules and buy insurance). Hence, this narrative, like the minister's, makes religion an intermediate territory between the private and public realms. Joe figures out a more appropriate orientation toward God and, probably, also toward business in general and fire insurance in particular.

Joe's anger indicates that he has developed a personal, rather than a contractual, relationship with God. He learns that the social contract model of his relationship with God does not work; God insists on surrender. But this surrender does not imply passivity or recklessness in business relationships. The riches-to-rags experience enables Joe to separate private spiritual practices from public economic practices. In this context, his business errors result from his confusion of the private and public realms. Just as surrender and trust are proper to his private, personal relationship with God, they are singularly inappropriate to his relationship with the human community.

Contradictions

The contradiction that Joe faces is between the demands of his religious convictions and the demands of the business world. The former urge trust and generous "giving," while the latter emphasize controlled investments to "get" profits. By giving money away, Joe violates the rules of competitive business practices. By not investing in insurance, he mismanages capital and it all "goes up in smoke." The story mediates the contradiction between the self-interested calculation of business and the trust and generosity that underlie good community relationships. Joe brings his excessive trust into balance by learning that what he owes God is obedience--"I shall never turn you down"--and what he owes his community is conformity to the norms of practical economic management. Even though he fails in business, Joe still wins a moral victory, so the future holds promise. By referring to the Job story, the narrator reinforces this hope since, ultimately, Job has all of his wealth restored to him. The narrative offers consolation to people who have lost their fortunes, suggesting that even such a devastating fall down the ladder might bring hidden benefits in heightened insight and the capacity for a better climb next time.

COMMUNITY BONDS AND BOUNDARIES

I shall present brief abridgements of the other four stories in this section and follow with an analysis that incorporates all seven stories. By looking carefully at these narratives, one can see a master story that tells both about how these citizens create the boundaries that separate their community from their families and from other communities and about how they form bonds with one another. To visualize the overall pattern in the plot structures, it may be helpful to turn to the table at the end of the chapter.

A Tennis Match of Mixed Doubles

The first narrator is a woman who works for the recreation department. She has a difficult encounter on the tennis courts.

> My husband and I had this tennis match last night. I practiced in the afternoon with a dear friend who told me, "Jo, you play better when you are relaxed, so don't try to kill the ball and ram it down your opponents' throats--just hit it back to them."
>
> When we got on the court in the evening, this lady and her husband were all down to business; they didn't show one emotion. When we first got on the court, my husband said, "Well, where am I supposed to stand now?" We are just beginners.
>
> And the lady said, "Well, if you don't know where you are supposed to be, I am not going to tell you, you know."
>
> I said to myself, "Oh no, I don't like this." It got to the point where it was just nit-picking stuff. I like to play and have a good time--on a happy level. I just kept saying to myself, "Stay relaxed," and I kept saying to my husband, "Just smile." We both went home and I said, "Well."
>
> He said, "We should have won that."
>
> "I know," I said, "but I had fun and learned an awful lot. Deep down we really did win, even though we lost, because we played fair. We were good sports and didn't lose our temper, and we played a close game." Later, we found out that they served out of turn in the tie breaker. We were novices and didn't know the rules.

Looking in the Mirror

A Catholic businessman finds that he must make a choice between securing profits for his own company and doing what he thinks is morally correct.

> My company has a very, very large contract here in town with the Chrome Corporation.[9] They are a multidivisional company and are pretty messed up in data processing. At the risk of losing the

contract, I was getting ready to go to New York and talk to the chairman of the board. They have a contract with us that is an absolute waste of money for them. I feel a moral obligation to tell them. I told some of the immediate people we work with in the Chrome company.

But they said, "Well, do the work anyway. Just don't bother me."

I was bothered by this, so I planned to visit their company president in New York. I was on my way to New York when I got the message, "That wraps it up." They had terminated our contract. It may have cost me a contract but, in the long run, I will gain more than I lose. If nothing else, I can look myself in the mirror and shave. I have to be fair to myself and do what I think is right.

They Can't Do That

A Jewish woman explains her surprise at the immoral behavior of a university.

The university sponsored a study in which people were told to go into a room and press buttons and when they pressed a button somebody would be hurt. Some of the people did it but with great reluctance. Only one man refused. But, it was just an act and nobody was hurt. They were testing how people, as in Nazi Germany, could do such unspeakable things.

One woman said, "I trusted the university so I did what I was told. I feel very sad to think that I did this, and yet, I thought it was for a good cause."

Another man, when he found out, said, "It doesn't matter that it was just an act. I almost killed a man. I have to live with myself."

The university had to go to trial because they are not allowed to do this by law. Even though it is an experiment, they have to tell people what they are getting into.

Family Justice

A Jewish father explains how he and his wife teach

their children about justice.

> We lived in Detroit and our kids were in the vehicle period. You could break your neck walking up our steps. So I called a meeting.
> "Here is the problem. What'll we do about it?"
> So the kids said, "We need a law."
> We decided, "The law should be that the bikes have to be parked on the grass."
> I said, "The law isn't finished. There have to be penalities for violators." The things they suggested were very severe. In our kitchen, we have a charity box that goes for the Jewish National Fund. We agreed that the penalty would be a fine which would be deposited in the charity box.
> One day, my wife and I came home and our son David's bike was in the driveway. I put it on the grass and wrote out a ticket. When he got the ticket, he said, "I want to be heard on this."
> I said, "Okay we will have a trial tonight, after dinner."
> I pounded the gavel and said, "Justice, justice, Stein family versus David."
> But he claimed he was innocent because he had loaned his bike to a friend who had parked it in the drive. I said, "He used your bike with your knowledge and consent so you are responsible."
> He said, "That is not fair, I take an appeal."
> Most middle-class families are afraid to go outside of themselves for help; his appeal went beyond family authority.
> We had a neighbor who was a superior court judge, and I asked him to come over. He heard the case and said, "I sustain the lower court because in this state ownership implies responsibility."
> The little kid went in the kitchen and put his penny in the charity box. This was a tremendous lesson.

POLITICS AND THE MASTER PLOT

To see the pattern that these stories tell through their plots, it is helpful to look at a master plot. The narratives unfold from the private realm, to the public realm and in some respects, this represents a rite of passage into citizenship in the community. While this pattern emerges in each of the seven stories, the minister's tale provides a concrete illustration.

Private Realm

1. The protagonist receives individual recognition.
The new father receives a job offer.

2. The protagonist asserts kinship ties and establishes a home.
The minister and his wife discuss the position.

3. The protagonist seeks support from his family.
His wife supports him.

4. The protagonist enters the public realm to gain resources.
He goes to the seminary.

Public Realm

5. The protagonist establishes public bonds.
The minister takes a position and begins work.

6. The protagonist meets a public challenge.
The minister receives the offer of a directorship.

7. The protagonist experiences conflict and loss.
The minister rejects the climb up the ladder.

8. The loss is transformed into a gain and the conflict resolved.
His ambition is transformed; he has found his niche.

The structure of this master plot should be kept in mind as the following interpretation of the political model underlying these stories is presented.

Oppositions

Each of the narratives constructs a tension between the private and public realms that involves an ethical or moral problem. In each of these stories, the protagonist loses. The tennis players lose the match. The businessman loses the contract. The experimental subject who did unspeakable things loses his self-respect. The child loses his case. In this respect, these stories echo the first series of narratives, in which Joe loses his home and business, the boys lose the game, and the minister fails to achieve his original goal. The tension that the protagonists in the present series of stories experience is between winning, that would bring public recognition for their achievements, and playing a good, honest game. For the tennis players knowledge of their honesty may be confined to the private sphere, and the businessman acknowledges that the ethical issues involved in the contract may be confined to his own conscience, since even the company which he hopes to help does not at first acknowledge that it is wasting its money by continuing its contract with his firm. His action will reduce his financial gain, but it gives him a sense of justice, even though he does think it might do him some financial good in the long run. Acknowledging this tension between ethical commitment and winning public reward, the protagonists come to see that their ethical commitments are important. In this context, what appears at first glance to be a loss becomes a victory.

In the tennis story, the boundary between the private and public spheres is embodied in the boundary between a friendly tennis game and a serious one. The narrator and her husband oppose the other team. As in the baseball story, the narrative addresses the problem facing the loser. Zealous competition leads to an unsatisfying game. The opponents were without emotion--"down to business." After returning home, she and her husband discuss the game and its ethical dimensions. When they discover that the opponents did not play fairly, they decide that they "really did win" because they "played fair." In this sense, like the businessman who attempted to cancel the contract, they have won a personal moral victory. They won where it "really" counts. The minister, the defeated baseball team, and the hapless Joe of the burning box factory win similar victories. The bicycle violator wins a moral lesson even though he, too, loses his case; and the subject in the university experiment learns, through his defeat at the hands of the researcher, that he must "live with himself."

In each of these cases, the losers consult their own consciences and reflect on the ethical commitments that they make to themselves as bases for judging actions in the public realm. The successful operation of the public sphere, the Essex community, depends upon the private personal ethical commitments of its members. The story of the bicycle violator best illustrates their interdependence. The parents teach the child very specifically about the law and his responsibility to it and are even willing to call on neighbors to be sure the lesson is well learned. It is appropriate for neighbors, even busy judges, to so respond because, if children learn the proper ethical behavior early on, the community will benefit. Both the bicycle story and the tale of the university experiment measure public actions by appealing to ethical codes. The tennis tale also fits this characterization, although the rules are in the game rather than in the community structure. Community order depends upon these ethical commitments. While a quick glance at the legal system might suggest a clear division between personal ethical commitments and the legal code, a second glance afforded through these tales reveals the interdependence of these two domains in the creation of a workable community. The individual connects these two realms, and so must reconcile his or her commitments to both. He or she must be able to look in the mirror and find grounds for self-respect in the reflection. To do this means never to turn down the "good" action. This is what Joe's story teaches, and it is just such private ethical commitments as these that impose restraints on competition.

In one sense, these stories sort out actions appropriate to the private and public realm. The boy who pursues his case through the appeal, and his family who encourages that pursuit, make the point that responsibility for ethical behavior in the public realm rests with individuals, whose values take shape in their family lives. The Jewish father explains that his family feels so strongly about its values that it is willing to risk its own reputation by calling on help from the public realm to teach those values to its children within its own domain--the family home. The bond that binds citizens together publicly, therefore, is a commitment to a watchful eye on public behavior from the privileged vantage point of the private sphere.

The opposition between the private and public sphere further clarifies the community's identity and the role it plays in the lives of its citizens. While family life is socially separate from community life, the community defines itself as a collection of families and, of course, it surrounds the family in the physical sense. It is important, therefore, for citizens to understand their own commitments in each sphere, because the family depends on the community for its needs while the community depends on the family to provide emotional and ethical support for its citizens. Since each sphere makes demands on the citizen's time and energy, the citizen needs to work out the connections between his or her roles in each of them. What emerges is that citizens conceive of themselves as sovereign individuals who play different roles in each sphere. Thus conceived, they can bring order into their private lives. The young math student becomes a professional minister in the public realm and a father and household head in the private realm. The private order of things provides the necessary condition for action in the public realm. Joe's lack of private order has drastic public consequences. Thus a condition for a successful community is that each family needs to have its own "house in order." It may even be appropriate, as in the case of "Family Justice," for the family to seek help in its efforts to establish that order.

Given an ordered family life, the citizen can take up a public position. It may be an economic position, as in the cases of the minister and the businessman, or it may be a social position, as in the cases of the tennis players and the Little Leaguers. The private realm is a base from which to wage the struggle for status and position and, in this sense, serves the liberal ideology of generating a "haven" from the competitive public economic realm.[10] The family is a base that shapes ethical commitments, that in turn foster emotional support and cooperation. While the public realm provides opportunities for ambition and competition, a genuine community requires cooperation. The public realm has a network of rules and a hierarchy of positions which orchestrate its many families into one workable community. Rules play a central role in this public order. The tennis story discusses how the narrator's opponents "really" lost because they chose not to observe the rules; the baseball coach subtly appeals to the rules to bring the father around. The university, which violates the rules (the law), finds itself in trouble; and "family justice" requires making family practices suit the public law even to the extent of calling in a judge, if need be. While kinship and mutual support form family bonds, rules (which include habits, customs, laws, and policies) forge community bonds.

The family offers one boundary to political life; the "larger" community provides the other. This is the community outside of Essex, including the urban area that surrounds it, the state of Ohio, and the nation. However, these larger entities constitute political organizations rather than political communities, and thus impinge less on daily lives and make far fewer emotional demands. Since commitments to this "larger" community draw citizens away from family life, they find it easier to define their commitments to these domains in purely governmental terms. Hence, they invest little energy in concerning themselves with the needs of these larger aggregations, while they are willing to invest time and energy addressing the needs of their community--Essex. In part, their lack of engagement with these larger political entities results from their relative satisfaction with the ways in which such entities are structured, as well as from the ease with which citizens can differentiate their own lives from them. It is also the case that intense involvement with these larger political entities would require citizens to spend less time with their families. The minister alludes to this in his rejection of the Eastern Division position. Such larger associations offer bureaucratic relationships, not community relationships. While the citizens of Essex affirm these larger units, they live their daily lives at the local community level, which makes possible a rich family life as well as a public life. This is what "community" means to Essex citizens. It weaves family and public life together.

Essex's central political problem as a community has to do with reconciling private personal ambitions, fueled by a competitive individualized ideology, with public needs for cooperation. By employing a private/public distinction that makes competition a private, individual virtue and cooperation a public virtue, Essex manages to embrace both competition and cooperation. The greater good of the community requires cooperation and "niche" finding, while the lesser commitment to individual ambition provides the energy for building and climbing ladders.

Metaphors

The metaphors in these stories help to illuminate problems. The comparison between baseballs and mortar shells dramatizes the threat not only of physical harm but of excessive competition as well. A similar metaphor appears in the tennis narrative when the storyteller's friend tells her not "to kill the ball and ram it down your opponents throats." The university experiment evokes similarly combative death threats, "It doesn't matter that it was just an act. I almost killed a man. I have to live with myself." In each case, the speaker worries about someone else's "death" not his or her own. Too much competition in the public realm leads to combative behavior and breaks down community relationships. Allusions to war and death dramatically express the loss of such relationships and the dues that have to be paid for being overly competitive. On the other hand, too little competition, as in the case of Joe Falkenberg means excessive generosity. The businessman who plans to deliberately lose business worries about this too, but he "gains" the ability to look himself in the "mirror," a metaphor for self-reflection and self-respect. It is not insignificant that the mirror is in the family home, the locus of ethical considerations, from which final judgements come.

The rung on the ladder metaphor suggests a way to think about the proper amount of competition and ambition. It asserts the importance of hierarchy and order within the community. In some sense, democratic values cherish equality, yet some citizens manage to reach higher rungs than others. What is important, then, is that, in climbing the ladder, citizens observe the rules and experience satisfaction at whatever rung they find themselves. The marks of wealth, as in the case of Joe before the fire, or of victory, as in the case of the nasty tennis players, do not necessarily indicate virtue or a proper order of things. What is needed is a balance between competition and cooperation--between attempting to win and playing the game fairly. The metaphor of the game itself illuminates the importance of winning in the right way and of losing without giving way to despair.

Transformations

Through the transformation of competition in the public sphere to ethical concerns in the private sphere apparent losses become "real" victories. The tennis players really won because they played fairly and the baseball team really won because the players were learning how to play the game. The corporate executive really won, even though he may have lost future contracts, because he could "look himself in the face." The private realm supplies the ethical commitments that, in fact, enable the community to run smoothly. Without corporate executives willing to take risks to do their jobs responsibly and without players who consider it more important to play fairly than to beat others, the public realm would be unable to function.

The two primary agents of transformation that

occur in the narratives have to do with learning and moral reflection. The minister learns about a different kind of ambition. The tennis players achieve a "moral" victory over the opponents who outscore them, and the partner who is the narrator is able to say that she "learned a lot" from the experience. The businessman gains a similar moral victory over the company whose employees order unnecessary work, even if it means losing future contracts with them. However, if an ethical or moral dilemma emerges in the family, as it does for the family whose son breaks the family rules, it can become necessary to call in outside help to resolve the dilemma, so that the family can continue to provide the moral material on which the social order depends. In the extreme case of the university experiment, the public realm may need to resort to law in order to restore order.

Contradictions

The underlying contradiction Essex citizens face calls for them to reconcile community norms that urge them to "climb up the ladder," to be successful, to win, and that at the same time require that some citizens remain on the lower rungs of the ladder. The community must have its share of losers. Because the social order also argues that citizens have the right to "pursue happiness," this contradiction presents a problem, especially for those who have ambition but do not occupy the top rung. In its collective manifestation, the contradiction produces tension. Citizens must compete with one other, and they must also cooperate with each other to keep the "game" in play.

Thus, a serious political problem Essex faces is that to the degree that it depends upon competition to motivate action, it risks loosening those bonds of community that commit citizens to each other. The ethics that guide this activity come from the family. In this respect, an orderly civic life depends upon the family's ability to maintain an ethical base for its members. The work left to government is not to inculcate public virtue but rather to protect citizens. In Essex, this means that the police and fire services represent primary government functions, which occupy much of the mayor's and council members' time. Supporting political institutions, like the family, friendships, and education, generate the underlying social structure that makes it possible to recognize Essex as a community.

The social political order offers a way to organize families and a rule structure within which to negotiate for resources. In return for such resources, the family socializes individuals into <u>good citizens</u> who, like the executive who does not wish to do unnecessary work even for profit, know ethical practices from unethical ones. At the same time, the community offers an arena for competition in which excellent performances will gain recognition. The opportunity to compete urges citizens to enter into the social arena with zeal. Only their ethical commitments to fair play curb their drive to excel competitively. The tension between winning and playing fairly generates the atmosphere that draws citizens together and binds them into a political game, whose rule structure not only maintains the order necessary to keep the game going but also serves to console those who lose. The winner takes pride in excelling. The loser takes pride in playing honorably. The game metaphor describes the political life of Essex citizens and fits easily into the "conservative-liberal" continuum, along which they are self-consciously arrayed.[11] Because Essex citizens understand themselves as playing the same social-political game, they are one. The game not only serves to sort out the winners from the losers but it also engages players with each other, inspiring a sense of unity and creating a corporate spirit.

TABLE 1. ESSEX   Private

	Ego Expression (1)	Establish Home/Domain (2)	Nurturing: Helping/Hurting (3)	Public Entry for Resources (4)
Becoming Minister	He makes job contact	Husband/wife discuss decision	She supports him	He needs job to support family
Baseballs	Coach identifies narrative as personal account, "I"	Father-son relationship; father upset at loss	Father tries to help son	Father enters public realm without authority
Joe	Joe: successful businessman, typical Essex citizen	Joe has wife, a daughter, and two sons	His wife is flamboyant; one son is spoiled, other is hippie; daughter is promiscuous	A friend visits Joe to discuss his financial practices
Tennis		Husband and wife form team	Friend helps wife with practice	Husband and wife enter tennis tournament
Looking in Mirror	He consults his own sense of ethics and acts as an individual			He owns data processing company
They Can't Do That	Individuals directed to press buttons to hurt people			University enters public by recruiting subjects for their study of authoritarian personalities
Family Justice	Father calls meeting (he narrates story)	They establish family meetings to make household rules	They make rules that prohibit parking bikes on walk and establish fines for violators	Son receives ticket; family court finds him guilty of violation; he asks for an appeal

Public

Bonding to Public Realm (5)	Challenge (6)	Conflict Resolution, Loss (7)	Gaining a New Community (8)
He goes to school	He receives challenge of directorship	He rejects offer	He finds a new ambition, a niche as parish pastor
Father coaches team	Coach challenges father's coaching	Coach explains father's coaching method is dangerous	Coach teachers father and identifies himself with the son and returns father's authority
Joe explains that the more money he gives away the more he gets	This position is challenged	Joe loses his business, his home, and his sons's health	Joe passes the test and establishes the proper relationship between his personal and public practices
They request a friendly game and ask for help	Opposing team challenges them and wants a "real" game	They lose	They really win because they were good sports and enjoyed themselves
Large company contracts with him for work, but he says they don't need this	They challenge his advice and tell him to do it anyway	He resists and they cancel contract	He may win in long run; he gains self-pride; he can look himself in the mirror
University conducts experiment by asking subjects to press buttons and shock "victims"	One man challenges this and leaves; others challenge the legality of this procedure	University's actions are exposed by media and legal sanctions are brought	The law controls university; one man still assumes individual responsibility for the event and asserts ethics as a private, individual action
Father requests help from a neighbor who is a judge	Son challenges father through the appeal in which judge presides	Son loses and must pay fine	Son gains a lesson in responsibility and places money in charity box; he returns to family

5
Community Bonds and Boundaries: *Kumu Aina*

> "I should see the garden far better," said Alice to herself, "if I could get to the top of that hill: and here's a path that leads straight to it--at least, no, it doesn't do that--"
>
> Lewis Carroll
> Through the Looking-Glass

KUMU AINA LEADERSHIP

Kumu Aina narratives lay out a path from which the view of "community" differs strikingly from that presented in the Essex narratives. The first story, which serves as a master plot, explains that building a community depends upon finding a leader. Kumu Aina binds its citizens to each other through a series of leaders, who become focal points for building community spirit, rather than binding members through a system of rules: a constitution, a moral code, a set of laws. While Essex citizens set themselves apart from others through their municipal government, Kumu Aina citizens, who enjoy the same strong sense of identity both internally and externally, achieve it in a different way. It is not so much that Kumu Aina adopts a different style because it has failed to achieve an independent governmental status, but rather that it has failed to seek an independent governmental status because it has a different image of what binds people together. This first story shows these bonds.

Lawrence of Arabia

The narrator, a native Hawaiian man, is active both in the multiethnic community of Kumu Aina and in the native Hawaiian Renaissance movement, which in the last ten years has revitalized Hawaiian culture and encouraged the participation of native Hawaiians in politics. For this storyteller, the film Lawrence of Arabia explains how the personal power of a leader creates the common bonds that give Kumu Aina an identity and coordinate the actions of its citizens.

Lawrence of Arabia was a savior. He began in the British Army and ended up a spiritual and military leader for all the Arab tribes. For the first time in the history of Arab countries, he alone got these nomadic tribes and nations together. This White English man who was not an Arab was taken in by the people. He empathized with them and felt so strongly about their cause that he became not only a military leader but also a spiritual leader.

One of the reasons he was so effective is that he was a rank-and-file man. The British officers, the colonialists, put him through some very humiliating sexual experiences that brought him near death. It caused his mind to snap, but it also brought out the genius. It made him even more dedicated in obtaining independence for the Arabs.

Tribal loyalties are very strong. Councils try to mediate disputes because those from one tribe do not trust other tribes. Somehow, he gained the trust of all the tribes. So, when he laid down the law, everyone was willing to live by it and not pull out their swords and guns.

He inspired them spiritually. He understood religion and was able to build a deep spiritual commitment down through the rank and file, which was, "No matter what, the last thing in the world that should happen is that we should fight among ourselves. The enemy is over there, not in this camp."

Arab countries revere leaders almost as gods. Lawrence became a leader; when he came, the masses fell to their knees and almost worshipped him because of what he was accomplishing. He backed up his action and philosophy with spectacular military achievements. He fought technology with swords and one-shot rifles. Militarily, he was a genius.

What is most amazing to me is that after all those years, when they finally won independence from the British, he left. The job was done. He went to England and was killed on a motorcycle. He spent all those years living among the people, absorbing their culture, providing leadership with a deep commitment, and he just left because the job was done. He did it.

He said,"Whew, it's over! I did my thing and I love you all. But I recognize the fact that I cannot really be one of you, because I am White. I have my own culture and my own people. Now I am going to go back there and see what I can do to attack the roots of the problem that occurs around the world."

Oppositions

The opposition between the Arabs and the British develops at three levels. There is a cultural ethnic tension between the British and the Arabs, a battle for national independence, and a class struggle, which appears in the tensions between a technologically advanced nation state, Britain, and a spiritually based tribal society, which lacks modern technology. The Arabs have only "swords and one-shot rifles," but their spirit is so strong that they prove victorious. Lawrence embodies both sides of each of these three tensions, and this makes it possible for him to become a mediator. While he was reared in the British culture, he identifies so closely with the Arabs that he becomes their spiritual leader. He is a British citizen but leads the Arabs to military success and political liberation. He is both upper and lower class, a rank-and-file man, yet something akin to an object of worship to the Arab people. In these ways, he is both insider and outsider with respect to both the British and the Arabs.

The first level of the tension manifested in ethnic and cultural differences reiterates a distinction in Hawaii between Caucasians or Whites of Euro-American ancestry, who are called haoles in Hawaii by all ethnic groups, including Whites, and "locals," brown-skinned people of Asian or Pacific Island ancestry. Some Kumu Aina citizens explain that haole means foreigner, people of a different breath or spirit.[1]

Lawrence's embodiment of crucial cultural differences helps him to blend them in creating the Arab state. On the one hand, he "lays down the law" to the people, which borrows from the liberal British tradition, but on the other, he "inspires" them. He breathes new life into them. As their spiritual leader, he gets them to make commitments to each other, helping to generate a bond among their various tribes. His leadership, which thus combines law and inspiration, shows that even those of a different breath (Whites) can contribute to the political liberation of people who have been oppressed by White nations. Even so, because he can never become "one" of them, Lawrence leaves the Arabs and returns to his home culture once his work is done.

The formation of community focuses on the boundary between the community (the Arab nations) and those outside it. The Arabs' political success depends upon generating community among their diverse tribes and establishing a clear boundary between themselves and the British. Perhaps it is because Lawrence is an outsider, with no tribal ties, that he can arbitrate tribal disputes and redirect attention toward the common enemy, the British.

What becomes central in the final resolution of this opposition between the British and the Arabs is Lawrence's willingness to respect that boundary himself. Even though he understands the culture of the Arabs and can lead them in battle, he does not become one of them. He has "his own culture" and he has no desire to obliterate cultural differences. In this sense, Lawrence transcends the liberal position that sometimes wishes to ignore cultural distinctions. Culture, in fact, is what makes it possible for him to belong somewhere, to say "my own people." Culture creates bonds and is, therefore, a resource for engendering community.

This emphasis on the boundary between community members and outsiders does not mean that no attention is paid to the boundary between family and community. Lawrence experiences alienation in his kinship family—the British—which itself distorts his affections. While this narrator's version varies from the film in this detail, the narrator has carefully constructed his version of the story in order to make this very point. What is important then is what the narrator wishes to explain by constructing the tale in this way rather than how closely this details follows the film or book. This is what is important about the story. In the narrator's story of Lawrence, sexuality, which normally binds the adults of the family together, alienates Lawrence from his ethnic kin. Of course, this is not quite a family, but it is important to know how Kumu Aina citizens define family. While in Euro-American terms the traditional Hawaiian concept of family encompasses the "extended family," for Kumu Aina citizens family is not constituted by blood ties. Families will adopt persons into their circle who are not related through blood lines. These persons may even be adults. With such adoption, in turn, comes the invitation to join in holiday celebrations and to share in the responsibilities and privileges associated with caring for children. The family bond depends upon a kindred spirit and a self-conscious commitment to support each other, rather than exclusively on genealogical lines.

This concept of family extends to politics and has recently been manifested in the political formation of the Kaho'olawe 'Ohana, a group of some 300 members. The term <u>ohana</u> means family. This group's purpose is to protect the island of Kaho'olawe, an uninhabited part of the Hawaiian chain, from damage by the U.S. Navy, which has been using it as a target for bombing practice. The island, which contains ancient Hawaiian temples, is regarded as a sacred place in the native Hawaiian tradition. At one meeting, a leader in the Kaho'olawe 'Ohana said to the entire assembly, "You can all call me Auntie." In this sense, the concept "family" denotes a large group of persons tied together by both blood and friendship not unlike a tribe. Having become aware of their common heritage, they form bonds based not only on that heritage but also on a shared vision of the future, including a political program for realizing that vision. Hence, the family serves as a basis from which to build common bonds that tie people into community with one another.

The story of Lawrence constitutes community as the unification of Arab tribes asserting itself against domination by foreign colonizers. The bonds that unite the community derive from a common spiritual and philosophical tradition. Once a leader able to draw on that resource can unite the people for political purposes, even if these include perilous military actions. Such unification displaces the tensions within the community and focuses them instead on the tension between the community and "outsiders," British colonialists in the case of Lawrence and the U.S. Navy in the case of the Kaho'olawe 'Ohana. Lawrence's successful leadership depends on his possession of both the spiritual aptitude for mediating among the Arab tribes and the military aptitude for bringing Arab interests effectively to bear against British power.

It is important to note here that there are some within the Kaho'olawe 'Ohana who have argued that the U.S. government actually has no jurisdiction in Hawaii because the islands were acquired through illegal military action by colonialists. Others argue from a less radical perspective and focus on the rights of the Hawaiians to this sacred island, using the U.S. Constitution and Hawaii's statehood as a basis for that argument. In either case, the U.S. Navy represents an "outside" force.

Generally speaking, in contrast to the citizens of Essex, Kumu Aina's citizens worry more about problems they encounter from outside the community than about those that they encounter as individuals trying to balance family and community commitments. For Kumu Aina citizens, a strong extended family structure makes possible the unity that is necessary to maintain the cultural identity of the community. Unlike Essex citizens, who assume that the "greater community" is like them, Kumu Aina citizens clearly perceive that the "outside community" is not like them and can, in fact, threaten their values.

Metaphors

Lawrence's spirituality "inspires" unity (community), obedience to the law, and collective action against the British. In this sense, Lawrence is a political "savior" for the Arabs. The mix of religious and political language in the narrative offers a different model of politics from that of Essex, for it underscores the leader's role in generating both spiritual commitments and military ones. The charismatic quality of Lawrence's leadership derives in part from the degree to which he has come to understand their cultural tradition, which itself becomes the basis for their collective action. Lawrence unifies the people under a single philosophical and spiritual tradition, and then implements the law to organize them for effective action.

This connection between religious discourse and political discourse echoes the concerns of the Hawaiian Renaissance movement. From the perspective of that movement the arrival of Captain Cook and the "discovery" of the Hawaiian Islands represents an invasion by colonialists, which is still going on. The military presence of the U.S. government, which holds some of the choicest beach property, serves as a silent reminder of the role an alien military force played in depriving the Hawaiians of their sovereignty as a people. Perhaps the most vivid example of the blending of religious and political discourse emerges in connection with the struggle over Kaho'olawe. This island traditionally has been a sacred site for native Hawaiians. For the native Hawaiian Renaissance movement, the Navy's use of the island as a bombing target is a poignant reminder of the problems caused by people outside the Hawaiian tradition who make very different uses of land. Not only has the Navy's bombing destroyed remnants of heiaus (ancient Hawaiian temples) and other archaeological sites, it has made it impossible for people to make pilgrimages to the island despite its spiritual significance for Hawaiians. For these Hawaiians, spiritual survival (the life of the spirit in both a religious and cultural sense) requires political action, and the movement has developed various political strategies aimed at stopping the bombing and taking control over the island away from the federal government. The Protect Kaho'olawe 'Ohana follows traditional Hawaiian practices in its meetings: opening and closing with a prayer, sharing mana'o (feelings and thoughts) and using ho'oponopono (a method of conflict resolution designed to "make it right"). By calling on these traditional Hawaiian spiritual practices, they recover their cultural roots while shaping community bonds and advocating public policies.

The Lawrence tale clearly suggests the Hawaiian Renaissance movement. The Navy represents the colonialists. The 'Ohana, even though it includes some members whose ethnic identity is not Hawaiian, represents a bond between those who are Hawaiian by blood and others who are Hawaiian by spirit. In this sense, the 'Ohana blends cultures (tribes) and corresponds well with Lawrence's united Arabs. The blend of people who make up the 'Ohana retains, however, elements of cultural diversity. The characteristically American image of the melting pot fails to capture its essence. Instead, the image of the rainbow, a frequent visitor to Hawaiian skys, more accurately symbolizes a unity that preserves diversity. In this sense, the entire Lawrence story serves as a metaphorical commentary on the Kaho'olawe struggle, which dramatizes the tensions between the culture of Hawaii and that of the United States mainland, between military-technical interests and cultural-religious interests, and between the wealthy Navy "class" with its solid economic resources and the poor native Hawaiians with their limited access to organizational resources.

Transformations

One of the most important transformations in this narrative takes place in Lawrence himself. In this narrator's version of the tale Lawrence is transformed from an enlisted man in the British army into a military genius who leads the Arabs to victory against the British.[2] Lawrence's political transformation comes about in part in the wake of a physical and psychological assault. By experiencing humiliation at the hands of British Officers, Lawrence shares in the Arabs' oppression. The officers physically oppress him and their oppressive acts affect his consciousness, causing "his mind to snap." As a colonial soldier Lawrence is the oppressor; as object of British brutality, he is oppressed. His humiliation paves the way for his exaltation in the eyes of the Arabs--he is "almost worshipped" by them. His departure from the Arab world and his final transformation, his death in an accident, leaves the work that he was to do undone, suggesting the need for a new leader. In this sense the story suggests a cycle, which calls for a new "Lawrence."

A second important transformation takes place among the Arabs, who discover the means of changing themselves from a collection of colonized tribes into a unified independent nation. With Lawrence's leadership, the Arab people are able to transform their political status, despite their inferior one-shot rifles. It is their spiritual and cultural unity that makes this transformation possible.

Contradictions

Lawrence's insider/outsider status presents an important contradiction. A colonizer becomes a liberator, and it appears that his status as colonizer is almost a requirement for his work as a liberator. His power to unite the tribes depends upon his lack of tribal affiliation and his military genius profits from a knowledge of the British military, which allows him to see the Arab's strengths.

A second contradiction lies in the fact that it is through a humiliatingly painful experience that Lawrence gains leadership. He moves from rank-and-file soldier to commander. Had Lawrence remained in power his elevation would seem less contradictory, but this "great" man returns home to death on a motorcycle. This emphasizes Lawrence's humble origins, and shows his return to the rank-and-file of those who have died, while the world waits for a new leader to take over the work. Greatness is mixed with humility, leadership with both affection (they "almost worshiped him") and alienation (he cannot become "one of them"). This is more than a commentary on the problems of cultural diversity. It is also an observation on the nature of leadership, in which affection is seen to be mixed with awe and alienation.

Horton Hears a Who

The next story reinforces the theme that political survival depends on spiritual unity and an effective leader who can mediate between different worldviews. The narrator is a Euro-American man who finds himself well integrated into Kumu Aina life. His casual dress and gentle open philosophy distinguish him from the stereotypic Euro-American professional.

> Horton, the elephant, was at his waterhole when he saw a little fuzzy thing fly by that looked like the top of a white dandelion. Elephants have good hearing and he heard a tiny little voice say, "Help! Help! Help!"
> He looks up and sees this little fuzzy thing headed for the water and he sticks out his palm and catches it. Holding it to his ear, he hears, "Help!" in this little tiny voice.
> He talked to the lions and his other friends around the waterhole and he said, "We got to help these guys."
> But they said, "Horton has flipped out. He is talking to the fuzz. Horton, you are crazy so we are going to get rid of you. You young elephants are all alike." They tried to smash it. They said, "We will boil it in water."
> Horton said, "You can't do that. There is something here on this fuzzy that we can't see because they are so small."
> They planned to trap him and take the fuzzy, but the wind caught it and it sailed over the mountain top and landed in a huge field of fuzzies. Horton knew that he had to help those guys. He looked over millions and millions of fuzzies and located the one he was after and took it back to the waterhole. He told the people on this fuzzy thing, called "Whos," to get everybody to yell at the same time. Then the others will be able to hear them. He says, "Get them out in the city square and everybody yell at once."
> They did, but only Horton could hear them. Then they said, "Wait, we will get

all our cymbals and make other kinds of noises." Again they tried with no success but then they discovered one little baby that had been forgotten. They all tried once more and with this addition of the one tiny voice, the animals heard them.

Oppositions

As in the Lawrence story, two different worldviews create the primary opposition. Although in this case they do not represent different nations, they symbolize different cultures. The waterhole realm threatens the survival of Whosville as the British threatened the Arabs. Horton, like Lawrence, belongs to the "threatening" realm and experiences humiliation at the hands of his own "people," his own culture. They mock him and consider him crazy. Like Lawrence, Horton's mind also "snapped." Horton's goal, like that of the Arab's leader, is to gain recognition for a new "state," Whosville, which has not yet been recognized by the powerful Waterhole animals. Like the Arabs, the Whos need unity if they are to succeed with their claim to existence as a separate "real" community. The Whos' primary political concern is creating a clear boundary between themselves and the outsiders, the Waterhole animals, so that they will no longer be invisible objects readily available for smashing. An outside force that nearly leads to their destruction. Without the animals' recognition of the existence of the Whos, and a legitimate border between the two communities, the Whos will not survive. Their community emerges by differentiating itself from the outside culture. For the Whos, yelling is the equivalent of the Arabs' military campaign; both struggle to establish their community's identity and sovereignty. The narratives chronicle their struggles.

Metaphor

Using animals to allude to a dominant culture and the tiny Whos to symbolize a minority culture articulates the situation in that Kumu Aina citizens find themselves. The urban Honolulu culture represents values which differ from theirs and make communication between the two areas difficult. Because developed listening skills are crucial to cross-cultural communication, Horton's special abilities in this area represent an important political virtue. Kumu Aina citizens make this point by censuring people who talk too much by saying that they are all "talk, talk, talk," which means <u>not</u> that they talk too much and do too little but that they listen too little. Kumu Aina mothers remind their children of the importance of listening by touching their child's earlobes. Good listening is a virtue that leads to greater community, but so is speaking up by the community as a whole--everybody yelling together. Good political communication requires both careful listening and persistent speaking up. And, even the smallest voice counts.

Sensitivity to the importance of listening has a special history for the citizens of Kumu Aina, who in earlier times were called the deaf people because they did not respond when people journeying through their region called out to them. Actually, their lack of response reflected their shame at having so little water that they were unable to offer any to passing strangers. Water is a central metaphor in the Horton story, and it also refers concretely to Kumu Aina's historical struggle. In more modern times, the struggle between the taro farmers (taro is the root used to make <u>poi</u>) and the big plantation owners revolved around the issue of water. The plantations drew water from wells (waterholes) rather than from streams in the traditional way, lowering the general water supply in the process. Taro farmers depend on stream water flowing down from the mountains. The plantations' extraordinary demands for water affected the entire area's water ecology and seriously threatened taro farming and its support for a way of life. This can be understood as a struggle between the native Hawaiian culture, with its subsistence agriculture based on taro, and the Euro-American culture, which organized agriculture industrially in the interests of producing cash crops for world trade. The "waterhole animals" have the power; water represents both a physical necessity and a sign of power and authority. Those who have plenty of it should learn to listen to the claims of others who want only a small place of their own in which they can be Whos.

Transformations

Like Lawrence, Horton undergoes humiliation before he is able to be an effective leader for the Whos. Like Lawrence, his ability to enter into another worldview, to empathize, makes him a successful leader. In Horton's case, of course, leadership derives entirely from his genius as a listener. Unlike Lawrence, he does not engage in military action. Perhaps, however, they are not as unlike as they may seem to be at first. The first narrative carefully explains that Lawrence was somehow able to learn about the Arab culture as the Arabs understood it, so he, too, must have had some talent for listening. At the same time, while Horton's leadership finally saves the Whos, in the process he puts their lives into even greater jeopardy than before. He draws attention to the fuzzy thing and places the Whos at risk. Lawrence's rally of the Arabs for united military action similarly exposes them to heightened danger as the price of ultimate recognition and sovereignty. And, despite the risks to which Horton exposes them, their outspoken unity, as nurtured by the big-eared mediator's listening skills, transforms the Whos from a state of existential "death"--political oblivion--into that of a recognized community.

A third transformative agent is the wind. At the most critical point, the wind takes the Whos out of the clutches of the waterhole animals. Kumu Aina's residents are likely to understand nature as a partner in cultural development, regarding as alien the Western understanding of culture as a struggle to control and "tame" nature. Some even talk about such natural phenomena as the sea, mountains, wind, and sharks as brothers and sisters.

Contradictions

The tale suggests that political success (gaining recognition is the first step toward exercising power) depends upon complementary skills between the leader and the people. Horton listens well. He really is not a persuasive orator, and at first, he fails miserably even to convince the animals of the Whos' existence. However, the Whos' power comes not from their ability to yell loudly but from their ability to yell together, to act in unison; and Horton encourages them to commit themselves to following this course. Their strength is in community not in this or that individual. Horton's political strategy is simple: He has faith in them and in their power as a community, even though as individuals they are as nearly invisible as they are inaudible. The contradiction, then is that the apparently powerless can have latent powers on which they can draw decisively. It may even be their lack of power (their smallness) that makes it possible for them all to come together in the town square and speak out as one.

A second contradiction exists in that Horton's

cultural difference from those he leads enables him to represent them. In this sense, the embrace of cultural differences is a source of power. In contrast to the liberal myth, in which in order to share power people need to be culturally homogeneous and leaders need to be "representative" of the people, the Horton narrative suggests that sharing power requires differences. The leader's power comes about because of such differences, and the leader does not so much represent the people as provide inducements and opportunities for them to communicate with each other and with outside communities that threaten their well being. Such a leader plays two roles: first, mediating differences within the community so that the community itself can unite (shout together); and second, mediating differences between the community and outsiders. It is because Horton is not really a Who that he is able to serve as their leader, and because he is not like them that he can help them. The deep structure of the narrative suggests that leadership requires very special gifts in the specific domain of cross-cultural understanding and mediation. In the perspective of liberal American culture, in which it is characteristically assumed that the leader embodies the best talents of the people and simply expresses them at a higher level of excellence, this is a contradiction.

A third contradiction lies in the fact that the Whos seek independence from the waterhole animals while at the same time they seem to want their help. Ultimately, they seek a cooperative relationship between the two communities. Like the Arabs, they want independence, because the waterhole animals not only refuse to recognize them as "real" beings but have the power to smash their world.[3] But, in their independence, they want to work out friendly relations with their erstwhile oppressors. This vision of ultimate cooperation may not be explicitly articulated in the Lawrence story, but the fact that the narrator tells us that Lawrence is going to England to work on the problem there suggests the possibility of cooperation, expressive of a general cry for help from the colonized to the colonizers in the interest of creating a different kind of world for all concerned.

Don't You Salute Second Lieutenants?

This next story demonstrates how a native Hawaiian can play a leadership role in the United States military. Caribou, the protagonist, is a native Hawaiian with remarkable talents in the ocean. He can swim unusually long distances and knows how to read the waves so well that he can travel on a surfboard from island to island in the Hawaiian chain, a feat involving distances of twenty-five miles or more. On first reading it may seem that Caribou is not a leader but a victim. A closer glance will show how Caribou has helped the U.S. Army gain some independence from its own bureaucratic structure. The story is told by a Chinese man who values Caribou's friendship highly.

My friend Caribou, by all standards, is poor but in another sense is richer than most of us. When he joined the Army, he had some difficulties.

One day, he was walking toward the PX and saw an officer on a bike. He thought it was a second lieutenant. He was looking at the PX wall when he heard the screech of bike brakes right next to him. A voice says, "Soldier, turn around. Don't you salute an officer as he goes by?"

He turned around, and it was a general, and so he saluted him. Caribou said, "I thought you were a second lieutenant."

"Well, don't you salute second lieutenants?"

Caribou says, "Ah, I really don't like to."

The general got so mad at him that he rebuked him right on the spot for not being military. Caribou wasn't military at all. In his simplest words he said to Caribou. "You are under arrest. Don't move, don't leave, don't run away. I am going to have you court-martialed."

Then, weeks later, they went to the courtroom for the trial. The charges were read. Caribou tells the story and says the guy said, "Blababababababababababab, do you understand that?"

"Yes, sir."

"Are you guilty?"

"Yes, sir."

Caribou's defense counsel said, "Wait a minute, Caribou doesn't understanding a thing you said." He explained that these Hawaiians get into the service and are very loyal Americans. If they are told to charge, they will charge and fight for their country. But they really don't understand these military procedures." He said, "Caribou do you understand what he is saying?"

"No, sir."

"Why did you answer, 'Yes, sir'?"

"I figured that is what he wanted me to say."

The courtroom and the judge began to chuckle.

"The charge is that you turned your back on the general and failed to offer him a salute. Why did you fail to salute the general?"

"I thought he was a second lieutenant."

Again the general was angry. Some Army people understand the Hawaiians like Caribou and defend them. They always get into trouble.

The judge said, "For your punishment you will spend two weeks in the stockade."

Caribou said, "Does that mean I can leave the PX?"

The judge said, "What do you mean?"

"Three weeks ago the general told me not to leave, that I was under arrest, so I stayed in the same spot where we had the confrontation."

"Everyday? Day and night?"

"Yes, my friend Fred got me clothes and Harry brought me something to eat."

The judge was very surprised. He said, "This is a loyal soldier. The general told him not to move and he hasn't moved. Nobody would do this except a very loyal and simple soldier like Caribou. The case is dismissed." The general was very angry and began yelling at the judge.

The judge said to Caribou, "We have to give you a job where you more fully understand the work." He moved him to the Haliewa Army Beach to work.[4]

Oppositions

In this story, as in the earlier tales, the primary opposition exists in the tension between two worldviews. The antagonist, represented by the general, embodies an ultramilitary culture, while the protagonist, represented by Caribou, embodies the Hawaiian culture. In playing out this opposition, the public political action culminates in the trial that incorporates three sets of actors: the bureaucratic structure, represented by the military, played by the general and the prosecutor; Hawaiians, represented by Caribou and his friends, played by the rank-and-file men, who help Caribou both in setting up camp at the PX and in his defense at the trial; the mediator, in this case played by the judge and the courtroom audience.

However, within this drama, a more abstract opposition is to be found. Caribou represents an authority structure alternative to that of the military. While the military bonds its members through a command structure with strict rules, Caribou creates bonds in a different way. His way is based on personal commitments and friendships rather than on rules and regulations. Caribou points out the difficulty of obeying the letter of the law by his exaggerated subordination to it--he remains exactly at the spot the general ordered. Once the courtroom laughs, it signals that he has taught those present something about the limitations and even the ridiculousness of attempting to base collective action solely on rules and regulations. At a political level, the opposition is between the community based on friendship bonds generated by Caribou and the community based on rules generated by the military.

Metaphors

Caribou's name itself invokes a metaphorical reference to an animal. This animal allusion itself creates a link between social life and nature. Anthropologists have studied totemism in a number of Polynesian societies, and today one encounters people in Hawaii, both native Hawaiians and others, who have special affinities with certain animals. This metaphorical link asserts the connections between human society and natural phenomena. The connection between the wind and animals in the Horton story, between animals and social structures, and even between Caribou and the ocean constitute a social political order that works cooperatively with nature rather than competitively against it in the interest of domination and control.

Transformations

Caribou's own inner discipline and commitment make it possible for him to confront the military system. But, he also needs others to help him, even though their help arrives without Caribou requesting it. His counsel defends him, friends assist him, and finally, the judge rewards rather than punishes him. The trial enriches Caribou not merely in the sense that he "gets off" but in the sense that he obtains a better assignment as a result of it. As with Lawrence, what begins as humiliation ends as exaltation, and both Caribou and the army are made stronger by the experience.

Friendship plays a major role in enabling Caribou to transform his situation from that of a disgraced soldier to that of an honored one, holding a choice assignment. In order for Caribou, and hence for Hawaiians, to gain recognition from the military realm, it is necessary for them to unite with friends. With his friends' help, Caribou wins over the judge and the courtroom audience. He builds these relationships on the basis of respect, which includes the recognition of cultural differences. His assignment at the beach not only makes use of his own talents but enables him to honor both his military commitment and his own cultural practices. Since work in and by the ocean plays a central role in Caribou's culture, the new assignment signals respect for that culture.

It may be helpful to know that, after his military service, Caribou continues to work on the beach where he has established himself as one who can take time to talk with people at length about basic philosophical issues and where he teaches young people and adults about the Hawaiian culture. In this respect, Caribou plays a role very similar to that which Plato assigns to Socrates. The public forum for Caribou is the beach. In itself, the beach represents the boundary between the island and the sea, the island culture and the cosmos; and, one can easily see how such a setting is conducive to asking general questions about the condition of humankind and its role in the cosmos.

Contradictions

While this story is in some ways an archetypical military tale, the Caribou version emphasizes the contradiction between two cultures. From the military perspective, Caribou's unusual loyalty appears to be contradicted by his disobedience in declining to salute second lieutenants. What is more, he successfully challenges a general. He creates a community of persons who, although they are not Hawaiians, begin to follow Hawaiian values by laughing at their own ridiculous activities, recognizing the value of friendship and taking steps to defend those who need someone to speak up for them. The forum of the courtroom provides a setting that encourages carefully listening to testimonies, which in some sense are stories. Caribou, with some special encouragement, is able to tell the story in a way that shows the weaknesses in the military system without undermining its basic values. At the same time, he acknowledges his own "guilt." By exaggerating military obedience, Caribou shows the contradiction between the spirit of the military, which requires unity and courage, and the regulations, which can create alienation and subservient cowardice. He shows it is possible to be committed to the authority of the military without becoming a slave to its regulations. In this critique, the court serves as a mediator between the strict military obedience model that the general embodies and the spirit of obedience that Caribou advocates. In this regard, Caribou becomes a mediator between the U.S. military and the native Hawaiian culture. Caribou's status in the military is not enhanced because he obeys the rules but rather because his loyal spirit enables him to go beyond the obedience of ordinary soldiers. In contrast to the Essex stories, Caribou does not climb the "military" ladder; he does not even recognize some aspects of its hierarchical order, although he does recognize hierarchies. He does not seek his own niche on the ladder. Instead, he seeks friends, who then find him a place at the beach. Unlike the Essex model of community bonding, this tale suggests that community bonding takes place through friendship rather than through establishing a position, an occupation.

LEADERSHIP AND HUMILITY

The next three narratives, told in abridged form, draw from well known tales to speak about life in Kumu Aina. These narrators quite self-consciously use these tales to describe political life in Kumu Aina and to show what can happen when leaders lose their humility.

David and Goliath

This next story develops this contradiction between power and humility while underscoring the importance of a spiritual dimension for building a political community. The narrator, a Japanese-American man, uses a biblical story to explain how a small and "powerless" person can "save" a people against gigantic powerful forces. He is an active community leader, who concentrates his energy on becoming aware of citizens' needs.

> The thing that sticks in my mind is that a lowly shepherd--a sheep boy--can challenge a monster, a Goliath. Because of the oppression and tyranny that the monster represents the youngster finds the courage to act. His people were fighting for the freedom to farm, to raise herds, to not be enslaved.
> No one dared challenge Goliath because he was so strong. No one would challenge what was happening until this young boy came along.
> In times of crisis, there is always someone who will come out to lead the people. It is at these times we find true leadership that guides our destinies. Today, we don't have any leaders, so we are in a similar situation. The world has no leadership and the Goliath of big governments, big bureaucracies, and multinational companies are the Goliaths of today.

The Secret of Beaver Valley

A native Hawaiian woman reveals the connection between society and nature in this tale. The story itself could easily be told though a *hula*, a dance that tells a tale drawn from the wisdom of the Hawaiian tradition. While this story originates in Euro-American literature, this woman's version carries a message that articulates contemporary Hawaiian concerns.

> All the animals live well together on this beaver pond. One beaver family is very happy because they have two new beavers in the family. One looks very strange because he has huge teeth; they call him Ernest. Each year, his teeth got bigger and his legs got bigger until he grew into a monster. Ernest had grown into a bulldozer.
> The other animals stopped working because he could do all the work for them. He got grapes for the fox, honey for the

bear, and so on. He ate trees; so they had to keep feeding him trees, so he would keep working.

Eventually, they built an entire organization with doctors, businessmen, politicians, and he is still doing all the work. He gets bigger all the time, and they have to keep working harder to feed him. Finally, there is only one tree left, called Big Tree. All the animals used it to play hide and seek; it symbolized pond life.

Now it was a battle between Big Tree and the beaver. The beaver tries to knock the tree down, and finally he does. Then, there is no more food for him; the snow comes and buries him. Ernest rusts.

But then in the spring, the tree has a new sapling coming from its roots so they know it is still alive. But, back at the dam, there is another family with another young beaver who looks very much like Ernest.

The Ways of Leaders

This elderly man, born in Japan, uses a traditional Japanese story to explain how greed destroys community and leads to the loss of political power. He has lived in Hawaii since before World War II and serves as a wise elder to many citizens in Kumu Aina, where he and his family have lived and worked for many years.

They killed the leader and then they became the leader. Because Tokugawa Yeasu wanted to be a leader, his family started a war and killed the leader Toyotomo Oshi. Side (pronounced seed-eh) Oshi was the first king in Japan.

Tokugawa wanted to be the king, so he killed Toyotomo. He could be a king like that. Tokugawa ran Japan three hundred years. He ruled for some fifteen years and then his son and his son, so for three hundred years they governed Japan. This is as long as many governments last.

He lasted so long because he wasn't too greedy. He wanted to control Japan, but

Tokugawa was like a businessman, and he controlled Japan to create business with those outside the country. That was wrong, because he didn't do what was good for the whole world but only what was good for Japan. We should make everything that we do good for the world. But he did make a government for three hundred years.

COMMUNITY COSMOLOGY: BONDS AND BOUNDARIES

In building community, the Kumu Aina stories argue that there are two barriers: First, the leader must find a genuine source of unity among community members; second, the community itself must secure its boundaries from "outside" dominating forces. A master plot from these six stories emphasizes ten functions that move the story from the private realm to the political realm. The Lawrence narrative illustrates the dynamics of the master tale. A table that charts the plot pattern for all the narratives in this section follows at the end of the chapter.

<u>Private Realm</u>

1. Leader's kinship identity established and family membership asserted.
Lawrence is a colonial soldier.

2. Problem of kinship relationships among new community members is raised.
Narrator explains tribal tensions and lack of trust.

3. Assertion of family unity and authority.
Lawrence is a rank-and file-man, a solid colonialist.

4. Leader experiences humiliation from his kin.
Lawrence sexually assaulted and humiliated by officers.

5. Moment of release.
Lawrence's mind snapped.

<u>Public Realm</u>

6. Protagonists leads a challenge.

Lawrence and Arabs challenge the British in war.

7. Mediation and unification.
Lawrence mediates among the tribes and then between Arabs and British.

8. Action produces a transformation.
Lawrence becomes spiritual and military leader.

9. Liberation experience.
They gain independence.

10. The leader "retires" and the cycle begins again.
Lawrence leaves them and dies before attacking the roots of the problem.

Oppositions

The analysis of oppositions reveals how Kumu Aina citizens create the bonds that make them a community. Unlike the Essex community, which locates that boundary in the struggle between responsibilities to family, on the one hand, and to community, on the other, the Kumu Aina community locates its identity struggle between the community and outside political forces.

One consistent tension in these narratives is that a modern technical bureaucratic society threatens a smaller community built upon friendships and long-standing commitments to a life that integrates nature and society. While the first four narratives--Lawrence, Horton, Caribou, David--are tales of victory for the community, the last two--Beaver and Tokugawa--tell of its defeat. The story of Beaver Valley most clearly dramatizes this tension. At first delighted by the mechanized modern society that comes to them, they finally collapse under its weight.

For the Kumu Aina citizens, this opposition expresses a very real issue. The citizens see the mechanized bureaucratic society of Honolulu encroaching on their borders, and they fight to maintain the rural face-to-face society that they prefer. However, there are young citizens in Kumu Aina who, like Ernest, earnestly want change and think that it will actually help citizens to live more comfortable lives. While many citizens prefer to settle disputes in the Hawaiian style, finding friends and neighbors to mediate, others seek lawyers and other bureaucratic means of resolving conflicts and otherwise ordering their lives. In this context, the story of Beaver Valley counsels caution in the face of the dangers inherent in modernization and in leaders who lack humility.

The tension between two worldviews is a fuller manifestation of this technical/traditional opposition. Each of these stories articulates such a tension, but as it turns out, it is a vital force, which helps to bring forth excellent leaders and which itself becomes the basis for community bonds. It helps to protect leaders from cultural pride and oppression. Lawrence does not become an Arab, and Caribou does not try to militarize himself. And because they retain their cultural identities, they are able to create a genuine community that not only recognizes differences but positively values them. Rejecting a melting pot image, which brings along with it a spirit that fosters obliteration of such differences, these stories assert that community thrives on maintaining its diversity. Its rainbow of colors supplies just the right hue to a community searching for a beautiful whole. While one color may dominate for awhile, the changing picture allows for a variety of combinations to emerge. The successful leader knows how to draw from this variety in solving problems and creating a coherent and satisfying pattern.

The unsuccessful leader does not have the benefit of this cultural tension. Both Ernest and Tokugawa give way to excesses--of greed in Ernest's case and ethnocentrism in Tokugawa's. Ernest even eats up the forest. Both become monsters, finally losing their positions because they become too interested in forcing their worldview on the entire world. They become imperialistic, excessively proud of their own accomplishments and correspondingly contemptuous of the needs of others and of other ways of life--other cultures. In this sense, they fail to respect diversity. In these narratives, the weak become powerful by constructing an intricate bureaucratic structure that eventually perishes and returns them to their original state of weakness. Unlike Lawrence, they do not have conflicting membership in two warring camps. Hence, they are more susceptible to cultural pride, which ultimately leads to their downfall. The stories tell us that after a victory over oppression, a community needs harmonious relationships with outsiders. A good victory is one like Caribou's, which gains power and recognition for the community with outsiders but does not then arrogantly assert monopolistic claims against them. This suggests that the <u>good</u> leader will embody a tension between insiders and outsiders and will refrain from attempting to dominate either element.

These narratives focus so intensely on leadership because the spirit of the community is articulated in the person of the leader. This spirit creates the bonds that make the community one. The bonds that shape these people into a community are forged by a leader. This does not mean, however, that the leadership is totalitarian or even what is commonly understood as charismatic. Instead, effective leaders are those who can mediate between the two different cultures because they live in both worlds at the same time. Unlike the Euro-American concept of leadership, such leaders wish to create an integrated political center, not a neutral one; they have clear roots in one culture, and they respect those roots, while at the same time, they know and have ties to the other. They recognize cultural differences and know that they have not transcended them.

In the culturally diverse context of Kumu Aina, extended families may represent different cultures, not unlike Lawrence's Arab tribes. At one level, this means that families may feud more that they do in a community like Essex, because they encompass larger numbers and a far greater diversity of people. But, through personal commitments to one another, families form a network of relationships. This means that families generate closer bonds among more citizens than can be the case in Essex because the level of commitment associated with family life extends more broadly throughout this network. Community cohesiveness comes about through uniting these family networks. Like the practice of adopting family members, citizens make a conscious commitment to the people of the community rather than to laws or written constitutions. If they were to dramatize their commitment in a political ceremony, the leaders would be less likely to pledge their allegiance to the law than to pledge their friendship to one another. An enormous feast, like a luau, at which attendance by three hundred people or so would not be unusual, might well serve as the proper occasion for making such a public commitment.

Comparing the bonds that bring together Kumu Aina citizens with those that unite Essex citizens illuminates a striking difference between the two. In Kumu Aina economic roles or occupations do not play a prominent role. Instead, a network of personal commitments, friendships, combine with the inspiration of a leader to become the basis for community unity. Those who listen well and make their humility evident, whatever their occupation or economic circumstances, can become leaders or otherwise contribute significantly to the success of a community effort; those who, like Ernest, work hard only to produce or acquire material wealth are dangerous characters not to be trusted, because even though they may become powerful in some sense, their power is essentially destructive. Caribou illustrates the proper leadership spirit in his integration of humour, humility, and discipline. These values create unity and draw citizens into collective action.

Metaphors

The narrators of these Kumu Aina stories mix spiritual language with political language. However, this spiritual imagery does not come from organized religion but emphasizes cosmological connections. The metaphorical use of animals and animal names establishes connections between nature and society. The beavers create a society; community members incorporate animal identities through personal names like Caribou. Kumu Aina citizens explain that natural phenomena, the land itself no less than plants and animals, are living beings. Citizens with sophisticated knowledge of Hawaiian traditions explain that rocks, land, and trees have spirits and can teach those who learn to listen to their messages. This is not a superstitious notion about talking rocks but an elaborate metaphysics, which teaches the connections between nature and society. Of equal importance are the connections between nature, community, and family. The reference to "shoots," which appears in the Ernest tale, signifies a spiritual connection between family and community. Native Hawaiians explain that family, 'ohana, relationships develop because all members spring from the same root. They use the image of the taro shoots to illustrate this point.[5]

In linking religious discourse with political discourse, water plays a central role. Water is a primary spiritual image for both the Christian and native Hawaiian religions, and it also plays an important role, as indicated earlier, in the political life of this community. It connects to both the spiritual and the physical life of the community, because Kumu Aina needs water for its agriculture and, hence, for the physical well being of both plants and citizens. Water plays a central role in both the waterhole story and the story of Caribou. It represents life itself as manifested at both the

spiritual and the physical levels. Ecologically, it links the human well being with the well being of nature.
Both the Goliath and Lawrence tales draw on religious allusions as a basis for challenging oppressive forces and, in that way, link politics with religion. In general, their language suggests that spiritual bonds are the primary source of community. The Kaho'olawe 'Ohana, described in an earlier section, clearly embodies this idea when it links kindred spirits together in a single spiritual "family" to bring about specific political changes aimed at creating harmony and new life for Hawaii's citizens.

Transformations

The most spectacular transformation in these narratives is the change in the protagonist from a humiliated, powerless figure into a powerful political leader. Not only do the heroes (Lawrence, Caribou, David, Horton) rise from humble origins but the greedy leaders (Tokugawa and Ernest) dramatically rise to power from humble beginnings. A difference seems to be that the greedy leaders rise by humiliating others, while the good leaders suffer humiliation themselves. Tokugawa kills his way to rulership and Ernest consumes the forest, nearly killing Big Tree. David comes from very humble origins but, unlike Lawrence and Horton, he does not directly experience humiliation at the hands of his opponents and we do not hear what happens to this "lowly sheep boy." He challenges the monster, but the narrator does not tell us if he is successful, perhaps suggesting that the challenge is still going on.[6]
The good leader transforms the community by creating greater unity. Perhaps, this is most clearly demonstrated in the tale of the Whos, but Lawrence's Arabs and Caribou's situation also make the point. Unification takes place by concentrating internal energy and by not giving in to outside forces. Even a leader such as Lawrence, who might have been able to negotiate a compromise settlement, avoids that strategy. In contrast, the leader succeeds by inspiring people to make strong commitments to the community on the basis of which effective collective action becomes possible. Through collective actions, such as warfare, yelling, or a trial, changes take place. In this respect, Kumu Aina is not understandable in terms of the liberal model suggested by the Essex narratives. Leaders neither negotiate

compromises nor resort to education as a means of transformation. Instead, they turn to the community's own historical traditions--its spirit. Caribou does not learn how to become a good soldier; he calls upon Hawaiian values to improve military life.

Hence, these narratives suggest that political transformation should be rooted in a community's own historical spirit and that it should move forward to realize that spirit. In this sense, the Kumu Aina community is conservative; not, of course, in the sense of the neo-conservatism of America in the eighties, but in the sense of the classical conservatism delineated by Edmund Burke.[7] The norm these stories express is that political action should attempt to integrate the human community with the natural environment, so that the two are mutually nurturant. Such an ecologically balanced society would produce a Beaver Valley with only ordinary beavers, "earnest," perhaps, but about using trees judiciously in order to protect the natural environment as well as to address human needs. It would also want to recognize and preserve cultural differences within the community. Caribou's new assignment represents a blending of both the military culture and the Hawaiian culture in a mutually beneficial way. But such blending can take place only after public recognition of such cultural differences and public articulation of respect for both worldviews.

Contradictions

The leaders embody a dual identification that itself represents a contradiction. Lawrence oppresses the Arabs as a British citizen and then liberates the Arabs from British imperialism. In trying to rescue the Whos, Horton endangers them and yet finally enables them to unite so that the other animals can hear them. In these cases, the leader is someone who embodies both the "outside" dominating culture and the "inside" community's values. Caribou is a native Hawaiian, an outsider to the military, but able to work within the Army and with Army personnel to gain an advantageous assignment benefiting both him and the Army. Because the leader, in some respect, lives in both cultures but makes a commitment to a particular political struggle, he unites one group while maintaining ties with the opposing force.

A second contradiction is between weakness and vulnerability, on the one hand, and strength and invincibility, on the other. In fact, power somehow develops out of weakness. Lawrence's humbling experiences make him effective. David's challenge against Goliath is important precisely because David is so small and vulnerable yet assumes effective leadership in a crisis. In some way, Caribou's humiliation by the general becomes the condition for his final victory over him. Meanwhile, Ernest the beaver is undone by his mindless drive for wealth and domination and the Tokugawa family finally loses its grip on Japan as the price of its own arrogance. These stories tell us that the contradiction between weakness and strength is mediated by the positive force of humility: With it, the weak can be powerful; without it, the strong are undone.

This marriage of humility and leadership is apparent in Hawaii's leaders at the national level as well as at the local level. United States Senator Daniel Inouye, referring to the defeat of his Democratic Party in the presidential election of 1980, had this to say: "It has never hurt anyone to go through a humbling experience. Whether you admit it or not, if you're in a position of leadership too long, there's a tendency to get a wee bit arrogant and a wee bit sloppy."[8] He, thus, placed emphasis on humility and, as may sometimes be necessary, the "humbling experience" as a condition for success in public life. Such an experience may strengthen the leader internally, by averting the pitfalls of arrogance, and externally, by showing the people that he or she remains one of them. In this sense, the experience serves a democratic function and publicly symbolizes the fundamental equality of a people and its leaders.

TABLE 2. KUMU AINA   Private

	Establish Kinship Ties (1)	Threat to Kinship Ties (2)	Assertion of Family Unity and Authority (3)	Moment of Release (4)	Humiliation (5)
Lawrence of Arabia	Lawrence dual identity: colonialist soldier & Arab savior	Tribes fight among themselves	Lawrence is rank and file soldier under military authority; Arabs like him	His mind snapped, because he was humiliated	Colonial officer humiliates him
Horton Hears a Who	Animals are all happy around the waterhole	Horton hears the Whos call for help, but other animals don't hear them	Animals unite against Horton	Whos are blown away	Animals humiliate young Horton
Don't You Salute Second Lieutenants?	Caribou is both a Hawaiian and a soldier	Caribou is separated from his people by the military	Caribou becomes a rank-and-file soldier	Caribou turns his back and does not salute	The general humiliates Caribou by placing him under arrest
David & Goliath	David is a shepherd boy	The monster Goliath tyrannizes David's people	People were fighting for freedom to farm		David was young lowly shepherd boy
The Secret of Beaver Valley	All animals live happily by the pond	A beaver child is born who has strange teeth	Ernest helps the other animals and gets food for them.	They experience freedom from work	
Ways of Leaders		They (outside family) want to be leader	Oshi first king in Japan		

		Public		
Issue of Challenge (6)	Mediation and Unification, Pulling Together (7)	Action Directed Toward Social Transformation (8)	Liberating Action (9)	Returning Home (10)
Lawrence and Arabs challenge colonialists	He mediates among tribes	He becomes their spiritual and military leader	They gain independence	Lawrence returns to England to continue work and dies there
He challenges them and tries to find Whos	Horton gets all Whos to shout at once so they will be heard	Finally, they all shout including the tiny baby	With the addition of this one voice, they are heard and saved	
Caribou challenges the military system	Friends mediate for Caribou at the trial	Caribou unites the courtroom through his honesty and humor; they all laugh together	Caribou is freed from the charge	Caribou returns home to the beach
David challenges the monster	David's courage leads the people in their struggle	David becomes their spiritual leader		
Ernest challenges the pond way of living	They form organizations with bureaucracies, businessmen, and politicians	They must work very hard to continue to feed Ernest; Ernest kills Big Tree for food	Ernest rusts and dies; the community is destroyed	Big Tree has a new shoot; a strange beaver is born with big teeth
Tokugawa Yenso challenges Side Oshi	Tokugawa wins and his family rules for three hundred years	He is not too greedy but limits his interaction with outsiders		He becomes greedy and loses rule

6
Transforming Institutions:
Participation in Essex

> "It's a great huge game of chess that's being played--all over the world--if this is the world at all, you know. Oh, what fun it is! . . . I wouldn't mind being a Pawn, if only I might join--though of course I should like to be a Queen, best."
>
> Lewis Carroll
> Through the Looking-Glass

Institutions and the customs and traditions that they give us make it possible for us to play such games as Alice has in mind. They even create roles, such as pawns and queens. Institutions offer us sets of rules, expressed as customs and traditions that govern us. The patterns that they provide enable us to interact in an orderly and meaningful way with each other, endowing us with a set of reliable expectations that manage our daily lives. In this way, our social institutions govern us more thoroughly than even government laws, because they guide and constrain us in all of our daily interactions, while government laws rule us far less comprehensively, even if at times we may be more conscious of their role in our lives. For example, college students know that they are to sit in chairs when they arrive in the classroom and usually teachers can count on them doing so, because it is so clearly "the way it is in college." Their experience with educational institutions has taught them what is expected of them and, at this point, they have come to expect it of themselves. But beyond providing such order for us, institutions give meaning to our social existence, making it possible for us to collectively share such complex activities as marrying, raising families, gaining educations, voting, making contracts, and passing laws.

However, the static structure of these inherited institutions, with their habits and rules, is challenged by citizens who act to alter them. Seeking changes in the institutions, they challenge them politically, and when successful, as they sometimes are, the institutions are re-formed. Thus, to understand a political community, it is important to examine the social institutions that regulate its daily activities and to examine the challenges that citizens bring to those institutions. Examining this nexus between the authority embedded in institutions and the political actions of citizens desiring to alter them, to organize their authority differently, reveals how citizens understand political change itself.

To understand how Essex citizens confront their social institutions, this chapter studies six stories in which citizens challenge their social institutions. A structural analysis, following each of the first two narratives, explores how Essex citizens challenge a central feature of Essex's political life--the institution of private property. The remaining four stories, presented in abridged form, reinforce the pattern laid out by the first two while offering nuances of their own.

PRIVATE PROPERTY AND PUBLIC RESPONSIBILITY

Since private property plays such a major role in this chapter, it will be helpful to begin with some background on Essex's residential structure. The home symbolizes private property and Essex, a suburban residential community, offers a show-case of homes. "Private" homes line the streets and neatly arranged yards clearly mark boundaries between families. Private property represents the private part of the private/public distinction and physically demarcates the boundaries between individual families and between the collectivity of families that makes up the public sphere. City government exercises some control over these homes through zoning restrictions and strictly enforced codes that specify standards for home maintenance. Private property, as it turns out, is more than a merely private matter. Participation in Essex depends upon the citizen's ability to "buy into" the community, and this means owning a home in a market that begins at about forty thousand dollars and moves upward to a quarter of a million. There are few renters. These owner-occupied homes publicly proclaim the economic status of their residents. The general appearance of the community makes a statement to both insiders and outsiders, and this statement is carefully controlled by the regulations that compel citizens to maintain their lawns, repair their garages, and paint their homes. This internal-external statement, however, creates tension between the sanctuary of the private family, which it publicly acclaims, and the affluent reputation of the community, which it also publicly acclaims, leaving citizens to struggle with the problem of how to maintain the community's reputation while protecting their private rights to live in any manner they choose or can afford. Such tensions as these, between the maintenance of particular institutional structures like private property, which represents the community's commitment to individual freedom, and the necessity of controlling those "private" properties so that they fit into the community and support its public life, require constantly altering and adjusting the relationship between private property and public order.

The first narrative examines the tension between private property as both a private and a public resource. As a public resource, it is a means by which the community can recruit citizens and continually renew its powers, as well as demonstrate to the world that it maintains the affluence for which it is known.

Alleys and Anger

Some citizens in northern Essex wished to have their alleys paved. This woman, a member of the city council, recalls the controversy.

> I was contacted about putting alleys in north Essex. The alleys were not paved and gravel was coming into people's homes. The northern Essex people said they did not think it was fair, because other areas of the city had paved alleys. So, the mayor told them to get petitions to bring to the council. They did this work.
> Whenever there was any controversy, there would be large crowds at meetings. Otherwise, no one except a reporter or two would come. This time, there was a big crowd. We had a gallery of about thirty chairs, which was not large enough. Even the larger room upstairs was jammed and people were furious. We were going to see if we could arrange to get the alleys paved, but it was going to cost the taxpayers some money, which would be calculated by the footage on the alley. Many people were on fixed incomes and one didn't want to say anything against them, but there were two

sides. We had several meetings and people were furious with us. The last one was right before the Fourth of July parade.

The council members were in the parade and, as I sat in the car waiting for it to begin, I recalled that one man had gotten so excited that he said he was going to get his gun out for us. Nobody was panicky and we weren't threatened but he was so emotionally keyed up that he expressed himself that way.

After the meeting was over, I thought we ought to try to help these people. If we had any little amount to cut the cost down, we should use it. Many years before I was in Essex, the council had done the alleys in central and south Essex for free. Now, we didn't have the money, but something should be done. I don't think that the citizens knew that I had proposed that.

The fun of the story is that when it was all done, the people loved the alleys. It was so much better for all the people and even those who were against it even told us they liked it. Often council members don't get any credit for their actions. But, then, for me to see all that anger and frustration turn out so well was one of my best memories.

Oppositions

The opposition between the pro-alley people and the anti-alley people comes before the town council, that is expected to mediate the dispute. However, this proves a difficult task which tests the strength of this public government institution against the institution of private property. If the city government cannot maintain order and prevent citizens from going for their guns, it fails. Hence, the opposition challenges the government because it articulates the contradiction between the public promise to provide civic amenities for its citizens and its responsibility for protecting the rights of private property owners to be secure in their individual homes. However, to fully protect homes, the government must keep the neighborhood property values up, which requires control over private property, for the physical state of each person's home affects the economic value of other homes in the neighborhood. Homes are not fully private matters.

But, in this case, protecting some peoples' property might force others to lose their property. The council faces a dilemma between protecting property values, which requires paving alleys, and yet protecting residents against "invasion" by government forces, that might cause them to lose their property. This dramatizes the difficulty of maintaining a clear private/public distinction, for the institution of the family requires public support and public good requires sacrifices from the family. The family home becomes the arena for the struggle between these two domains, for the choice of wholly rejecting any imposition of public interests over the purely private interests of home owners is not a real alternative. The narrator explains that even the gravel from the alleys actually invades the private property of citizens. Certainly the assessments needed to pay the cost of paving the alleys will invade the private economic resources of the community's homeowners. The two institutions, family and government, are intimately intertwined even though Essex citizens strive to keep them separate.

Metaphor

The storyteller takes pains to explain that the reference to the gun was not meant as a threat but rather as an expression of frustration; hence, it was a metaphor that articulated violent feelings, not a sign of possible violent actions. The Fourth of July parade itself symbolizes the independence and, in the same moment, the interdependence of community. The allusion to the Kennedy assassination shows how connected all citizens are and how vulnerable they are to each other. This vulnerability requires a careful balance between private and public interests. The narrator's own contribution to this ultimate resolution demonstrates a careful managing of this private/public balance, for she privately negotiates for public funds to help the people of north Essex. Eventually, the costs of paving the alleys are shared between the two constituencies, the city and the taxpayers whose property most directly benefit from the work. This is not a compromise solution, however. It is an "adjustment" that, she explains, is necessary to create equity between the north section, which had to pay for the paving, and the other two sections, which were paved in earlier times when the city paid for the expense. Since no homes were lost as a result of the assessments, the balance turned out to be proper.

Transformation

The primary transformation in the narrative has two levels. The council meetings become crowded scenes of controversy rather than their usual sparsely attended routine business meetings. The second transformation turns the controversial, almost "explosive," event into a party (fun), which overflows with love--"the people loved the alleys." The institution of city government provides a regulating mechanism between too much concern, controversy, and too much complacency which is shown by the unattended meetings. As long as the meetings provide this context for resolving issues, the city council protects its citizens and serves its purpose of providing a neutral forum in which competing interests can solve common problems.

Contradiction

A contradiction that faces the narrator, the council, and the citizens is that the city government cannot merely provide a neutral forum for the resolution of conflict; it must make a decision. Its decision goes against the anti-alley people, but the narrator is able privately to find assistance for them and so helps to ease their defeat. Thus, in some respect, the city council can begin anew as neutral territory, having mitigated its apparent favoritism toward the citizens of central and south Essex by finding some public funds for the new alleys. The story, therefore, reassures citizens that, even in making a controversial decision, the council can remain in some sense neutral. However, the story also lets it be known that this friendly neutrality is not necessarily recognized by citizens and that often the council fails to get credit for what it does, because whatever it does will disappoint some constituency. This problem of maintaining a neutral image in the midst of partisan struggles gets emphasized because the council rests its claims to leadership on the presumption of its nonpartisan orientation and the entire city government takes pride in its transcendence of partisan loyalties. Despite these claims, however, it must act in partisan ways. Hence, the narrator emphasizes that in this case even those "violently" opposed to the paving plan, because of the drain on their own resources, eventually "came around," acknowledging the wisdom of the council's action. It becomes important then, in the context of this contradiction between city government as a neutral forum and as a partisan force, that its decision satisfies the interest of the public. In this case, even those opposed finally saw that what was good for Essex was also good for them.

At another level, the contradiction that the narrative articulates is the tension between the public sphere, represented by the city government, and the private sphere, represented by the frustrated citizens. While, on the surface, these two spheres represent different elements in Essex life, at a more fundamental level, they are intertwined. No neat separation can be maintained, for the city government must constantly deal with those who feel that it may threaten their homes and property rather than provide protection for them. If such tensions could not be resolved, the legitimacy of the city government would be threatened or undone. This story resolves the tension between private property and public civic services, while suggesting that it does not always turn out this way. The story shows us that private property and public matters are intertwined.

Squirrels and Families

In the next story, a young professional man, who grew up in Essex and lives with his elderly parents, explores the tension between private property and civic order. As an active participant in an Essex Protestant church and in various community improvement projects, he has encountered the problem of integrating private interests with public needs. In this case, it is not the city council but a neighbor and some squirrels that pose a threat.

> We had a new family move into the neighborhood who were a little stand-offish. If you want privacy, the people here respect that and leave you alone. That was fine, except for one problem.
> Two doors away from there was a lady who took a great deal of interest in nature--especially our marvelous allotment of squirrels, which includes an albino squirrel. The squirrels are very fast and fun. Unfortunately, the population has been growing, extensively, and there is no real natural enemy for the squirrels except car wheels.
> She was concerned for the squirrels and so started to feed them. She put nuts all

over her yard. They took to that quite well and that attracted squirrels from other neighborhoods.

It got to be a serious problem with squirrels everywhere. When you reached for the newspaper they would think that you were bringing them nuts and would come. She became a little eccentric. She was painting the nuts different colors so the families would know which was theirs. Unfortunately, I discovered that squirrels are color blind. The thing got involved.

The stand-offish lady took serious offense at the entire thing and decided to curtail it. She began to talk with the neighbors and everyone became aware of the problem.

She went to the State Department of Natural Resources to borrow some squirrel traps. The traps would not harm them but would only cage them and she could take them out in the country and set them free in the natural environment.

She arranged with a number of us to place the traps in our yards. The traps would trim the population a bit.

The woman who was feeding the squirrels was incensed. Not only did the idea of catching the squirrels upset her but this would break up squirrel families.

At night, one woman would set the traps and then later, under cover of darkness, the other woman would come around and spring them. Finally, the traps were effective. They kept moving them and concealing them. It turned into a minor feud. The lady who was upset about the squirrels actually began spraying defoliant all over the other woman's front yard, which killed the bushes so that she could not hide the traps. It ended up in court.

So, fortunately, they are all still living here but they don't speak. Other than that, everything is back to normal. The squirrel population is in line--though I must admit that the rabbit population is getting out of hand. Something ate all of our marigolds, and I don't think it was the squirrels. But that will probably be another story.

Oppositions

The opposition between the squirrel feeder and the squirrel trapper takes place because the institution of private property is insufficient to the squirrel problem. Squirrels do not recognize property lines. One woman's excessively "stand-offish" perspective, her passion for privacy, encounters the excessive public generosity of another woman who insists on feeding both her "own" squirrels and others as well. Like the alley tale, one family's action threatens another family. The solution does not lie in simply protecting private property, for either way someone's property will be "violated." Even the population control plan requires crossing boundary lines in order to capture squirrels. Although the woman who executes the plan asks permission to set the traps on other people's property, this strategy only accelerates the problem. Settling the dispute involves the stand-offish woman in the politics of the neighborhood and even beyond, as she seeks help from outside political institutions, including a state agency and the courts. While private property boundaries confer a measure of protection, they are insufficient for maintaining an orderly community life. Such order requires negotiations among neighbors and even legal action in order to find satisfactory solutions to problems. Such order requires a healthy, even active, public life.

Metaphors

The use of terms like "normal" and "eccentric" evoke psychological images of these women. The emphasis on the albino squirrel echoes the tension between the "normal" and "unusual." Normally, the squirrel situation is not a problem and private property separates families. However, in this circumstance, a problem necessitates participation by the entire neighborhood and two social agencies. The metaphor "getting out of hand" suggests that ordinarily the situation can be handled. This also recalls the alley tale, in which an "out of hand" situation evoked violent language. The language about car wheels as natural enemies of squirrels adds an ecological note. Neighborhood life has a natural balance that ordinarily requires very little political effort. The allusion to war under the "cover of darkness" and the use of a defoliant heightens the tension by suggesting the potentially damaging aspects of this event. The image of a neighbor "killing" private property with defoliant is suggestive of the problem that occurs when the institution of private property does not work adequately. In this context, interpersonal or interfamilial problems legitimate intense public activity by citizens. <u>Normally</u> public life operates automatically, without citizen assistance.

Transformations

The squirrel problem transforms the newcomer into a "normal" neighbor. By protecting her privacy, she becomes involved in public discourse and abandons her "stand-offish" perspective. The squirrel protector, who has become "eccentric," returns to "normal" as she becomes less excessive in her public activity. The story itself addresses the problem of interfering both with the balance of nature and with private property. Both types of interferences challenge the institution of private property because, no matter which side either the public or the government takes, private property will become subject to public regulation. However, because the problem disappears, the story can reaffirm private property in its conclusion. It then can keep neighbors within the bounds of "normal" behavior without too much neighborliness (inviting squirrels into your property) or too little neighborliness (being stand-offish). Property buffers differences, and by maintaining its boundaries, a community can preserve peace. When property cannot do this, political institutions such as public administrative agencies and courts can.

Contradictions

The exaggerated features of these women--too much and too little involvement with others--illuminate the tension between private concerns and public peace. In this story, private property serves its traditional symbolic function of creating a haven for individual variation, but when that variation goes too far, it becomes a battlefield--even with night defoliation maneuvers. To maintain her <u>privacy</u>, the stand-offish woman must become intensely involved in <u>public</u> life. Essex considers itself a "conservative" town, in which government "interference" in private life is to be kept at a minimum, but even in this context citizens advocate public controls over property; they advocate "interference." Hence, citizens must continually confront the tension between the sanctity of private property and the need for public political controls to maintain the particular model of privacy that they prize.

PUBLIC STATUS AND PRIVATE FUNDS

The next two narratives also concern the institution of private property but go beyond looking at tensions among families and between families and the city government. The first tale explores the problem of private property inside the home; the second examines the issue of whether an "outsider," whose values do not fit Essex's norm, should be permitted to own a home in the community. These two narratives illuminate the problem of setting limits on the community's regulation of the institution of the family and its locus of power, the family home. The third narrative investigates the tension between public needs and services and private, even egocentric, interests in power. It serves as a summary to this section on institutions.

Fifty Cents Found

The narrator of the next story moved to Essex shortly after her marriage. Her story recalls her childhood experiences on a southern Ohio farm in the fifties. Small towns like the one in which she was raised are to be found every few miles along the highways of Ohio. On Saturday nights, the towns fill with farmers, who come to shop and otherwise entertain themselves. Town streets become public forums with the overflow retreating to the single local bar or coffee shop. Small truck farms produce considerable revenue and serve as reminders of the intimate association all Ohioans once had with the land. Rural farming arts appear in Essex itself in backyard gardens, which offer these residents therapeutic and recreational, if not economic, sustenance. The narrator's story draws upon farm life as a source of values, especially honesty and simplicity, which Essex citizens find very appealing even though they have long since left the farm.

> One time, my Dad had lost fifty cents down an old sofa. He knew he lost it and we all looked for it and couldn't find it. We would have given it to him if we had found it, for we were taught this. If we swore, lied, or stole, we were beat. We just didn't do these things.
> One day, I happened to be playing and I found the fifty cent piece. I thought,

"What do I do with it?" I didn't tell my dad that I found it. We didn't have any money, but that was no excuse.

That next Saturday night, I tried to hide it. If you ever try to hide something that you aren't supposed to have, your conscience won't let you. But I kept it hid. We went to town every Saturday night and went to church on Sunday. This Saturday night, I took that fifty cents with me and I thought, "How can I best spend it so that no one would know?" I went into a dime store and bought three pair of socks. Then I bought two or three different items that couldn't be noticed. I don't know why I thought those socks would not have been noticed. Then I thought, "Oh it is my chance to buy me some candy all for myself."

I hid it very carefully. When I got home, it was that hard cake decorator candy that cannot be eaten. It taught me a good lesson; you never get away with it.

The Publisher Purchases a House

The publisher of <u>Trickster</u>, an erotic magazine, bought an Essex house for $375,000. A number of citizens came to a meeting.

They said, "What are we going to do about this terrible thing?"

Sam, the mayor, and I talked about it, and I said, "Sam, you have to resist them. Anybody has a constitutional right to buy a house. If he trespasses on the law, the law agencies will deal with him. If they don't, it means he has not done anything wrong. Why should anybody be on his back?"

I don't want <u>Trickster</u> magazine in the school and, of course, the students will want Leonard Ross, the publisher, to address them. My response will be, "If you can get three or four journalists and publishers who have different points of view and Leonard Ross is one of them, that is fine. If you want to get Leonard Ross to hassle the school administrators, forget it." This is the kind of incident which creates conflict.

Budgets and Facts

There were two areas in the council budget--recreation and planning--where we did not have enough facts, but we had to pay the workers, so we agreed to pass the budget and reevaluate these portions later. We were allocating a sufficient sum of money to the Recreation Board. Everyone agreed, because we could not respond without the facts.

A couple of council members took it upon themselves to go to the recreation director and start hammering him with facts. They exposed themselves to facts no other council members had. In addition, they promised not to do this. They came to the next council meeting to try to make themselves look good.

I do not see the Essex council as a forum for ego building. The three other council members agreed with me and they were turned down flat. They wanted increases in both recreation and planning.

We met with the Planning Commission and the Recreation Board and they said the budget was fine.

Oppositions

In each of these three narratives citizens want so much to enhance their private property and the services that support it that they are willing to violate the rules to accomplish their ends. The young girl is willing to "steal" from her father; citizens are willing to attempt to prevent the publisher from living in their community even though such action violates public law; and some council members are willing to violate an agreement with others in an attempt to secure the budget outcome they desire. In this respect, the narratives reveal a tension between private desires for control and the community's rule structure, which is designed to limit and control desire. Because these citizens act on private desire with a disregard for public good, they fail. Hence, the stories argue that even on self-interested grounds it is better to obey the rules and not give in to unlimited self-centered desires. The young girl's candy is too "hard" to eat. The mayor will resist the citizens who wish to prevent the publisher from purchasing a home, and the clandestine budget advocates lose their bid for power. Citizens like those opposed to the publisher engage in excessively public activity and control, which is very similar to the case of the squirrel protector with her defoliant. Leonard Ross cannot be prevented legally from purchasing a home. The council members who wish to increase public recreational services also find themselves confronting limits. Such limits on public activity help maintain a balance between public and private spheres. It is only with great deliberation and difficulty that a public city government finally decides to increase its services (the alley story also makes this point); the government is moderate in fulfilling its desires. This is a model for citizens who should also be moderate in pursuing their own desires.

Metaphor

The presence of metaphors of violence suggests that when the private realm experiences challenge it responds with a threat. The clandestine council members "hammered" the recreational director with facts. The young girl knows that if she is found out her father will "beat" her. Short of violence is the force of law that both protects and limits rights. The publisher's privacy must be respected but, if he "violates" the law, "the law agencies will deal with him." Sweet victories turn into hard lessons, just as the sweet treat became hard cake decorators candy. Because Essex citizens believe that the public good requires prevention of excessive pursuit of pleasure by private citizens, they see public law and custom as means for regulating citizens. These laws and customs create a balance between private pursuits, which private property symbolizes, and public needs. When citizens become excessively selfish they become excessively active in public affairs, in an effort to gain greater power. As the little girl who wanted more needed to take it from the household, so the private family that wants more needs to take it from the public realm. This makes it necessary for other citizens to engage in public activity to counter their purposes. Normally, however, the rules--customs, agreements, laws--curb these excessive desires, which would otherwise infringe on the rights of others. In this sense, these stories take the problem of ladder-climbing one step further. They deal with excessive self-seeking (excessive ambition) and its consequences for public life.

Transformations

These narratives portray citizens who begin with a narrow self-interested view of the world but who acquire a broader public view, a moral consciousness. In "Fifty Cents Found," the young girl said she wanted to do something for "myself." This excessive me-ism ignores the benefits of obedience to social institutions, in this case represented by her father. Her ego, however, turns out not to be served by her action and she learns, that even from a personal perspective, it is necessary to observe the moral code, which in this case takes the form of respect for private property. In the case of the publisher, the narrator argues that citizens must respect both the law and their own moral codes in regard to private property. Since the moral code clearly states that "anybody has a constitutional right to buy a house," the citizens must observe this principle.

The deep structure of the narrative relies upon a private/public distinction to explain how it is that citizens can justify doing nothing about a notorious pornographic publisher who lives in their residential city. The narrator explains that despite their personal feelings, egos, they must be guided by constitutional principles. To emphasize this point, the narrator introduces the protagonist first as the "publisher of Trickster," which places him in his public economic role but, later in the story, refers to him by name, Leonard Ross. This language represents a transformation in Ross's identity from his public role to his private role. The last narrative most directly addresses the problem of ego. As the story progresses, the original issue of the budget gets lost in a clash of egos struggling for preeminence. The narrator explains that this violates the purposes of the council: "I do not see the Essex council as a forum for ego building." So this case is not a matter of different policy values but rather an attempt by some to gratify their individual egos at the expense of the council's public responsibilities. Their efforts fail and the narrator uses their failure to explain the importance of honoring public principles and agreements. "Everyone agreed because we could not respond without the facts." But these people sought the facts privately in order to "make themselves look good." Selfishness and duplicity, whether about recreation budgets or ill-gotten candy, brings only hardship in the end. These various transformations show the importance of using public moral codes to discipline private selfish desires against temptations to extremism. Honoring codes that protect and preserve private property serves this end.

Contradictions

Citizens in these narratives confront a contradiction in their dual commitment: protecting the private realm, private property, and "invading" it to provide for the community as a whole. Alley assessments and attempts to prevent certain citizens from purchasing property in Essex demonstrate the reality of this tension. The stories show public activity in terms of protecting the community as a whole, which makes it easier at least to consider invading the private realm. The community's moral principles--rules, customs--can resolve most tensions. In the case of the alleys, the solution comes through a public open meeting, and in the case of the publisher through the application of legal principles. However, both stories show the contradiction between the public's responsibility to protect private property and the public's responsibility to protect its interests as a collective entity. The narratives painfully remind citizens that the city does invade and that, in the wake of such invasions, some interests emerge victorious while others go down in defeat. But, as long as the rules themselves "win," the defeats are tolerable. Then, the "hard" candy becomes a lesson in moral behavior, providing a means of transforming individual ego needs into a public moral conscience oriented toward doing what is best for the community as a whole. This protects the social institution of private property itself, rather than satisfying only the individual's needs of the moment. The publisher story makes this point by explaining that, if the citizens throw Leonard Ross out of his home, they will also jeopardize the security of their own private homes. Simply put, this requires adherence to moral codes--not stealing, lying, or otherwise violating the rules of fair play in the game of community life.

SOCIAL CHANGE AND POLITICAL INSTITUTIONS

From the narratives in this section, a model of Essex emerges, in which citizens move back and forth between the privacy of their lives, represented by their private property, and civic concern, motivated by a desire to maintain a high quality of public services and an attractive image of the town in the minds of outsiders. This produces tension between the desire to protect private families from excessive "intrusion" in the form of taxes or other threats that might lower property values and the desire to maintain Essex's reputation as a upper-middle-class community with fine homes and excellent services. When a problem arises, citizens, like the woman invaded by squirrels or those whose homes were invaded by alley gravel, come out of their private spheres to participate actively in public life. Normally, people restrict themselves to their private lives. Political scientist Mark Roelofs describes this "crisis model" of politics as a serious problem for the American political system.[1] Roelofs argues that this means that only temporary quick-fix solutions are sought to problems, leaving them structurally intact and ready to erupt again. Essex citizens, through these narratives, present a different model. What is important to them is that political participation is possible. When there is a problem, citizens can find a public forum for their greviances. The council makes room for crowds and council members listen to the crowds. Because the political system in both its formal rules and informal customs disciplines its citizens, it takes care of most problems and, hence, citizens do not need to participate frequently. In this sense, the tales assure that the institution of private property works and that families are secure against threats from their government or from their neighbors. The institution of government and the institution of private property constitute a balance that assures justice. From time to time, however, that balance requires some adjustment at the hands of citizens, who play their role in helping to maintain the institutions that govern their lives.

The narratives repeat the loss-gain pattern of the stories in Chapter Four. Citizens who lose the battle gain alleys and finally their own happiness. The little girl who "gained" the fifty cents in fact lost because it brought her more pain than pleasure. Each narrative, by showing that those who try to "win" by violating the rules of the institutions actually "lose," affirms the value of these institutions and their ability to regulate citizens as long as a "little" help comes from the citizens themselves. Thus, the stories support the myth that what makes America work is not deep social transformations but small adjustments on a case-by-case basis that maintain basic institutional structures. Citizens are always there, ready to come to a meeting, ready to discourage fellow citizens from violating constitutional rights or to encourage children to respect property. They continually maintain their institutions by respecting the rules and customs that structure them and by participating in politics when other citizens' excessive public activity challenges them.

TABLE 3. ESSEX

	Private			Public
	Ego Expression (1)	Establish Home/Domain (2)	Nurturing: Helping/Hurting (3)	Entry for Resources (4)
Alleys and Anger	Protagonist contacted about putting alleys into north Essex		Citizens who want alleys follow mayor's direction and work on petitions	Alleys would be paid for by assessment of bordering properties
Squirrels & Families	Stand-offish woman moves into neighborhood	She maintains her privacy, which others respect	Eccentric woman begins feeding squirrels	Squirrels begin coming into neighborhood from all over
Fifty Cents Found	Father loses fifty cents in old sofa		Family teaches that there should be no stealing, lying, or swearing	They cannot find money; later daughter finds the money and hides it
Publisher Purchases a Home	Publisher of erotic magazine buys a house in Essex			Number of citizens meet to stop him
Budgets and Facts			Two areas of budget-recreation and planning-lack data; cannot make decision, but pass them so workers will get paid	Council agrees to pass budget and reevaluate budget by meeting with Planning Commission and Recreation Department

Public

Bonding to Public Realm (5)	Challenge (6)	Conflict Resolution, Loss (7)	Gaining a New Community (8)
Controversy over paving alleys brings large number of citizens to Council meeting	Fixed-income citizens challenge "tax"; one man threatens to "get a gun"	Council decides to pave alleys	When it was done, all the people loved the alleys.
Stand-offish neighbor begins to talk to people to correct this problem	Trapping squirrels leads eccentric woman to destroy foilage in yards where traps are concealed	The neighbors go to court, and these women do not speak	Neighborhood returns to normal
She buys herself things in town—white socks and candy	She challenges her own actions	The candy cannot be eaten because it is only for decoration	She gains a lesson: you never get away with it
The mayor protects individual rights to property and resists citizens pressure; he backs mayor and upholds law	Students will want publisher to speak at high school and will challenge principal	He will allow publisher to speak as long as other views are also represented	While he may be outraged by publisher, he will protect his rights
Everyone agrees to pass budget, get facts later to adjust it	Some council members meet privately with Recreation Department; he challenges them	They wanted to increase budget; they lose	Everyone agrees that it is fine the way it is

7
Kumu Aina:
Challenges to Social Institutions

> However, there was the hill full in sight, so there was nothing to be done but start again. This time she came upon a large flower-bed, with a border of daisies, and a willow-tree growing in the middle.
> "O Tiger-lily!" said Alice, addressing herself to one that was waving gracefully about in the wind, "I <u>wish</u> you could talk!"
> "We <u>can</u> talk," said the Tiger-lily, "when there's anybody worth talking to."
>
> Lewis Carroll
> <u>Through the Looking-Glass</u>

Alice's experience with the tiger-lily reminds her of how important it is to be a receptive listener in a conversation. Because she is open, although it is her unusual Looking-Glass experience that creates this openness, she is able to listen. In Kumu Aina, citizens seek such openness, and when it is found, it becomes the basis for deeper relationships and new vistas. In challenging their social institutions, these citizens hope to create deeper relationships with each other.

INSTITUTIONAL DEMANDS AND COMMUNITY COMMITMENTS

In the structure of social institutions, Kumu Aina citizens experience a conflict between their own cultural traditions, which structure primary commitments around family and friends, and the demands made by institutions shaped by the Euro-American tradition. The following story, told by a native Hawaiian, describes his experience of this tension in the school system.

To follow his story it is helpful to begin with some background information on the educational system in Kumu Aina. While in most mainland U.S. schools, the local community administers the school system, in Hawaii, the state bureaucracy makes all school administrative decisions, including personnel decisions. Many teachers assigned to Kumu Aina come from other areas of Hawaii or the U.S. mainland and are unfamiliar with the Hawaiian culture. Although many within the school system are Japanese-American, these Hawaii residents, like their Euro-American counterparts, also often lack knowledge and appreciation of native Hawaiian practices. This means that the school system in Kumu Aina represents an institution imposed from the outside and often fails to reflect the interests and concerns of community parents and elders.

This native Hawaiian storyteller describes a turning point in his life that reflects the problems such an external institutional structure generates. As he explains, it is customary in his Hawaiian tradition to display modesty about one's achievements, so as not to create the feeling among one's friends that one person is better than another. Friendship is a basic component in the structure of community and requires a sense of genuine equality. Boasting about individual accomplishments or publicly stating that some people are superior to others weakens the community. While this may seem to inhibit individuals, they experience it as a benefit that gives them a strong sense of commitment to one another. Native Hawaiians joke that Hawaiians are like a bucket of crabs. When one tries to get out the others try to pull him back. At first glance, this appears to be a humorous way of pointing out the shortcomings of this emphasis upon modesty, but reflection reveals that this is a way of explaining the importance of the community and the willingness of Hawaiians to give their lives to support and be with others. They value each other and the community very highly.

Learning About Injustice

I first realized the magnitude of the injustice in the fourth grade. I was a good reader even when I was young but nobody knew about that because it wasn't something to talk about. You didn't go around saying I am a good reader. You just read. It was no big thing. I liked to read. Other guys like to surf.

We didn't do that well in school because for us it was a social trip. Eating lunch was what school was to me, but it was also interesting and I learned things. I also didn't learn some things. We did not have high marks and were in a half-half class, a class of average ability.

One day, we had a reading test. We had a Japanese teacher, and I think she was racist. She was always talking about her Japanese boys. I guess she was from the plantation and had finally made it in the system. She was an old lady and I still remember her name.

I never tried that hard on tests. The reading test was very easy for me, but she didn't know that. She thought that Hawaiians were ignorant and that all they did was steal. Anytime anything was missing she looked at us. We used to cheat on tests because that was being a friend. Everybody takes care of everybody else. Hawaiians take care of everybody else. If they knew the answers, they shove the answers down. All the Hawaiians sat in the back and on a math test we helped each other. If you know the answers, you don't cover them up. If you do you will get a lickin' afterwards. So the Japanese kids used to get a lickin' after school, because they wouldn't share their answers.

I scored the highest in the class. After she corrected the test, she called me to the front of the class. She said, "I want you to tell me how you cheated."

I said, "I what?"

She says, "I want you to tell this class how you cheated."

"I didn't cheat."

"Don't lie to me. You are going to stand in front of this class until you tell me how you cheated."

She couldn't' figure out how I "cheated." Everybody had a different test so it blew her out. When you are young and don't know about prejudice you don't understand. I was holding back the tears and she says, "You are going to sit there until you tell this class how you cheated."

That was a turning point. She could not accept the fact that Hawaiians had intelligence and simply didn't respond to her system. If we didn't want to study, we didn't. I didn't want to stick out and be a brain.

Oppositions

An opposition articulated in this narrative is between two cultures--Japanese and Hawaiian. But at a more fundamental level, this opposition evolves into an opposition between the local Hawaiian culture and the imposed Euro-American culture to which the Japanese school teacher already has adapted. From the Hawaiian perspective, this becomes an opposition between friends and the educational system, because Hawaiians take pride in taking care of friends. They say, "Everybody takes care of everybody else." The school system, whose structure and curriculum represents the Euro-American culture, emphasizes individual achievement and values individual competition over friendship, particularly the kind of "taking care" of each other that is so central to the Hawaiian way. Ironically, the test the teacher gives reveals more about her attitude than about the student's performance. She shows herself to be either ignorant or unappreciative of the cultural values and practices of her students. Her failure helps to explain the tension between the Japanese students who, from the Hawaiian perspective, selfishly cover up their answers and the Hawaiian students who "punish" them after school. The narrator does not take a neutral position in the tale but takes a stand. He shows how the educational institution fails to meet its goals because of its inability to integrate the two perspectives. In addition, the school creates tension among its students and, because of the teacher's own ignorance of her students, fails to educate them. Because the Hawaiian students fail to understand the nature of the prejudice involved, they withdraw from the institution. However, the narrator does not romanticize the Hawaiian perspective but gives an honest account that shows flaws on both sides. He knows well that the "lickin's" given the Japanese represent unfair actions on the part of the Hawaiian students and that sharing math answers represents "cheating." His story does not condemn the school but instead calls for it to incorporate some aspects of the local culture into its structure.

This tension between the educational institution and the Hawaiian culture need not exist. In Kumu Aina, some teachers make use of the value of friends helping each other, encouraging students to study together so that their pride in their friendship commitments will make them work hard and perform well. However, because part of the problem is the teacher's racism, overcoming it requires a new way of thinking. It cannot be overcome by the mere application of new teaching techniques. This is why the narrator, who himself has excellent teaching skills, does not offer a quick solution but instead draws attention to the cause of the problem. "She could not accept the fact that Hawaiians had intelligence."

Metaphor

By suggesting that, for some students, school is primarily "eating lunch," the narrator shows the importance of social relationships. Rather than build on the social network, the school frustrates it by ranking students and making them compete against each other. In picturing the group, he does not use hierarchical images. He does not say that he did not wish to be "above" others, but instead that he did not wish "to stick out." The test itself, an instrument for ranking students, becomes an interesting metaphor, for while it begins as a test to measure the students it ends up measuring the teacher and the school system.

Transformations

This narrative challenges the authority of the school. Given its mission of education, the school reveals itself as flawed by ignorance and insensitivity. What the boy learns in the fourth grade is the magnitude of injustice. The story shows the importance of challenging such unjust institutions by revealing their racial and cultural bias. Telling the story in terms of cultural tensions rather than in terms of the teacher's personality, the narrator shows the politics of the situation. He even explains that her response came out of a structure of injustice from the plantation days, in which Japanese were exploited for labor and were discriminated against racially as a means of facilitating their exploitation.[1] She learned her prejudice under an unjust system, but once she "made it" within the system, she also embraced its racism and/or cultural imperialism. In this sense, the tale gives two models for dealing with such injustice: working within the system, which brings forth additional unjust activity in the form of "lickin's"; or challenging the system straightforwardly, as he did, which results in personal pain. He must hold back the tears, but he does not give in to her demands that he lie.

Contradictions

A contradiction this tale confronts is the difficulty of structuring an institution so that it responds to contrasting cultural perspectives. It is easy for the teacher and the school system to go astray, since both Japanese and European cultures attach high value to competition among individuals while the Hawaiian culture favors cooperation and community solidarity over competition. The narrator, however, does not respond to this conflict by embracing a kind of neutral cultural pluralism. He represents racism and cultural ignorance as negative forces in the system, pointing out the injustice they produce. The teacher failed to be open to the possibility that he had intellectual talent and, therefore, was unable to see it even when it was clearly displayed. When he played honestly according to the rules of her system, she still rejected him, insisting that he tell the class how he had "cheated." Since, apparently, he was not supposed to win in the system, she actually insisted that he lie in order to protect her belief that Hawaiians were unintelligent; she needed her own "lie" protected. Her ignorance brought pain to the young boy, the class, and even to herself.

Accepting

The following narrative elaborates on how Kumu Aina citizens challenge the school system and so improve it. The narrator, a Euro-American from the mainland, has lived in the community for a long time and his family has been adopted by a Polynesian family, which indicates his full integration into Kumu Aina society. On the edge of the community, not far from the school, is a beach park where citizens camp.

We went camping at the beach park the year it was dedicated. We were the only tent down there. At that time, this community was so small that the second morning we were camping our morning newspaper was delivered right in front of our tent.

I had been asked to serve on a panel to speak to incoming teachers, because about seventy-five to ninety percent were new. One of the biggest problems was the cultural shock. Teachers walked into the school system from a different social-economic level as well. They came to our quiet town and it took them months to put on the brakes and slow down.

When we first got here, driving to and from Honolulu, I was ready to tear my hair out. I drove 50-70 miles an hour in California and here I was reduced to 35 miles an hour on a windy beach road. After we were here for awhile, we slowed down and began to see things. We saw all the things we missed by going so fast. We began to watch the mongoose cross the road.

The morning I was to sit on the panel we had been at the beach for a week and I had a week's beard growth. I said to my wife, "I think I better run home and shave. I better look half-way decent to sit in front of all those learned people."

When I got home the phone rang and I had to spend quite a bit of time helping someone in trouble. I only had time to change my clothes and didn't get a chance to shave. When I walked onto the campus the principal said, "Are you dropping out?" That was the time when people were doing that, and we all laughed a bit. I walked into the room and sat with the panel. I was third.

I was watching the people and they would steal a glance at me and on their faces said, "Who is that funny looking guy?" You could read it as plain as if there were a neon sign flashing. When the moderator said, "I would like to introduce the Reverend Timothy," their mouths dropped open.

I stood there for a second because the whole thing had unnerved me. I said, "The look on your faces and what is going through your minds right now is exactly the thing I want to talk about. Never judge a book by its cover. If you came to this town to judge the kids that you teach, just as you are judging me, you are in trouble. Go home, because you will not be successful. Nobody here is taking the time to ask me if there is any reason for the beard." I told them why I had not shaved, and then I said, "All I want to say to you is take people where they are--be open."

A fellow came up to me afterwards and said he wanted to come to my church. I said, "Well, I am glad you feel that way, but I didn't come for that purpose, I came to share with you my understanding of this community." He became one of the most effective teachers here, but he has gone back to Oregon. He said the system here didn't work, but he did a tremendous job of accepting the kids where they were and developing programs for them. He could take nonreading high schools students and teach them to read and write.

Oppositions

In his first few lines, the narrator lays out the opposition between the fast-paced urban mainland middle-class culture and the slow-paced rural local (Hawaiian) working-class culture. One political effect of this contrast is that it is difficult for fast-paced people to see what is really happening in Kumu Aina. They miss things. The tempo image helps make the point that newcomers need to observe more carefully and be wary of rushing into judgements before they have taken the time to discover what is really going on. At another level, this is an opposition between the educational institution, based on the Euro-American system, and the local culture, which is largely Polynesian and Asian-American in its cultural roots. The teachers come from middle-class urban Euro-American backgrounds, in some cases modified by their own Asian-American subcultures, and so they have a hard time understanding Kumu Aina customs. Kumu Aina is aware of this problem and has organized to address it. Since officials in Hawaii's state educational bureaucracy make personnel decisions for the community's school system, Kumu Aina citizens have very little say in the governance of the schools their children attend, at least in any formal sense. The orientation meeting described in the following narrative shows how they have informally dealt with the problem of introducing teachers from "outside" Kumu Aina to local customs.

Metaphors

The tempo metaphor provides an excellent way of speaking about cultural differences. The narrator mixes it with a geographic metaphor, in which he argues that teachers should "Take people where they are." The delivery of the newspaper illustrates this. It arrives where the person actually is, not at his address, his property. Even the newspaper delivery constitutes a connection among persons rather than among formal statuses or physical structures. Mechanical metaphors also help explain how Kumu Aina differs from urban areas. Cars are driven more slowly, for example, so that even the pesky mongoose, who like the squirrel can sometimes be annoying, can be a source of pleasure. The image of the flashing neon sign indicates that, while outsiders may not know what is happening in Kumu Aina, citizens know about outsiders and can read their faces, which show their real thoughts. Such careful observation makes it possible for the newspaper deliverer to find someone who has gone camping and for students to know when teachers accept them and when they do not.

Transformations

Like leaders in other Kumu Aina stories, this narrator experiences humiliation. The humiliating event furnishes the very thing that he needs to transform his audience. It is a genuinely humiliating experience; he was "unnerved" by it. Like Lawrence, his consciousness was assaulted. But then he turns the tables on those who unnerved him by suggesting that their pride may be their undoing in Kumu Aina, reminding them that they should not "judge a book by its cover." This gives them the opportunity of humbling themselves and, thereby, reaching a new level of understanding. They then may be ready to accept their students and work effectively within the cultural context of Kumu Aina, because they know something of Kumu Aina's spirit. It is not insignificant that the narrator is a minister and, hence, pays attention to spiritual matters. The teacher who first responds to him does so in spiritual terms; he wants to attend his church. The inclusion of spiritual conversation in the community discourse represents an important dimension of Kumu Aina social life, for it introduces a reflective element. The narrator portrays his own transformation from a rushed urban person to a rural person able to take time for careful observation and reflection. This invites the teachers to consider educating and changing themselves as well as their students. The fact that the system finally doesn't work--even the successful teacher thinks so--suggests that it needs to be changed as well. In any case, the transformation needed by these new teachers is one of mind and spirit. It is this spiritual dimension that the Japanese teacher in the previous narrative lacked, for she was unable to create a genuine bond with her students because she couldn't clearly reflect on her own situation.

Contradictions

Being humiliated, the minister gains the power to transform others. It is also important that the most successful teacher, who was able to respond to the students, left the school because its system was inadequate. It is as if his very success made it impossible for him to stay in the system, to continue to accept working in a system so fundamentally flawed. Like Lawrence, he goes back to his original community. While, in terms of the narrator's personal situation, the story has a happy ending, it also has an unhappy ending, in what it suggests about the seriousness of the community's problems. The struggle continues; the roots of the problem still need addressing.

POLITICS TRANSFORMS INSTITUTIONS

These next three narratives deal with citizens who challenge social institutions, other than education, in an effort to get them to appreciate their worldview and, in general, to become more open to cultural perspectives other than those of the Euro-American culture.

A Sewing Machine

This narrator, a Euro-American, runs a social service agency in Kumu Aina. While her cultural heritage is from the Euro-American tradition, she grew up in a small farming community on the mainland and, therefore, her experience makes her feel more at home in Kumu Aina than other Euro-Americans, who grew up in urban areas. In depicting how communication works in Kumu Aina, she points out the problems faced by a culturally diverse community that receives offers of assistance from a social agency modeled on an urban-middle-class value system. The story shows how the agency has adapted to local cultural patterns, while meeting the requirements of the large parent bureaucracy on which it depends and whose demands emanate from those in the downtown Honolulu office who have little awareness of Kumu Aina culture.

> Our office loaned a lady a sewing machine. Then I received a message that it had been stolen. The message came from the lady's cousin to the cousin's grandmother and then to me. It went through two people before I received it. She didn't want to

confront me because she didn't know what my reaction would be. This is a common technique. If someone has information that the other might not want to hear, they use an intermediary to avoid confrontation. When people get angry, it can be very violent. This way, no one is put on the spot and it gives time for working out other kinds of resolutions. The intermediary was carefully chosen.

Then, I said to her, "That is all right; these things happen. The only thing she has to do for me is to report it to the police. Once that happens, I can report to the Honolulu headquarters that it was stolen and there will be no problem.

I sent the message back. If there is something that I have to talk to the person about, I can say enough to remove the threat so the person will come in and talk with me.

My Home

In this story Gladys MacDonald, a Euro-American woman who has contributed many years of service to the community by raising children and working to support them, has become a welfare recipient. However, she finds the welfare department's policies unrealistic so she challenges them. Housing is quite expensive even in this rural area and the welfare agency allows up to $250 per month for rent. She pays less than this on the mortgage on her home. She wants to keep her home, but the rules are against her. As she nears retirement, she worries about her own financial security and, of course, wants to live out her life in Kumu Aina. She and others know many citizens, including native Hawaiians, who have been forced to leave Hawaii because of the high price of housing and relatively low-paying jobs. Those who secured land before the rapid inflation of land prices have been able to stay, but those without this protection have had to leave because of high housing costs. She fears that this will be her own destiny as well.

I am a welfare recipient and I brought my property back in 1955 when it was cheap--$9500 for the house and lot.

Artificial inflation has made it valuable. Over the twenty years, I owe just about $3000 on it. When I look at what I could sell it for, there is tremendous equity.

Welfare says I must sell but I will not. Where would I go? In the meantime I have incurred debts to friends of about $6000. If I were to come into money from the sale of my property, I would have to pay them, which would leave me very little to live on. Then, in no time I would be back on welfare. They would have to pay rent for me that would be higher than what they pay right now. It would cost them more money if I sold the house. But the state doesn't agree, so I am challenging them through Legal Aid in court.

Next month I shall not be low income, I shall be no income. Everyone says, "What are you going to do?" Until it happens, I don't really have a way to deal with it. In desperation you can always find a way--at least so far--knock on wood.

One Dollar Down

The narrator of this next tale challenges a bureaucrat on the staff of a low-income government housing project. When his challenge is unsuccessful, he is forced to leave his home. But he finds another home in Kumu Aina, where he is able to work with a private corporation willing to make some adjustments to meet his needs. This Black man finds that the Chinese corporation and the White woman who is its secretary respond to his situation. Like the social agency that loaned the sewing machine, they are flexible and adapt their procedures to the situation.

Those of us who came in the fifties to Kumu Aina came for other reasons. I came because a woman died in the other half of the house I was living in in Honolulu public housing. I was county committeeman for the Democratic party, and I knew the people. They wanted to take up a collection to bury the woman because they didn't want a cheap county funeral. The manager of the housing told them they could not take up a collection, so they came to me. I called up downtown and the head of housing said the manager was in error. But, then, I made my mistake. I told the women, "Go ahead and take up the collection and if he says anything to you, you tell him to see me." I was playing the big shot, which was wrong. I was angry with him for stopping them.

We had a nice burial for the woman but I had an enemy.

One day he came over to my place and said, "Well, Mr. Wilson, you have some things under your house. You have three days to move it out or I'll send a truck over and move it out and give you the bill for it."

At that time, I was making a dollar and a quarter an hour. I had just spent four years in the Army, and I had to start all over when I came to Hawaii. I looked at him calmly and said, "You do that and this world will have gotten too small for the two of us. I will hunt you down like a mad dog. I paid my rent for a month. Get out of my yard and if you want to come over here again, send me a notice at least three days in advance." He left.

My wife, in the meantime, dug out the contract that I had signed, and there in fine letters it said, "You will not store anything under your house."

I always made decisions and action followed fast. That was Friday, and on Sunday, I put my family in the car and drove out here to this land--nine cents a square foot. I had a dollar and eighty-five cents and I figured that would get me a few feet. But when I got here, they were selling it by the acre and they wanted a thousand dollars down.

All the way, driving out here, I kept passing this _haole_ _wahine_ (White woman). Finally, we ended up at the same place and we smiled and spoke. She was Chu Lai's executive secretary--Lucy Mae Turner.

I got my whole family and we looked at

the land. The salesman asked me if I wanted it and Lucy Mae Turner was standing there.

I said, "I don't have a thousand dollars."

He said, "Well, we can swing it for six hundred."

He might as well have kept it at a thousand, but then she spoke up. She said, "Mr. Wilson, you look like you want land bad. Why don't you tell me what you can do, and I will see if we can go along with it."

I said, "Friday I can pay you $100 down and then I can pay you $75 per month until I get the down payment paid."

She said, "All right. Do you have anything that you can put down on it to make it binding?"

"All I can put down is a dollar right now. I didn't expect to buy any land today."

She said, "Okay."

I borrowed $100 from my credit union and then I paid it. In about two years, I was having a hard time because I hadn't thought about the interest, which brought it to $90 per month. I always faced her and she would say "Let me see what I can do, Mr. Wilson."

She cut it down. Later, I was paying $32 per month and I got $850 behind on the payments. Then, I joined the credit union at Pearl Harbor and borrowed $6000 to pay it off and it became a mortgage deed. So I came out here because the manager in public housing was riding me and I wouldn't take it. I have a family to look out for.

Becoming a Nurse

This next narrative shows a young Euro-American woman confronting the institution of the family, which demands that she adjust to the future they have planned for her. She feels called to nursing, while the family wants her to marry and raise children. As it turns out she accomplishes both, but to do so she has to begin by challenging her family and striking out on her own. It is her grandparents who make this possible. In Kumu Aina, grandparents play an important role in providing children with an alternative set of parents with whom to interact and from whom to receive guidance and support. It is not unusual for grandparents to play a central role in child rearing. While the narrator's childhood was spent on the mainland she experienced something like her own version of an important aspect of the local culture, insofar as her grandmother was a central figure in her childhood years.

> When I was sixteen I had an appendix operation. I was a rebel at that time and didn't know what I wanted to do. When I saw the nurses and the care they gave the patients, I was convinced I should be a nurse.
> My grandmother who raised me was a nurse, but she didn't want me to go into nursing. When I graduated from high school, I was too young to go into training. My family thought it was a horrible decision. That was probably part of my rebellion, too. They thought girls should marry and have children, and so they practically disowned me when they found out about my plans. My grandfather who died had left me $500 and that was what the training cost. So I took that money and went to school. The first year my family never talked to me they were so angry with me.

Oppositions

The narrators in these stories find themselves confronting social institutions. However, in each case they constitute this opposition as a struggle that involves shortcomings within themselves or within Kumu Aina citizens, as well as within the structure of the institution. The dollar-down man outrightly declares that he made a mistake in the way he proceeded. He admonishes people always to confront problems but here suggests that one should be careful about how the confrontation is conducted. The nurse explains that part of her own motivation was simply to rebel against her family, not in itself the most admirable of motives. She is now a grandmother herself. The sewing machine incident focuses on the social agency's problem. It is so severe that citizens the agency is supposed to help are hesitant about coming in. In this case, nevertheless, the client does not ignore the lost machine but finds a way to ease the confrontation through an appropriate intermediary. Unfortunately, the young Hawaiian boy who experiences racism in the classroom has to do without the services of such an intermediary, but he, too, acknowledges shortcomings on his part as well as in the structure of the institution. The minister who teaches the teachers concludes his story with the departure of the successful teacher, making the point that even with the best of efforts to make them work, the schools still need structural change.

Metaphor

In American culture, the home has become the symbol of the family. As such, it is wrapped up with the dream of having a healthy happy family. While Kumu Aina residents share this dream, they add something to the symbol of the home. For them, the home also is a symbol of membership in the community. It is more than a "castle," a "haven" to escape from the pressures of the world, for it offers the security of a "place" in the community. If Kumu Aina citizens are unable to keep their homes, it is quite possible that they will be forced to leave the community. Some who experience financial hardship attempt to live on the Kumu Aina beach in order to see themselves through their hard times, but the government has made this quite difficult. Two of these stories deal directly with threats to homes, and ironically it is a social agency designed to provide homes for the needy that threatens these citizens. A threat to a home not only puts shelter needs at risk, but it also threatens continuity in community relationships. The Black man loses such continuity and must build for himself a new community in Kumu Aina. He shows just how dehumanizing this experience is by explaining that the manager would "ride" him, treating him as an animal. He himself threatens to become a "mad dog." The home, because it provides shelter and a place in the community, represents his humanity, his social being.

In a similar way, the welfare agency threatens to rob Gladys of her public social life, by putting her out of her home. The home is her tie to Kumu Aina. Although she is not Hawaiian, she has adopted an Hawaiian understanding of the sacredness of the land, and her home ties her to it. It links her physically and spiritually to the past history of Kumu Aina. It is more than shelter or property; it is a place within Kumu Aina that makes her part of it. It gives her something in common with those who have lived there for many generations. Because she shares their land, in some sense, she shares their heritage. She does not so much want to own it as to remain on it, and the only way she can do that is to retain ownership. If it had financial value to her she would simply sell it for profit, which is what the welfare agency urges.

Transformations

In their stories, Mr. Wilson and Gladys MacDonald wish to resist the transformations the public agencies want to impose on them. The sewing machine client also fears a transformation. The nurse, on the other hand, actively seeks a radical transformation in her status. At another level, however, each protagonist seeks to transform the structure of a social institution. The nurse wants to change the family's orientation toward her future. The director of the social agency sufficiently transforms the communication norms within her own institution to adapt it to Kumu Aina communication patterns, which rely heavily upon the use of mediators. Mr. Wilson attempts to adjust public welfare housing practices to enable the residents to give the woman a decent burial, but it costs him his home. He is able, however, to get the Chu Lai Corporation to adjust its rules so that he can keep up the payments and eventually purchase his own home in Kumu Aina. Both Mr. Wilson and Gladys MacDonald use their own creativity to find appropriate mediators to inspire adjustments in the system, so that they can transform threatening situations into promising ones. Kumu Aina institutions that are able to make adjustments, that are genuinely open to modifying their own policies, genuinely serve the community. However, as suggested in the two earlier stories about cultural problems in the schools, institutions may also effectively resist making any such adjustments, insisting instead on applying alien models insensitively to local cultural conditions and, therefore, failing to "work."

By showing not only the weaknesses in the institutions but their own failings as well, these narrators show that they have the power to make changes if they proceed carefully and self-critically. They do not need to wait for institutions to fix themselves up. They can challenge them and critically review their own challenges, so that when they fail, they can develop new strategies that have hope for success. They are part of the action.

Contradictions

While these institutions threaten citizens, they also provide genuine assistance to them. Social agencies lend sewing machines and the welfare department offers financial support. Even the family, which rejects the young woman's aspirations for a career in nursing, gives her an inheritance that finances her training. Mr. Wilson articulates this contradiction when he explains that he came to Kumu Aina because of the "manager in public housing." While the manager drove him out of his former home, that humiliating experience led to his move to Kumu Aina, where he emerged as a community leader. The difficulties that these institutions sometimes create for their clients are also challenges that inspire them to creative public action. As Gladys says, "In desperation you can always find a way--at least so far." The institution generates desperation and citizens find creative responses to move the institution to fulfill its own purpose, even though this might require it to restructure its rules.

KUMU AINA AND THE POLITICS OF CONFRONTING INSTITUTIONS

While the citizens confront the social institutions that fail to adjust to Kumu Aina, they also see themselves as active negotiators who, like Mr. Wilson, through thoughtful politics can reshape those institutions. Sometimes apparent "errors"--unshaven faces, students for whom school is primarily lunch, items stored illegally under porches--are the keys to social transformation. Through their struggles, and even the consequences of such "errors," they find power.

In some respects, each of these stories represents a small personal incident. The reader should not be deceived, however, because in that incident the narrator is revealing a serious social problem that makes institutions less effective than they might be in Kumu Aina, producing pain for many citizens. Of equal importance, these narrators argue for confronting institutional structures not passively adapting to them. As in the sewing machine case, they can adjust the institution to suit their needs rather than simply adjust their needs to fit the institution. This may mean recruiting a mediator or getting Legal Aid to take the welfare department to court. This confrontation does not mean that they wish to eradicate these institutions and build alternatives from scratch. For the most part, they are not looking for institutional revolution or even major reforms. Instead, they are on the lookout for adjustments that can make the institutions more responsive to local conditions, while still staying within the spirit of the institutions' general purposes. For example, the story of the young Hawaiian boy does not argue that the school should restructure itself in accordance with early Hawaiian educational practices or even in accordance with contemporary Hawaiian values, but that it should deliver to its students in Kumu Aina what it promises in the Euro-American tradition that it embodies. It should give equal education to all students, respecting their talents irrespective of their cultural orientations. The welfare recipient does not argue that citizens have an unlimited right to free minimum housing or basic necessities; she argues that since they are giving her money for housing, they should do so in a way that saves both her and them the most money. Like Mr. Wilson, the Kumu Aina citizens ask the institution "to see what they can do" under the particular circumstances in Kumu Aina. This requires sensitivity, humility, careful observation, and reflection.

Thus, these citizens hope for, even demand, that such institutions as welfare agencies, schools, land development corporations, and social service agencies make adjustments to the particular needs of these citizens and life in Kumu Aina. Since these institutions reach into Kumu Aina from outside, they do not always suit local circumstances. However, these citizens neither wait passively for the institution to adjust itself nor assume the role of powerless victim, because they locate power both in institutions and in themselves. The citizens form an educational committee to educate the new teachers about Kumu Aina. The director of the social agency embraces a different communication network in order to deal with such issues as "lost" sewing machines, honoring the possibility of negotiation and adjustment through the use of mediators. Acting in concert with institutions, citizens help them to adjust to Kumu Aina political life.

In this model of shared power citizens are expected to be self-critical as well as critical of the institutions with which they deal. Because citizens see themselves as powerful persons, they can take measures to alter institutions and they can also acknowledge their own errors and learn from them. Mr. Wilson's story illustrates this point. He makes a mistake in his first housing situation, but corrects this mistake in his second one. In both cases, he fails to fulfill the terms of his contract. In the first case, he stores things illegally under the house; in the second, he falls behind in his payments. In the first case, the consequences of the error were magnified by the fact that he had made an enemy of the manager. Acknowledging this error, he deals more effectively in Kumu Aina, where he finds a friend in the secretary and then is able to deal effectively with the development corporation despite his departures from the "rules." In Kumu Aina, people publicly say "I was wrong," and through that acknowledgement they gain power, because the capacity for self-criticism enables them to see themselves as actors who affect outcomes. This opens up to them new strategies for acting differently so that they can win more satisfying outcomes from the institutions that govern their lives.

Another strategy that enables citizens to gain political power is their ability to use mediators. In the "lost" sewing machine story, the client is fearful of any direct confrontation with the agency because such confrontation could lead to violence. For example, the client may end up in jail because she did not take proper care of the machine. Citizens in this poor community experience violence on a regular basis and many report that they are as fearful of violence from the police as from their fellow citizens. So, it is not surprising that such care is taken in dealing with unpleasant issues. In this case, the client's choice of a mediator to deal with the institution on her behalf acknowledges the potential threat that such institutions represent but also suggests a way in which the community can deal with such threats, by taking deliberate steps to adjust social institutional practices to its own needs. Violence erupts among Kumu Aina citizens, and the strategy of using an intermediary to deliver negative information and lay the ground work for reconciliation works not only in bureaucratic situations but also in interpersonal and interfamilial relationships. The use of a mediator is one strategy that enables citizens to politically challenge the formal institutions without directly confronting their policies. Since mediators often represent groups, their pleas direct attention away from the single case to a pattern of cases, an institutional practice. Thus, individuals avoid the charge of the obvious self-interested pleading of their own cases. Leaders who continually play mediation roles become familiar with the problem areas and can discuss the problems as patterns rather than as isolated cases. At the same time, this mediational approach avoids the more costly or complicated business of bringing legal challenges or appealing to authorities higher up in the institutional structure. Such authorities are apt to be unfamiliar with the particular issues Kumu Aina citizens face. The social mediation model suits the people of Kumu Aina. It does so by supplying a mechanism for challenging institutions, which develops out of their own creativity and their own sense of power, rather than relying upon the formal procedures and policing functions of the state. It also enables citizens who play the mediating roles to take care of each other and, in doing so, to enhance community solidarity.

TABLE 4. KUMU AINA   Private

	Establish Kinship Ties (1)	Threat to Kinship Ties (2)	Assertion of Family Unity and Authority (3)	Freedom Experience (4)	Humiliation (5)
Learning About Justice	Importance to friendships at school	He is a good reader	All have their special talent; his is reading		They would all not do well in school
Accepting		Slowing down in new enviornment, Kumu Aina, was a problem at first	Begins to see more as he slows down; new culture of Kumu Aina gains meaning	He moves freely to beach and still gets newspaper	Beard makes him look like drop-out
A Sewing Machine			Family network used for communication; grandmother delivers message		Does not want to confront someone with bad news and experience humiliation
My Home	She bought home in 1955 in Kumu Aina		She receives help from welfare		Welfare tells her to sell her house
One Dollar Down	All living in public housing together	Woman died and they had trouble taking up collection	Women told to go ahead according to Housing Authority Rules		Narrator humiliated by manager, his enemy.
Becoming a Nurse		Leaves family for appendix operation	Grandmother downgraded nursing	Rebellious teenager	Family does not want her to go into nursing

Public

Issue of Challenge (6)	Mediation, Pulling Together (7)	Unity and Action (8)	Liberating Action (9)	Returning Home (10)
Teacher challenges him on reading test	He mediates by showing that Hawaiians are intelligent	He learns of her prejudice and is free from her stereotyping		
They challenge his legitimacy and he challenges them	He mediates by explaining new culture to teachers	He cautions them against prejudging; asks them to accept students	One teacher responds positively and develops programs	This teacher returns home to Oregon
Avoid challenge	Family and police serve as mediators	Unity and good feelings preserved	Woman is freed of problem with lost machine or threatened relationship	
She challenges them in court	Legal Aid mediates for her in court	She is taking no action; will wait		
He seeks new home in country and tests his ability to purchase land	Miss Turner mediates for him to buy land from Corporation	He always goes and deals with her	He buys land and gains his independence	
She challenges family authority	Inheritance from grandfather pays for nursing; grandparents mediate	They refuse to talk to her	She gains her independence	

8
Essex:
Creating Unity and Freedom

> Alice thought to herself "Then there's no use in speaking." The voices didn't join in, <u>this</u> time, as she hadn't spoken, but, to her great surprise, they all <u>thought</u> in chorus (I hope you understand what <u>thinking in chorus</u> means—for I must confess that <u>I don't</u>), "Better say nothing at all. Language is worth a thousand pounds a word!"
>
> Lewis Carroll
> <u>Through the Looking-Glass</u>

Thinking in a chorus or collective action of any kind seems to bring with it an ominous loss of freedom. But, of course, to speak at all requires submission to a language system, and if we were unwilling to do that, we indeed would be able to say "nothing at all." The political questions that this tension between authority and freedom brings to contemporary America is how to reconcile personal freedom with the need to unify and control citizens. Essex citizens also encounter the difficulty of enticing citizens to participate in public life. Because citizens begin with an understanding of the individual as primary, they see participation in community and government—membership in the body politic—as a secondary activity. Simultaneously, since the body politic has powers that far surpass those of individuals, citizens see it as a threat. Liberal theory, shaped by both Hobbes and Locke, historically has provided the philosophical basis for explaining government institutions as "necessary evils." On the other hand, since people are essentially social beings, they stand in need of community. Essex citizens address this problem in the next set of narratives, in which they attempt to challenge institutional arrangements that fail to provide a healthy context for individual development. In this sense they assert their individuality against the body politic and the social institutions that maintain it.

Essex: Unity and Freedom

INDEPENDENCE AND COMMUNITY

The story about founding the historical society presents a dynamic model that combines community spirit with individual freedom. The narrator, Mary Ann Wilton, lives in Essex at a time when the community has lost some of its pride. Roads, homes, and other buildings are showing some signs of deterioration. Although these signs do not alarm most residents, to the watchful artistic eye of the storyteller they signal trouble. She fears that they are signs of declining community spirit, portents of civic lethargy. Perhaps, she is able to read these signs because of her own long-term residency in the community. She grew up in Essex and has raised her children there. Her father, an active community participant, also grew up in the town. Hence, she has a real sense of Essex's history derived from her personal experience as well as that of her father. Mary Ann Wilton is active in one of Essex's Protestant churches and also in a number of community organizations. She serves as a mentor for many young women who are beginning to provide volunteer civic leadership.

Founding the Historical Society

What this community needed was an appreciation of its heritage. Some of the pride was deteriorating. I went to different people all over the community to find out if there was a knowledge of our history. I went to the Board of Education, to City Hall, to Trinity College, and to the Recreation Department.

Everybody said, "You know, you are right. We need something like this and we will be glad to help. Let's get something started."

At this point I felt inadequate, so I went back to school to get some training. I went to the Ohio Historical Society to find out about the greater community. I got so interested that I decided to take a course up there and became a guide for the Ohio Historical Center. All the time, I was still thinking about Essex.

I went to the mayor and said, "Hey, how can we excite the community and get them interested in this kind of thing?" I came up with the idea that I could do drawings of what Essex used to look like and maybe we could publish it.

He said, "Why don't you put it in the *Essex Voice?*" which is our community newspaper.

It only comes out twice a year but I thought that was a good start. I did a drawing of the old school house and it appeared in the *Essex Voice.* I had hoped that people would be interested and I wrote a little about the first school house and asked, "What do you know about it? Would you write and get in touch with me?" I could not believe the response I got. It was very exciting. It started to snowball and I felt like I had a tiger by the tail.

More people were interested in giving me information than in helping me organize. So, I found myself organizing a historical committee. I got a neat idea. I thought, "What we really need is to get some of these people together to reminisce. We could find out a lot this way."

So, we got a couple of people together--with somebody to do refreshments, somebody to send out invitations, somebody to prepare a list of people who might have something historical to tell us. We sent out the invitations. The Ohio Historical Society heard about it and the oral history gentleman called me and said, "I hear you are doing oral interviews."

To show my ignorance, I said, "Oh what is an oral interview?"

He told me and said,"I am head of oral interviews and I would like to come out to your party and tape them for you."

I thought, "Oh taping is a neat idea." I found out we had an innovative idea to do the interview in a group rather than on a one-on-one basis.

The advantage was that you get two opinions. If there are diverse opinions you can come up with a better answer because you can resolve disagreements. For instance, we did have a difference of opinion on how Essex was named. One person told it this way and the other another way. If we had talked to them alone in a single interview, we would never have resolved that question. But these two talked about it at our first reminiscing party and the majority rules, so we had a better basis for our history. We had more than one opinion to answer that question.

Another advantage to this kind of interview was that one story promoted somebody else's reminiscence so it evolved into a group. I really think we were innovative with my dumb luck. But it has grown and the reminiscing parties are fun. But more people want to come to the parties than to do the work. But the number of workers is growing too. We have opened our office, hired a part-time secretary, and have gotten some excellent people on the board of trustees. Now I am hoping I can hand over the administrative part and get back to the part that I really love, which is the oral interviews and the research.

Oppositions

In thinking about Essex, this narrator argues that it is important to know the past in order to take pride in the present. Learning about the past has a present political purpose in improving Essex' community spirit and, indirectly, its physical appearance. She diagnoses the problem as a lack of pride derived from a lack of historical consciousness. Attempting to restore the link between the past and present, she begins with the power centers--the Board of Education, City Hall, Trinity College, and the Recreation Department. All of the leaders in these positions are professionals in the sense that they hold paid positions. She, on the other hand, is a volunteer. While visiting these agencies acknowledges their power, it also gives them notice of her activity. In addition, it links the average citizens that she will involve in her project with these professional community leaders. This reestablishes the necessary connection between the professional civic leader and the citizen. While the opposition between the past and present serves as one dynamic in this tale, this second opposition between professional leaders like the mayor and volunteer community leaders like Mary Ann Wilton affords another dynamic. A third opposition emerges between Essex and the "greater community." While this latter one plays a minor role in the narrative, it nonetheless serves as a reminder of Essex's boundaries and the resources that the "larger" community has to offer Essex. The final party dramatically resolves this opposition because the group finds a better answer to its questions, a better method for conducting interviews than the "greater" community could provide.

Transformation

To establish her project she seeks "outside" legitimation, which leads her to take courses at the Ohio Historical Society and to gain experience as a society guide. She takes five steps in developing her project for the community's transformation. First, she consults with and enlists the support of key community authority figures--the mayor, the educational institutions, and the recreation department director. Because the recreation director runs the country club facilities provided by the city he plays a role in organizing Essex's social life. Second, she acquires professional training, which transforms her own abilities. Third, she moves into the public realm by publishing her drawing. This third step incorporates her natural artistic talent with her professional training.

The fourth step calls upon her organizational skills. She draws citizens out of their private lives into the public world by organizing meetings and activities aimed at bringing collective wisdom to bear on the project. She discovers before long, however, that she has herself become excessively involved in public life. But, she sees this "tiger by the tail" period as a brief episode, after which she will return to the quieter activity of doing research. What begins as concern over excessive privatization in the community--even citizens in public authority positions do not know their heritage--leads to an excessively public life. Ultimately, she hopes to be less intensely involved in the administration of the organization. For the time being, she willingly assumes a prominent leadership position in order to create the institutional structure that will preserve a connection between the past and present. The administrative work involves her in planning and management, which deals with policies rather than people. Like the minister, she prefers to work directly with people, which in this case is the interview work. This tension between administration and research echoes the problems confronting the minister in the first tale and reiterates the values to which he finally gave priority in his own life.

Her fifth step involves generating a solid institutional basis for the Historical Society. While she has brought a new organization into being, she does not create a new organizational form. Like the city council, the Historical Society has a policy making body, a staff, and an office, located in the same building as the city council. Within this structure, she creates a new organization whose staff is composed primarily of volunteers. Hence, the organization offers a public activity in which volunteer citizens can take up professional roles in the public political life of Essex. Because its purpose is historical, it has a conservative tone even though it is clearly meant to revitalize Essex's public life.

Metaphor

Business and economic metaphors predominate. The narrator's final sign of success is the establishment of an office, secretary, and board of trustees. Her project acquires tokens of legitimation similar to those of the official organizations she first visited. Political metaphors also figure in her story. The reminiscing parties are occasions for sharing opinions and making decisions, including voting to adopt a single historical interpretation of their city. While historians may not find this an acceptable model for determining historical truth, students of politics will recognize that the voting procedure follows the liberal democratic model and holds promise for creating a community that can move forward because it agrees about its past. While this is not quite rule by the consent of the governed, it is a process of constructing a history that affirms both the importance of their existence as a community and the importance of the average citizen,s continued participation in preserving community values. The construction of an agreed-upon story about the past is the basis of community pride and of hope for the construction of an agreement about the future. The narrator recognizes that such an agreement inspires unity and pride.

A third set of metaphors comes from nature. She says, "It started to snowball and I felt like I had a tiger by the tail." These metaphors develop from a cosmology that sees civilization as being under human control and nature as being "out of hand." Her success depends on a blend between that which she can control, hard work, and that which she cannot control, dumb luck.

Contradictions

A central contradiction in this narrative exists in the requirement that citizens achieve independence while enjoying community and interdependence. The narrator in this story sees that Essex has gone too far in honoring independence and has neglected to nurture the interdependence that maintains the community. To restore this balance requires the cooperation of many different citizens--those in authority who acknowledge the problem, volunteers who organize the parties, a paid staff member who serves the organization, and elders who contribute information.

However, for this organization to function it must create an independent existence. That independent existence builds upon the diversity of its membership, a diversity of organizational talents and, more important, opinions about Essex itself. Competing opinions about Essex's history create excitement as long as mechanisms exist for solving the controversies they entail. As in a baseball game, the outcome provides a final resolution of the tension. Someone wins; a common historical understanding wins out. Competition is not open-ended; it draws to a conclusion. The independence that she shows in creating this new organization, and the independence in the diverse opinions of the elders, play important parts in generating the energy that makes this organization a success as well as a source of satisfaction to its members. The diversity and disagreement vitalize the meetings. Hence, the historical story they come up with is a better expression of their community spirit. Independent thinking produces group discussion and ends by finding a common collective past. Together they build an organization that tells the story of their independence and their interdependence.

These next narratives follow the Historical Society model. Each narrator explores ways in which citizens can move from their private lives into collective public community. Each presents a slightly different model for generating a richer, fuller public life.

Community Pool

The next narrator, Robert Shaw, has served as a volunteer in many civic activities. The project he describes here illuminates how he and others generate a social center for Essex. Like the Historical Society, this center provides a public forum that augments government institutions. In the early part of the twentieth century, the Zettle family donated an estate as a town park and recreational center. Since that time, improvements have been made to make it suitable for community activities, such as summer programs, parties, meetings, and recreation, including hiking and tennis. In the early sixties, Essex citizens decided that they needed a new project to give the estate more life so that it would become even more attractive to citizens as a town center. In creating this new facility, they, too rescue Essex from its privatized life.

> The Zettle family gave the mansion and surrounding acres to the community for recreation. I served on the board and we decided to build a pool on the site.
> We contacted the city council and mayor to get their approval. Three or four us worked to persuade them. Many people objected because they were worried about a loud speaker system, which would disturb the neighbors. We found out about those objections. What that loud speaker system provides is a baby sitting operation, but we had no intention of having such a system.
> We sold $100 bonds to pay for it, and when we had sold about $70,000, we felt that we could go ahead. With solid planning and two weekends of promotion we raised the money and opened the pool in June of 1963.

Dancing in the Streets

This narrator, Jane O'Neill, wanted to throw a public party to celebrate the local community as well as the nation on the Fourth of July. Her goal was to make public life enjoyable--fun.

> We wanted something fun for the Fourth of July, so at the last minute we did it. We blocked off the streets, got a band, had a concession man, and charged fifty cents admission.
> It started one night when I said, "Wouldn't it be fun to have a street dance?"

Somebody said, "let's do it." So two, actually one and half of us, did it. We publicized it in the town newspaper, made posters, and sent a flyer home the last day of school.

We had about eighteen hundred people there. I think, that if we have it next year, we will have twice that many. Everybody had a good time and we had all ages there.

The Recreation Department ran a few games for us on the tennis courts. If we do it next year, we will expand that and start a little earlier. We couldn't start as early as we liked but it was a successful venture.

Senior Citizens' Club

Because of the professionalization of civic services, it has become difficult for retired members of Essex to participate in the community. Yet they can provide a rich source of volunteer workers whose long-term residence gives them a strong sense of Essex's community feelings as well as the expertise and personal networks that make projects work. While this organization has not actually directed its energies toward specific political projects, it offers that potential. The narrator, a woman who is a long-term resident of E sex, works closely with the staff of the recreation department.

Several times the Recreation Department tried to start a senior citizens' club. We had programs for preschoolers, kids, and adults but nothing for senior citizens. Then Mr. Salinger, the director, hired someone to create this program. But nothing came of it, so we decided to go about it in a different way. Mr. Salinger invited some of the retired school teachers to a meeting and asked them what kind of program they would like.

They got together and said to us. "We don't want you doing anything for us except providing the building. We want to do it ourselves. You provide a newsletter each month, the building, and set up the tables and chairs for us."

We provided the coffee, tea, and sugar

and one part-time worker to compile a newsletter and take the minutes of the steering committee meetings.

They started with a nucleus of about sixteen people and now they take three or four trips each year and have monthly pot luck dinners. They have 189 paid members. They have a ball. They have theater parties at the country dinner play house. They go to restaurants for dinner. They get guest speakers. They have a three-ring circus and they do it themselves. This fall they are taking a five-day trip up to New England. They limit the trips to one busload of forty people, and we pay our staff coordinator to be sure nobody gets left behind or some little old lady doesn't have someone to pal around with. This and our preschool program have been the two most successful; we worked hard with the preschool but the seniors work hard for themselves.

The King and I

While this story seems to wander far from Essex, the story of Anna is a story of how a solitary individual can become part of a co munity and how that community can integrate European traditions into its political structure. The narrator is a woman whose civic activities include participation in the Essex Women's Club, an Essex Protestant church, and many hours of volunteer work for Essex community projects.

Anna is a tutor who lives in England. She is hired by the King of Siam to tutor his son. She leaves England for a foreign country, Siam. The story describes a man who is really trying to be an intellectual of Europe but who is from the Far East. Then s flict between Anna and the King; she tries to tell him what he should do but he is very strongheaded. He is the King. The conflict is between the values of England in the 1800's and this developing but fairly backward country. This gentle English woman tempers this very masculine, very authoritative king. The king dies at he end and she faces many frustrations because of the barbarianism in Siam.

Dove

Like the story of Anna, this protagonist wanders far from home to find himself and to finally find a place hat he can call his community. It is a very small community, but his solitary voyage has made him yearn for home and a family. Even hough he retains his love for nature, he makes a clear statement about the value of ociety. The narrator, a professional woman who served many years in Essex's public sector as an administrator, obtained her position at a time when few women held such professional offices.

>A young boy of sixteen got bored with school and decided to sail around the world by himself. His Dad and Mom agreed that this was the best thing for him. He was an outstanding sailor.
>He had many experiences with people on ferent islands. He took only cats with him but he returned married. On one of the slands, he ied a girl he had known back home. She went from island to island where she knew he was ₃ ing to be landing and finally they got married. Out in the ocean, he had to face all the problems by himself--working with the water and the s ils to manipulate the boat. His wife and he decided that they would never go back to a city. They decided to build their own home out in the open with nature. He learned so much more than what anybody could ever have taught him in college.

Paddle-to-the-Sea

This story, perhaps even more than the others, shows life as a quest for community. Beginning as a solitary individual on a mountain, this boy, as he mes a man, begins to make connections with a variety of persons, forging community bonds. The narrator, a Jewish man who grew up in Essex and raised his children there, is a successful businessman and ic ial who is especially dedicated to Essex's public welfare.

>A little Indian boy living up in far northern Canada built a little wood canoe, about twelve inches long, with a little man

in it. The canoe traveled from way up there to the Great Lakes and finally ended up in the ocean. This little wooden figure meets twenty-five or thirty different people. It is caught in a forest fire and icebound and finally he is picked up by a fishing boat off Newfoundland.

The current takes him everyplace. One day, a log man finds him on a logging chain about to be cut up and takes him out. A boat picks him up and repaints it and refinishes it.

On the bottom of the boat is a plate saying "I am Paddle-to-the-Sea." A boat picks him up in the Atlantic Ocean and it gets into the newspaper. By this time, the little boy has grown into a man. He remembers how he put the boat on the top of a mountain and when the mountain melted, it ran into a stream and the stream into the lakes and down to the ocean. The boat never comes back to him, but he reads about this young boy of sixteen who was fishing off Newfoundland and pulled this boat up in his fishing net. I read that story when I was young and I have read it to all of my kids.

Oppositions

The oppositions in this third set of narratives illuminate the tension between the private and public spheres, while showing how a public life can emerge that does not threaten citizens. Each narrator argues for an expansion of the public sphere, and, in some sense, explains how this will not diminish the private sphere. In the pool case, what might have become a burden on the community turns out to be an unadulterated benefit. The project gains approval from various private familial arenas--the Zettle family approves the project, individual citizens give financial support, and nearby residents agree that it will not invade their homes with noise. In addition, the project is self-supporting, so it does not draw on the private funds of any family except those who willingly participate. While organized under the structure of Essex government, it has private funding and a private administrative apparatus. Continuing costs of operation are covered by membership fees. Since the fees are relatively low, the facility is genuinely open to all Essex residents who wish to use it. This gives residents the best of both worlds:

private funding with an "independent" business operation, and a public facility that both extends civic services and provides an attractive hysical addition to Essex, thus enhancing its appearance and the pride that goes with it. Unlike the alley situation, it is unlikely that elderly citizens on fixed incomes will want to use the pool, so the membership fee is not a problem.

"Dancing in the Streets" offers a similar solution to the problem of how to expand the public realm without threatening the private realm. While the event is staged on the public streets, its financing remains the responsibility of those attending, the users. So the public provides the space and private users supply operating costs. The "Senior Citizens Club" makes the same arrangement, except that, in this case, there is an additional public contribution in the form of a staff person to assist in the operation. While the pool's membership fees pay its staff, the seniors do not quite "do it for themselves" even though this is the way the narrator characterizes the club. The emphasis upon self-reliance versus public reliance indicates how important it is that the participants themselves supply part or even all of the financing for these public activities. Hence the narrator points out that the seniors' club has membership dues. This makes them official participants as individuals. Their financial independence gives them the authority to govern their own organization even though it is a part of Essex public service.

The "Dove" story adds an additional dimension to this private/public authority pattern. While Essex prides itself on its public education, which also incidentally helps to support its high property values, the Dove skipper acquires his own education. He proceeds by gaining experience that, according to the narrator, teaches him more than he could have learned in the school system. However, it is important to note that it serves to socialize him into a different world than Essex. He will not reside in an urban city like Essex but will change to a rural setting. While his education does meet his needs, it does not provide him with access to Essex's social structure. In a world of upwardly mobile people reaching for their niches in the world, he selects a lateral move into the country. The Dove's skipper sails far from Essex, recognizing perhaps that his extreme individualism is incompatible with life in such a community, even if Essex goes to great lengths to minimize the intrusion of the community into its citizen's private lives.

In a similar way, "The King and I" demonstrates the difficulty of forming a community among individuals who, like Anna and the King have "stubborn" views of what the social order should be. The "Dove" narrative draws a clear boundary between nature and urban society and points out that, while value, delight, romance, and experience await those who seek to embrace nature, those who seek to participate in the social structure of Essex need a formal education and a different set of skills. Similarly, Essex can tolerate neither the excessive public control that a King seeks nor the excessive individual authority on which Anna insists. Together, these two tales illustrate the problem of integrating individualism with the public realm, showing it to be a difficult thing at best, impossible when individualism is carried to extremes. Family commitments limit public life, but this rugged natural individualism is not a commitment that is consistent with life in Essex, and most families need a community for support. While "Paddle-to-the-Sea" displays a similar affection for adventure and nature, the canoe finally does return to civilization. Although civilization is not a totally benign force, for the logging operation nearly industrialized the canoe, Paddle-to-the-Sea, like the boy who made it and the other boy who found it, belongs to civil society, not to nature. It may be exciting to be free of one's "niche," but it is gratifying at last to find another. Paddle-to-the-Sea's adventure does not end at sea but on shore. While the story shows the importance of a solitary quest, much of its importance lies in its revelation of the centrality of community. The newspaper connects the two boys, who play their roles at opposite ends of the journey. The canoe's builder and its rescuer have a bond that is publicly manifest in the canoe and its story. At this point, even though they do not know each other, they are a part of a community that made the event possible. Perhaps, in a similar way, Essex citizens are not fully aware of the various things they do that contribute to helping other community members complete their various journeys.

A second level of opposition exists between youth and maturity. The Indian boy grows into a man and comes down from the mountain top to join the industrialized world. The boat never returns to him but remains with him as a memory. Paddle-to-the-Sea reaches his goal, the sea, with the help of many people. As the canoe grows older, it makes more connections with others. In fact, its ability to survive depends upon these connections. Hence, for Paddle-to-the-Sea, the freedom to pursue its goal depends on a spirit of interdependence and mutual assistance. People give it assistance, doing so not because they know him or have a commitment to him personally. They offer help when they see it is needed. The success of the project depends on these volunteers. The dance, the pool, the seniors' club, and the Historical Society similarly depend on volunteers who choose to offer their services. Because there is no obligation to help these organizations, like the canoe, they carry on their own journeys without set plans or guaranteed financial bases. They must make their projects work independently, just as the canoe must somehow find its way to the sea by itself. Its lack of financial resources and their lack of dependence on city government signal the fact that "they do it themselves." The pool, the seniors' club, the Dove, the Historical Society, and the dance--all retain financial independence. Citizen volunteers create the space for the public activities that enlarge and strengthen the bonds that make these people a community. They are not obliged to carry out this work, and they do not receive pay for it. It does not place a drain on public resources but, instead, is a genuine public service.

Metaphors

The stories about the pool, the street dance, and the seniors' club each refer to the establishment of an official administration as part of the project. This mixing of business metaphors--boards, committees, publicity people--with these leisure activities certify them as official public activities. While this organizational structure obviously has such practical benefits as assuring the continuity of the activity, it also has metaphorical import. It shows that the power of the organization is not maintained by personal energy, individual "egos," but is tied to its status as a part of an organic bureaucratic structure that transcends individuals. In contrast to the Dove skipper, who sails by himself, these organizations need many workers, even though as organizations they are intent, like the skipper, on being self-reliant. The street dance provides an image of the mixture of business and leisure, for streets that are normally dedicated to commerce become settings for recreation. The celebration signifies

that there is more to public life than business. The
playfulness of the dance, however, reminds citizens
that until the next Fourth of July the streets will be
used for the conduct of everyday business, which is
the primary Essex public activity. Admission tickets
and concessions remind the participants that an
important meaning of Independence Day is financial
independence. In case this point should be missed,
the seniors' club story makes it even clearer. These
people demand financial independence and insist on
membership dues so that they will "be a member."
While, at the one to two-dollar level, the dues
represent a metaphorical token, the token symbolizes
the importance of financial independence. In
addition, they "work hard" for themselves to establish
their club, and such work in part establishes their
right to govern the organization. The central
importance of financial self-reliance echoes as a
chorus throughout these narratives.

As in the minister's story, travel refers to the
boundary between Essex and communities beyond it. The
Dove skipper travels beyond Essex; while the young
Indian boy does not travel from his own land, the boat
does it for him. None of these stories show travel
per se as a means of climbing the social ladder, even
though for many Americans it serves that purpose.
Upward mobility ordinarily involves travel, which
results from promotions and professional advancement.
In these stories, however, travel is a romantic
interlude that fulfills youthful desires but, more
important, accentuates the benefits of community that
Essex has to offer citizens right in their hometown.
Adventures come in the form of establishing new
services and activities--creating a pool or staging a
street dance--that enhance public life. Such
activities bring home the romance of the seas and
travel, as the pool brings swimming to Essex, a
landlocked community with only a small creek on its
border. The organizations create more public space
and so enrich the lives of Essex citizens.

Transformations

The primary transformation in these stories is that
public spaces--streets, an estate that has become a
community recreational facility--take on new life and
incorporate new activities. These activities expand
the public realm but do not transform its character,
because they add very little additional authority to
city government. Something is added to the public but
little is taken away. The park now has a swimming

pool, the streets have an occasional role as a dance floor, and the city hall has an Historical Society office. These physical artifacts symbolize new life for Essex and make it clear that the new activities do not represent momentary enthusiasms that will quickly fade. Next year, there will be another street dance. The pool and the Historical Society have boards that will look after their continued life.

To create this transformation citizens find public spaces and discover new purposes for them rather than taking private property or expanding their boundaries beyond Essex. In doing this, they adjust the myth of the expanding frontier to suburban conditions and reassure fellow citizens that the public realm can experience regeneration within its own boundaries. Essex citizens call the leaders who establish these organizations trail blazers. They chart new directions for community achievement. Their trails lead not into the wilderness but into set patterns of Essex's public life, which they open to new forms of expression. In the process, these leaders use educational skills to embellish public life with organizations whose visible components say to the community "Here you can come together" and "If you work hard for yourselves and pay your dues like the seniors do, you can contribute to the public realm and you too will find that work fun." Public activity will be a delight both to them and to their fellow citizens. Such public services bring their own rewards, for like the boy who made the canoe, the citizens who extend public life in Essex can bask in the proud knowledge that others derive pleasure from their projects.

The full development of a spirited public life is these leaders' goal. Its accomplishment has three aspects: First, the transformation requires cooperation to make fuller use of "interior spaces" that already exist. The pool is located on public land already within Essex's geographic territory and its financial base does not drain public resources. Second, they provide social services that give citizens greater opportunity to engage in collective leisure activity, which is culturally enriching--swimming, dancing, exploring Essex's history. Third, because this community activity is leisure activity, an activity to be enjoyed for itself, it can become the basis for a rejuvenated political life, for it provides citizens with a place, a forum, in which they can pursue questions about community life in a relaxed, thoughtful way, without the demands of an immediate policy decision. Unlike either the public debate format of the city council or the exchange model of business, leisure time offers the possibility of engaging in the process of building community. These organizations offer possibilities for the pursuit of common understandings that can become the basis for a greater sense of genuine community. The activities that they foster are goods in themselves and not merely means to other valued ends. In this sense, they offer the participants a sense of a shared common good, which is itself the ultimate purpose of political community.

Contradictions

The tension between the individual and society requires citizens to display independence and self-reliance in a context in which they are indisputably interdependent and reliant on others. Because citizens view human existence as fundamentally composed of individuals who form societies, they need to explain the conditions under that they make such affiliations. Because genuine community requires commitments that go beyond short contractual terms, these citizens generate potentially durable social entities which entice people into communal relationships. They do this in part by making participation voluntary. This quiets the liberal who, believing that power corrupts and that the least government is the best government, fears both the power of the state and the power of the group. In the Historical Society, the narrator's independence gives her the creative energy to create a new institution. However, as the work mounts, she realizes that she cannot do it alone and that it is difficult to get others involved in the volunteer effort. While these organizations appear independent and self-reliant, they depend upon the city government for their maintenance and on citizens for volunteer work. While they begin with the creative initiative of one or a few citizens, they involve the support of all the citizens. So the contradiction that these organizations embody is that, even through they are in some measure self-reliant, they depend upon public resources and the work of dedicated citizens for their existence.

This tension emerges more dramatically in the senior citizens club, which begins its operation as a service provided to seniors by others. Constructed on this premise, the project fails. The seniors want to "do it themselves," and once they have managed to get themselves placed in charge, the club becomes an organization with "real" members, who work cooperatively for their own group. Since their resources do not meet all their needs, they welcome participation from the public realm, which includes supplying their meeting place and a "chaperone" for their long trips, so that no little old lady is left alone. The public realm fills the gap, indicating the final interdependence of even the most independent. In somewhat the same spirit as that which informs welfare policy in America at large, the "independent ones" take care of themselves and the government takes care of the "left overs." This kind of government in the gaps attempts to solve the tension between independence and dependence. Of course, all Essex citizens depend on the city government for services--fire, water, police, and education, among others. They do not do these things "themselves."

From this perspective, the public realm is understood as a government of gaps, which should put in its appearance only when problems emerge, whereupon citizens move in to solve them. After finding solutions, the citizens return to their "ordinary private lives." But the citizens, in these stories, return only after they have enlarged the public realm. A more accurate model, therefore, would suggest that citizens continually lead two lives, one private and familial, the other ever ready to work on maintaining their community and enlarging its public scope.

When citizens contribute work or money (dues) to an enterprise they have power and authority in it. Once they organize the enterprise, the city government can provide auxiliary services. The city provides the land for the pool, although it can do so only because the land had been donated by a private citizen. The city sees that the seniors have a chaperone, a newsletter, and a meeting place. This picture of the relationship between these activities and city government articulates the liberal American hope that the primary flow of life will come from private initiative and the private sector, with the public realm supplying only minimal structures of support.

PUBLIC LIFE AND INDEPENDENCE

The problem for the citizen is to find the proper balance between public and private life. At the opening of the Historical Society story, the narrator finds Essex in a situation in which there is too little public spirit, but in discovering a way to generate more spirit she has taken "a tiger by the tail." The story's conclusion anticipates a balance between a very private life lacking in public involvement and an intense, time-consuming public project like founding an organization. A great deal of work has to go into creating these community enterprises, but the enterprises themselves are fun. Participation in them is a reward in itself. One way of enticing citizens into public life is to make it playful in the sense of recreational. One could argue that this limits the political force of this activity, since once it begins to address serious issues, citizens may withdraw. But it may also become the occasion for political discussions because it permits the inhabitants of a very privatized society to meet on terms other than those of the business world and thus to discover a basis for their collective existence. This sense of their collective existence, this genuine commitment to a common existence, is fundamental to political community. The seniors' club, the pool, and even the Historical Society promise to become forums for leisurely exploration of common interests. Freed from the demands of the market and from the intensity of city council policy decisions, citizens can use these forums to reflect on their collective concerns and to contemplate the common good for Essex. Thus, these organizations provide a corrective to the extreme individualism that could lead to the disintegration of the community.

The extreme case of independence is the Dove skipper. In some sense he does "do it all himself." Like Paddle-to-the-Sea, a young man enters upon a rite of passage to adulthood, discovers and celebrates his independence, but in the end finds that he needs community and a home, even if it is not in the suburban city from which his travels began. The seniors undergo a rite of passage of a different nature. While they work hard to establish the club and their rights to authority in it, one of the payoffs of club membership takes the form of travel. Like the Dove skipper, their traveling is temporary. Unlike him they travel in a a group and invariably return to the same shared hometown. Rather than a solitary quest, theirs is a collective celebration of their life together. On their various "trips," they do not so much leave Essex as take Essex along with them. Rather than "getting away" from the community, they intensify their experience of it by traveling together and getting to know one another in more intimate ways.

Citizen independence is a fragile myth, since all citizens depend upon each other and the city government. Yet, the stories stress the independence of the organizations to which they refer and the underlying self-reliant nature of their participants. If they did not make this declaration, it would be difficult to see their independence. The point is not that this claim to independence is false but that it bespeaks the tension citizens experience between their image of American life as independent and self-reliant and their daily experience of it, which demonstrates how citizens depend upon their connections to the community for their survival and happiness.

On the other hand, the liberal caution against excessive government and social control is not without merit in these narratives. Mary Ann Wilton finds herself too intensely involved in organization and citizens worry that the pool may "invade" their private lives. The tension between private and public life requires a balance that these citizens cherish, even though at this point in their lives the private sphere has crowded out much of public life. Because the organizations they propose are small and because Essex itself has a small government apparatus with a minimal police force, they are less concerned about the possibility of it overwhelming them than they might be about the federal government. In some respects their perspective is similar to the notion that "small is beautiful" which E. F. Schumacher has proposed.[1] However, while they like the ease with which they can participate in public affairs, they also enjoy the limits placed on the government itself. This means that political life is not merely government activity but is more importantly a social experience, an experience of community. Community emerges in the activities that these citizens create. Their participation is not so much designed for protesting public policy as for enjoying one another. Their impulse to political activity does not come about as a response to harsh government policies but as an expression of the loneliness they experience when their lives are lacking in this community dimension.

Small as it is, however, the city government, like the state and federal governments, tends to focus on policy decisions, evoking a debate model of interaction that does not address this common need for a collective experience. In this context, the organizations that are the occasions for these stories constitute first steps in the formation of bonds that could generate a genuine collective identity. This contrasts with the merely legal and territorial identity to which citizens are entitled because they reside within the geographic boundaries of the city. Genuine community identity requires intimate relationship with other citizens and collective activities in which citizens can form projects together, so that, in relatively leisure circumstances that foster interaction and shared reflection, they can explore their common visions of the good and just social order. Such organizations provide precisely the kinds of structures needed for such collective contemplation and reflection. In this respect, they offer promise for politics in Essex, because the most authentic basis of political action is a quest for the good and just in the immediate daily lives of citizens.

TABLE 5. ESSEX   Private

	Ego Expression (1)	Establish Home/Domain (2)	Nurturing: Helping/Hurting (3)	Public Entry for Resources (4)
The Historical Society	Narrator saw town needed pride	She talks with authorities in town about the problem and they encourage her	She goes to school to develop her talents	She publicizes the idea by drawing the little red school house
Community Pool	Narrator identifies his role as member of the board	Zettle family approves of pool	Pool will not be baby-sitting operation.	Gains approval from city council; they propose self-supporting financial plans
Dancing in the Streets	Narrator gets idea for the street dance		Two people work on project	They organize event: block off street, bank, concessions, admission fee
Senior Citizens' Club	We try to start a senior citizens' club		Citizens reject the idea because it invaded their privacy	The recreation director consults with senior citizen leaders
The King and I	Anna is a tutor	She lives in England	She is hired by King of Siam to tutor his son	She leaves England to work as a teacher
Dove	A young boy sails alone	He buys a boat that will be his home	His parents help him prepare for the trip	He leaves school to sail around the world
Paddle-to-the-Sea	Indian boy is alone on a hill	He builds a canoe with a wooden man in it		The current takes the canoe many places

Public

Bonding to Public Realm (5)	Challenge (6)	Conflict Resolution, Loss (7)	Gaining a New Community (8)
Many people call to give her information about Essex's history	She and others organize Historical Society	Reminiscing party celebrates their success; outside professionals attend to witness this event	She gains office for Historical Society and plans to return to doing research and interviews
They sell bonds pay for pool	They are afraid they won't get enough money and plan two-week bond selling campaign	They get financial support	They build the pool that becomes a summer public forum
They publicize event through flyers, posters in stores and at pool	They work at it	People come and everybody has a good time	It is successful and may be held next year as part of fourth of July celebration
The senior citizens form the club and the Recreation Department helps them	They challenge the recreation director's control and demonstrate fiscal responsibility	The senior citizens and Recreation Department work together and the club becomes successful with dues paying members	The senior citizens work hard for themselves and gain independence
King desires a European education	Anna challenges the King	She teaches the King and he learns from her	They form bonds of affection
He gains experience of other cultures and becomes citizen of the world	The winds, water, and boat challenge him	He learns more than if he had gone to college; he proves he is self-reliant	He and his wife decide to raise family in rural America
	Nature and civilization threaten the canoe's life	Finally, it reaches the sea and a young fisherman catches it in his net	The boy, now a man, reads about his canoe in the paper

9
Kumu Aina:
Barriers Unite Citizens

> "When I use a word," Humpty Dumpty said, in rather a scornful tone, "it means just what I choose it to mean--neither more nor less."
> "The question is," said Alice, "whether you can make words mean so many different things."
> "The question is," said Humpty Dumpty, "which is to be master--that's all."
>
> Lewis Carroll
> Through the Looking-Glass

To Humpty Dumpty, freedom is the power to work one's will on anything and anyone without restraint, even without purposes beyond that of mastery. Like the citizens of Kumu Aina, as we shall see, Alice has her doubts about this notion of freedom and about the notion of power that goes with it. The Kumu Aina narratives presented in this chapter address the issue of how citizens can acquire freedom and power but propose its resolution in terms quite different from those supplied by Humpty Dumpty. Somehow, instead, they suggest that freedom and power come from participating with humility in the collective struggles of a community.

TROUBLE, FRIENDSHIP AND POLITICS

"Pilikia and Friendship" is a rich example of this political model. In the Hawaiian language pilikia means "trouble." The narrator, a native Hawaiian, explains the trouble her son encounters and how he finds his way through it to overcome both his own rejection of the Euro-American school system and the rejection he faces in the racism that confronts him on the U.S. mainland. Ultimately, he becomes a community leader, able to work within both cultural traditions, native Hawaiian and Euro-American. This Hawaiian mother describes how her son acquired his leadership skills.

Pilikia and Friendship

Came this one time, when he had a friend who didn't care for school. He was a Hawaiian boy and a good friend but they started cutting classes.

There was a time he didn't come home for one night, then two nights. I was frantic. I got some of my friends, who went all over looking for Kimo. One friend said that she was afraid, because there was a fellow who was peddling dope. She thought maybe the kids got into that. Another friend said, "His friend has a grandmother who lives way up in the valley." He said, "Maybe, they are there."

So we went up there, and on the front porch there they were as big as life. The boys were sitting playing the 'ukulele for the grandmother. I walked up to this woman and told her that I was worried about my son because he had not come home.

"That's okay, That's okay," she said in Hawaiian. "Don't worry, he is a good boy. He only came up here because he likes to play music. No pilikia. No trouble."

I told her that was trouble because the law said he was supposed to go to school. I brought him home. We decided that we couldn't let this go on because we both had to work and his love for music was going to really take him off. So we sent him to Washington to his older brother, who was teaching in Seattle.

While up there, he went to school. Just about the end of the school, he wrote and said he wanted to come home. He said it was very hard for him at first. There aren't many Hawaiians there. There aren't too many Blacks to begin with--no dark races because of where the state is. They really made him feel unwanted. This is maybe why he behaves the way he does. He has gone through racism, and that is why he is so very gentle when that kind of thing happens. He said that they made fun of him in school.

But, he finally won them over. He found a friend who took a liking to him. They didn't know what a Hawaiian was. Through this friend, he was introduced to other haole (White) kids and they found out that he was an alright kind of guy.

By the time they had elections for class officers, they wanted him to run for office. It had just reversed itself, but he was not eligible because he had not been in the school for a whole year.

He said, "Well, I will be manager." He was real game. "I will be manager for whichever guy is going to run." He was manager, and they won. So that built up his confidence.

He came home and we put him in school. Then, after two years, he went to the mainland to a university to study music. After that, he was really alright.

Oppositions

The Kumu Aina narratives in this third set describe the development of a new authority structure that vests power in a person who embodies the community and serves as its leader, unlike the liberal tradition which vests power in the law. This does not mean that the leader is above or beyond the law, rather that the fundamental representation of the community is in a person rather than a constitution or written legal agreement. The leader then inspires social change and collective actions which express community values. Considering the structure of the community that this narrative displays, there are five sets of oppositions in which leaders find power.

First, there are opposing cultures that together present a group of insiders and outsiders. In Hawaii, Kimo represents his Hawaiian side by visiting the grandmother. Traditionally, Hawaiians gained an education by studying with a wise elder, so by going to the grandmother's house, he follows this earlier educational model. However, he also attends a Euro-American school and so has access to this culture's tradition as well. Because he has emphasized his Hawaiian side and violated state law by missing school, his mother sends him to the mainland to develop his Euro-American ties. In Seattle, he moves from being an outsider who experiences racial ridicule to being an insider who assumes a leadership role, displaying his ability to balance both the Hawaiian and the Euro-American traditions.

Within this cultural opposition, it is important to take note of the role that music plays. In contemporary Hawaii, music most spectacularly revives native Hawaiian traditions. One of the key founders of the Hawaiian Renaissance movement was George Helm, who worked as a professional musician and whose music spoke about the politics of native Hawaiians. Thus Kimo's interest in music and in spending time with the grandmother indicate an interest not only in the Hawaiian tradition but also in its contemporary political life. Much of the music represents a critical review of Hawaii's history and of the loss of traditional Hawaiian values. By sending her son to live with his elder brother, which exposes him more fully to the Euro-American culture, the narrator also asserts Hawaiian values, because in the Hawaiian tradition, parents often send a boy to stay with an elder brother. It is important to note that, while the mother is well aware of the legal requirement that Kimo attend school, she does not ask the law to help her find him. She turns instead to her friends.

This leads to a second set of oppositions, between friends who, although they are genuine friends, represent ties that hold back leaders, and other friends who represent ties that facilitate leadership. A friend helps the narrator find Kimo when he fails to turn up at home and a friend finally brings Kimo into the Seattle school community. Friendship and extended family ties constitute an alternative authority that in this story, surpasses the legal authority both of the police, on whom she does not even bother to call for help, and of the school officials in Seattle, who cannot prevent racism from penetrating their system.

A third layer of opposition exists between the special skills and norms needed for creating community institutions. What Kimo first learns in the mainland school is the pain of rejection, but at the same time, he acquires the skills needed to participate in the Euro-American culture. This repeats the pattern established in the earlier stories. The school presents the first test for the students, who seek a way to emerge as leaders rather than simply to acquire cultural techniques. Kimo acquires two different cultural consciousnesses and develops ways of acting within each one. His musical talent is insufficient for his full development; he must acquire skills that will enable him to use his various talents in both cultural contexts. At a more general level, Kimo acquires both insider and outsider status in each of these contexts. This facilitates his development as a leader because it enables him to serve as a mediator, as he does in managing the election. His mediation does not derive from the neutral liberal model but rather from a specific commitment to a set of values. In this case, the values he embraces include the rules of the school, which forbid him from running for office, and regard for his friends, who want him to work with them. Hence, he resolves his earlier tension between obeying the law and sharing himself with his friends.

One facet of Kimo's commitment is that his ties to the community exist primarily as manifestations of friendship, which are more compelling than legal ones. It was a friend who "took him off" from school even though it violated the law. Even though the school environment is required by law to provide equal educational opportunities for all its students, the Seattle school fails Kimo because of the racism he experiences. Again, however, because "he found a friend," he is able to become a part of this community. The opposition that this articulates is the tension between one community based on friendship ties and another based on legal or contractual bonds.

A fourth layer of opposition is the tension between a society formed through agreements expressed in terms of contracts and a society formed through spiritual commitments expressed in terms of values that transcend the individual. Kimo's interest in music represents a transcendental commitment because it establishes links with the ancient Hawaiian heritage, including its religious practices, in which music and dance were central elements of worship. Kimo's devotion to his new Seattle friends comes to life in political participation, for it is this form in which community commitment manifests itself within the Euro-American culture, where religion is a private matter and electoral politics is public.

A fifth theme of this opposition exists in Kimo's status. He moves from being a rejected, humiliated citizen in the Seattle school system to being a popular leader. Indeed, the very experience of humiliation makes his leadership possible. According to his mother, that is why he is "so very gentle." The combination of gentleness and power makes him a leader. He is willing to take a back seat in the elections, which for him is not a defeat but evidence of true leadership ability. "He was manager, and they won." He won them over, playing an important role in the creation of a "we" who could win the election. The creation of this we, the articulation of collective identity and energy, makes him a genuine leader.

Metaphors

In these narratives, language plays a central role in allocating power. Kimo's mother knows both Hawaiian and English, even though as a child she was forbidden to speak Hawaiian in the schools or on the streets of her hometown on the island of Maui. Nevertheless, she acquired both Hawaiian and English. Kimo's musical skills underscore the importance of language as a form of communication. Music, especially singing, plays a central role in teaching the people of modern Hawaii about Hawaiian culture, Hawaiian language, and Hawaiian values. Music leads him to the Hawaiian grandmother and music leads him to his university studies. Music here is the medium that helps him create his own harmony between both cultural traditions.

Transformations

Two transformations that confront Kimo come about through friends. In the first case, a friend "takes him off," which leads his parents to send him to the mainland; in the second case, a friend "took a liking to him," finding out who he was, both by discovering the Hawaiian culture and by getting to know Kimo as a person. Without being acquainted with his cultural heritage, it is impossible for the Seattle students to know Kimo, because he is not simply an individual but also a part of an elaborate and ancient cultural tradition. Kimo is not bothered because they think he is Black; he is bothered because they do not know what a Hawaiian is. Hence, the story explains that transformations in relationships begin with genuine knowledge, not only about an individual person but also about that persons's cultural heritage. Such friendship then can serve as an agent of political transformation.

Contradictions

Kimo also encounters pain when his Seattle classmates reject him. His humiliation, like that of Lawrence, leads finally to leadership. Also following the Lawrence model, Kimo leaves Seattle and returns to "his people" in Hawaii. Kimo's leadership, however, is effective with both the Hawaiian and Euro-American people, so he moves between the two cultures playing the role of mediator and leader. As a participant in both cultures, he is in some sense outside both of them. Unlike his mother, whose primary identity has been within the Hawaiian tradition although she has become an effective leader in Euro-American situations as well, Kimo must strive hard to appropriate both his Hawaiian roots and his Euro-American roots. The center of this narrative's political contradiction lies in the powerful leadership that a mediator possesses. While Kimo does not run for office in Seattle, he is the hero of the event. He has been humiliated but is now exalted. Leadership requires both humility and exaltation and necessitates knowledge of various cultural traditions. This is not to suggest that Kimo's kind of leadership is in any sense "neutral," as the liberal tradition would have it. Kimo does not move outside of cultural tradition into some tradition-free space; instead, he makes a commitment to two different traditions from which he can draw values and insights for political action.

The other stories in this third set elaborate on the pattern expressed in Kimo's story. They also reveal the energy that makes politics in Hawaii an exciting arena for exploring cultural values and alternative political futures.

Margarette

This story, told by a Euro-American political activist, shows that a young girl can exercise considerable power. It also explains the connection between spiritual power and political power in a way that gives credit to both by showing how they support each other.

>Margarette was a young wealthy girl in France who lived with her uncle. She was his pride and joy. She lived on a big estate where everybody in the whole compound was really evil. Everybody wanted Margarette to be their special friend. They went to her and almost drained her spiritual power and everybody complained to her about everyone else.
>But Granny was the big one. She wheeled herself all around and she had a bunch of keys that could open any door in the manor; she held on to those keys. Margarette tried to restore her physical and mental health. One day she said, "Granny, you are not ready to meet God yet." Granny said she was because she had done this and

that. Margarette said, "There is one thing that you haven't yet given up. You have to give that up before you are ready to meet God."

They had called in a psychiatrist to work with the Grandmother and a Catholic priest as well. None of them seemed to be able to get near her.

Margarette said, "Granny, I want those keys. When you can give me those keys, then you are going to be all right. Those keys are enslaving you."

Eventually, she handed the keys over to Margarette, and just closed her eyes and died. She surrendered herself completely into the future to God.

One particular servant who was in charge of the others was after Margarette to love him. He said that miracles just dripped from her fingers, but she said, "I have no miracles. I have no power of working miracles. I am simply a child of God, and I just have nothing." He hated her and at the end of the story he came into her room and killed her by pounding on her.

In the house was a priest who Margarette knew had no faith. She prayed for his conversion. After Granny's death, he made his act of faith. They asked Margarette, "Aren't you afraid to go out alone with all your beauty and your charm? Aren't you afraid that something will happen to you? Aren't you afraid of falling from those heights?"

She said, "Where would I fall to? I could only fall into God no matter where I was."

Pulling Together

This narrative, told by a native Hawaiian, reflects his integration of the Christian religion with the native Hawaiian religious tradition. He often explains to his friends that, for him, the commandment not to have any gods before the Lord God explicitly suggests the possibility of paying respect to other gods as long as God is first. He also emphasizes the connection between genuine community and spiritual phenomena. In this narrative, rather than arguing for religious <u>tolerance</u>, he argues for <u>respect</u> for the religious convictions of others.

The high school took nineteen students to Kauai to camp out. We stayed at my cousin's place; he is a single man with a small shack. When we got there he said "Mai, mai, mai,[1] come, come, sleep on the bed. Don't sleep outside." We had one boy who was very religious. I said, "Kauai is a very superstitious island. So you people watch out what you say to the people here because they take offense if you make fun of their beliefs. One kid said, "Aw, I don't believe that kind of stuff because I am a Christian."

"Well, Fred, what you believe is your business but don't criticize the people here."

That night there were six or seven of us sleeping under the tree. Some were sleeping in the bus and some were in the house with my cousin Kainoa. I woke up and I heard sticks hitting--clack, clack, clack, clack. We were close to the roadway and there were street lights there. We looked up and there was no air blowing. The coconut trees were still and there were no stars. That is the sign of pokane--the night marchers night. Then one of the girls got up and said, "Kai, you hear that?"

I said, "Just keep quiet. Keep quiet."

A football boy got up and said, "Kai, somebody just stepped by my head."

I said, "Okay, people, if you feel anything pushing you, move."

I don't know why I wasn't scared. I guess I was trying to be the rational brave teacher. The hedge went "shuuuuu" like someone was moving near it. There was no wind.

Two girls got up and said, "We are not going to stay here and they got in the bus. Then the bus started shaking and they all came out and were scared. One girl was crying.

I said, "Okay, just keep quiet."

Then, up the road, we heard a dog bark and it stopped. Then, further up the road, we heard a rooster crow and it stopped. Something was traveling up the road.

Then, I saw this black figure hovering by the road. We said, "It must be a rock." Then it got up and moved and crouched again. We didn't sleep the rest of the night and in the morning we asked some people about it.

I asked another cousin there about it and she didn't believe us but some other people said that road is the pathway where the so-called dead carry their dead up to the mountains to bury them. The sound was the clacking of the stretchers they use.

The next night all nineteen kids were right around me. We had a word of prayer and then everybody got a good night's rest.

I said, "Well Fred, what do you say now?"

He said, "I'm not going to say nothing."

I said, "You have experienced it and you can say what you feel about it but never make fun of people. We experienced something and that makes us believers now."

A Community Grant

An area of land designated as special homestead land for native Hawaiians raises problems for these residents, who find that the government agency that administers the homestead lands does not provide them with needed services. The narrator, a native Hawaiian, helps coordinate social services in the Kumu Aina area, but, more important, her long-time residency and feisty spirit inspires other residents to experience their own efficacy and to cherish Kumu Aina for its own special qualities.

Sue, myself, Bob, and his wife met one Sunday afternoon and decided to write up a project for the Interagency Council to get money to create an official advocate for the people living on the homestead lands. The advocate would find out what the problems were and act as a liaison between the residents and the state Department of Community Homes. The state Department of Community Homes wasn't too enthusiastic about it, but we continued with it. We submitted it to the Neighborhood Task Force.

In the meantime, the homeowners

themselves found out about it and started screaming that we had not contacted them. We tried to meet with them to apologize for not checking with them, but we learned that there were only five on the board and they were all part of one family. They were very hostile to us. They said it was their project and they had thought about it even though they didn't put it down on paper. They they started in on the four of us. They criticized Sue because she was a <u>haole</u> and ran a health center that did not <u>fulfill</u> its mission which was to keep kids from getting involved with drugs.

They said, "Sue, you should stay with the counseling center because those kids need you."

Then they started on Stella because she was a <u>haole</u>, and then they turned to Bob because he was Japanese and worked for an organization that had not done much for the Hawaiians. I was getting pretty angry and wondered what they would say to me.

I said, "While it is not my turn yet, I don't know what you folks will do when you get to me. I am Hawaiian and my Grandma and I have spent a lot of time here."

At the end of the meeting, they asked that the reports be turned over to them and that it be scrapped. Everyone in our group wanted to scrap it because of the problems. But I wasn't willing to do that.

I stayed with the homeowners and met with them to see that the project did go through. The same family, however, is still controlling it and it has not been turned over to the residents.

Search Your Own Heart

As mentioned earlier the Kaho'olawe 'Ohana, a native Hawaiian political action group, works toward ending the bombing of the island of Kaho'olawe and restoring it to the Hawaiian people. As a part of their politics, many members have occupied the island from time to time to dramatize their opposition to the bombing. Some of these citizens were arrested and, just before the trial, the 'Ohana met to decide what would be their role in it. This story takes place in the context of the 'Ohana and its internal dynamics. The narrator, a native Hawaiian, has both official and unofficial leadership responsibilities in Kumu Aina. She also has played a leadership role in the 'Ohana, which draws its membership from the entire state.

> The Kaho'olawe 'Ohana asked me to sit and share <u>mana'o</u> (feelings, thoughts). The trial for the alleged trespassers was coming up and we were talking about how to give them support. We planned to first meet at Iolani Palace and have prayers. We did not want a drum beating, yelling type of demonstration but we wanted a humble, peaceful, quiet demonstration. No matter what the decision was afterward we would march to Kawaiahao Church to pray and give thanks.
> In these discussions one of our young <u>opio</u> (young people) gave way to her own personal thing. She has been going to school at the university for some time. She has been exposed to different political theories, and the way she was coming across was shades of Marxism. She said the people on trial should not feel that they are better than the grassroots people. After some discussion and her own <u>mana'o</u> about what had happened in the past, I was asked to give my <u>mana'o</u>.
> I said, "Sometimes a lot of people do things and they need 'attaboys,' and 'atta girls' every day. So you look at that and ask why are you doing things--for the cause, for somebody else, for yourself? If you are doing it for yourself, you need to be complimented because you are insecure. If anybody owes something, it is we who owe those defendants because they put their ass on the line. They are the ones whose lives will be affected by the trial. They are <u>koa</u>, soldiers, in the front of this effort. At forty-six years, I am a lousy soldier. I cannot live on the island because there are no cigarettes. Weak individuals need 'atta girls' and 'attaboys.' Search your own heart and see what you can contribute to society without anybody even knowing what you have done. You don't need for everybody to know because then you will feel good inside."
> She said she learned from me and felt embarrassed. But I said, "No need to feel

embarrassed but once you understand then you do things differently. That is what is important."

FREEDOM AND COMMUNITY

Oppositions

The insider/outsider distinction that illuminates the tension between two different cultures appears in a somewhat different form in "Pulling Together," because it represents an opposition between the spiritually connected insiders, who are even connected to those who have died, and political outsiders, who take their values from a rational, individualist, Judeo-Christian tradition. The story presents two different cultures, in that Kai specifically talks about the cultural differences between his students on Oahu and those who live on Kauai, an outer island. He expresses this cultural difference in terms of their spiritual orientations. The students represent Christian rationality, while Kauai residents represent a more intense spirituality to which he initially refers as superstition. However, through their experience, the visitors acquire an appreciation of this so-called superstition and begin to see some of its spiritual significance. They also discover that it empowers them, for they now have their own experiences and their own personal stories. The spirits have visited them; they have intervened in their lives and made them special. They have become insiders, and as they have done so, they have strengthened their own political relationships with each other and with the people of Kauai.

In "Search Your Own Heart," the Hawaiian activists, in planning their trial demonstration, make a similar connection between spiritual life and politics. They wish to discover the Hawaiian way of expressing political positions and that way has a spiritual dimension to it, including prayer and a discipline that requires them to give thanks even if they do not win. In this context the importance of their political work at the trial is not in its victorious outcome but rather their ability to commit themselves to the values of the Hawaiian tradition--their ability to conduct themselves according to their own vision of the good. Hence, the opposition between the two cultures--the Hawaiian tradition and the modern American demonstration model--represents for them an opposition between an integrated virtuous course of action and an inauthentic course of action, which does not represent their values. This helps explain the problem the homesteaders confront. The Interagency Council obviously has created a grant that will help them but, because it comes from "outside" their tradition and does not embody its values, they are put off by it. The grant is written to "win" money not to further the spiritual and political values they represent, so they reject it. It is not their pride which causes them to reject it, nor is it their own racial bias. It is simply that the collective commitments of the community are more important than the material benefits individuals members would receive. Being and meaning are found finally in the collective political life of the group, not with the individuals. If the homesteaders are not together as a group, then the improvement of their living conditions is irrelevant; the group's integrity comes first. Hence, the narrator, whose kinship ties make her a part of the homesteaders' group, continues to work with them even though they have insulted her friends and at times act in ways detrimental to the needs of the homesteaders. In the struggle between the individual and the society, society wins. But this is not a victory for the state. It is a victory for the network of relationships that fundamentally constitute that society. In this case, that network is better described as kindred spirits, kinfolk, than as parties to a contract.

Alongside this opposition between spiritual and political commitments is an opposition between professional expertise and personal cultural experience. While the Interagency Council members certainly have professional expertise, they lack concrete personal experience in living on the homestead lands. The narrator, on the other hand, has such personal experience as well as professional expertise, so it is appropriate for her to continue working on the project. A similar point is made about the opposition between professional expertise and personal experience in "Margarette." While the priest has the professional expertise, Margarette has the genuine spiritual experience. Her experience not only helps her grandmother to detach herself from material goods (symbolized by the keys) and make a spiritual commitment to God but also enables Margarette to bring the priest to a genuine conversion. In dealing with this professional/personal opposition, the story asserts that personal experience, with a genuine commitment to a personal relationship, has greater power than professional expertise and vocational status. The Kauai tale echoes the same theme, for it is through a personal experience that the students acquire their genuine education rather than though the instruction of their very knowledgeable teacher. In the homesteaders' decisions, personal relationships are so much more important than the professional expertise of the Interagency Council that the people willingly sacrifice the success of their project in order to maintain these relationships. In the Kaho'olawe trial, the narrator explains that, while the young woman has a university education, without the integrity that comes from knowing that you act in order to help others rather than for recognition or praise, action becomes hollow and ineffective. This type of understanding comes about through a personal political relationship that reveals the young woman's shortcomings to her. Professional expertise, which brings with it public recognition, can hinder action rather than facilitate it, because it tempts one to act out of a desire for "atta boys" or "atta girls" rather than out of a desire to strengthen community bonds. Such prestige can interfere with a leader's humble status which is the primary path to power.

However, leaders need more than knowledge about opposing cultural values; they need a sense of the good. The Hawaiian grandmother says that the mother is not to worry because Kimo "is a good boy." The Kaho'olawe elder explains that the primary criterion for taking action in the group, must be an inner sense of goodness, not the external praise and status that may flow from it. Margarette's final victory is in winning another soul for good work, not in a physical victory over death or evil actions. In the Kauai story, the students acquire respect for the good in persons rather than in their ability to represent the dominant culture's values. The dead who bury their dead manifest community commitment and a desire to do good. The ethic that these narratives articulate calls for primary commitments to persons rather than abstract principles. In burying the dead, the night marchers display their commitment to one another; in trying to save the grandmother and the priest, Margarette demonstrates an affection for persons rather than a call to subscribe to missionary principles or even a call to a religious vocation. One is called first to a person and then to the work of determining what actions are appropriate to that commitment.

Thus, an underlying opposition for these citizens involves distinguishing appropriate and good action from inappropriate and bad action. Cultural awareness is one aspect of this process, not because one culture is more clearly in possession of virtue, but because a lack of cultural awareness produces a bias that makes it difficult for one to see the proper course of action. Therefore, good leadership, like that provided by Lawrence, Kimo, Horton, Kai, and the narrator of "Search Your Own Heart," requires knowledge of cultural differences so that decisions will genuinely mediate among differences rather than simply assert one culture over another. Such decisions will then be made on the basis of commitments to particular persons rather than on the basis of commitments to abstract principles based on the values of a single culture. It means that, in each action, the participants need to discover the good for the collectivity and then embrace that good, so that it becomes the basis for public action.

Metaphor

The word "right" appears in many of these narratives and its presence speaks of the importance of linking conceptions of the good with the immediate reality that faces a citizen. In the Hawaiian tradition, disputes are resolved by a process called ho'oponopono, "making it right." While this process is complex, two of its more important components can be brought out in this analysis: its spiritual dimension; and its focus on establishing just relationships among persons. It proceeds with a healer or wise elder, who leads a session that can easily last an entire day. Its purpose is to discover underlying tensions and injustices so that participants can deal with them and "make it right." What is important here is the emphasis upon "rightness." This refers to redressing past wrongs, to finding the correct action in the present circumstances, so as to account for the past and reestablish a historical relationship freed of the guilt and burdens of such past wrongs.[2] In this context, when at the very end of her story, Kimo's mother says of him, "After that he was really all right," she suggests that after that he understood what was appropriate to each cultural context. She does not speak about him in merely a psychological way but suggests that he has matured politically. He has developed a center from which he can draw on his own knowledge of the good and just.

Within the Hawaiian tradition this suggests he has strong mana, a sense of himself that gives him the peace and presence necessary to deal with challenges.

One leader explained _mana_ in terms of an internal energy that enables a person to confront challenges, even challenges that threaten life itself. This inner energy develops through relationships with others. The students on Kauai confront their fears together, which suggests a model for others. Once the students come together in one place, and pray together, they are able to acknowledge their experience and, finally, to incorporate it into their life stories. Together, they help each other to develop their _mana_ and to find a way of acknowledging and then making use of the mysterious powers that reside in the connections between the living and the dead, between present and past political life, and between both of these and the mysterious forces of the universe.

Hawaiians define _mana_ as mystical power.[3] This power, however, is different from the power of imposing one's will on others; it is a power that entails an "inherent quality of command and leadership...a reservoir of strength."[4] In this modern context, _mana_ manifests itself when Kimo, through his struggle and humiliation, comes to know his own inner strength; he has access to his _mana_, and from that point on, he is able to transcend his struggle and act out of a sense of justice--to do what is "right." He is in touch with his own sense of "right." He is "alright." In a similar way Margarette implores her Grandmother, "When you can give me those keys, then you are going to be alright." The Kauai narrative describes this experience, and the narrator explains that one of the most important things that happened to his students was not that they acquired some tolerance for people different from themselves, but that they acquired their own experience and their own story, which, in turn, will enable them to preserve and communicate that experience. Rather than acquiring _tolerance_, they acquired a common experience that helped them to _identify_ with the Kauai residents. This is the basis for genuine community, for such feelings of community, of being bound together by common experiences, common stories, constitute the basis for public political action. Such stories work at a sophisticated level of communication that preserves both the linguistic habits of a people and the meaning of their experiences and their history. This story goes so far as to transcend life itself and to connect these people with the night marchers--the dead. Its political basis unites not only persons living in a single locality under a single government but also people of various traditions, including their ancestors--their founders. The story argues for what many Americans seek, elusive as it often is, a link to the founders of the nation.

Another aspect of the link between communication and community appears in the message that the animals give to the students on Kauai. The dogs and roosters announce that the night marchers have passed by their homes, so that the students know they have moved on. For those who know their language the animals give reassurance. In Kumu Aina, animals announce the travel of visitors up and down the valleys and provide a system of communication that provides protection for those who know how to listen. This represents a cosmological bond between humans and animals. Those who understand this bond possess a spiritual power that makes them more effective as political leaders. They understand nature and culture as cooperating forces that preserve and protect human life.

But, language has its dark side as well. The story of the trial shows that some people need verbal incantations in order to sustain their pride. Those who need these "atta boys" and "atta girls" serve as metaphorical opposites to the Kauai students. These prideful people lack genuine experience and commitment, so they must be sustained by such empty speech. Those who have deep experience can open the way for a new understanding, which integrates Hawaiian tradition and language in the sharing of mana'o with the Euro-American tradition of political demonstrations and "grassroot" movements. "Grassroots" itself brings together the Hawaiian commitment to land and the importance of "roots" as an image, of the unity of a people with the Euro-American image which has its own origins in a people whose lives once depended upon land and agriculture.

The Hawaiian way, however, goes beyond bringing new words like mana'o into modern American politics. It brings a new, quiet, peaceful consciousness. The center of that consciousness is displayed in the relationship between the members on trial and the demonstrators, and that is why the group and the two women, both younger and elder, must work out the proper understanding for this relationship. Without this, victory is probably impossible and certainly empty.

The type of power that these narratives articulate is not control over others, but rather surrender to the proper order of things. The story of Margarette makes this clear by reversing the traditional Euro-American image of "keys." Normally, keys signify power over others. For example, God gives to Peter the "keys to the Kingdom of Heaven." However, in this case, the "keys," which unlock and lock the various rooms in the mansion, actually imprison the Grandmother. If she is to become free, she must surrender them. Like the Kauai students, she must become open to the spiritual dimension of life, which in turn will open to her the possibility of surrendering to experience and appreciating others. Freedom depends on surrender to concern for persons not on separating oneself from them in organized domination and submission. It is through interdependence and connectedness to others that one can gain true freedom.

Transformations

After their experience, the young campers have their own story to tell and find themselves better able to move between the rationalistic Christian tradition and the holistic, spiritual orientation of the native Hawaiian tradition. Evidence for this is to be found in Fred's response, that in the future he will not say anything when people make claims about their spiritual experience. He moves from seeing Kauai as superstitious place to knowing it as a spiritual place. The transformation takes place through an experience, and the story that embodies that experience makes it possible for them to continue to share it with others by simply telling their story.

Two levels of transformation generate political action. The first takes place at the level of consciousness. It resembles Plato's story of the cave which involves a turning around, a transcendence or what modern Western Christians call conversion and psychiatrists call a new level of consciousness. This new understanding transforms people and makes it possible for them to transform their situations. The young woman who had been motivated by "atta girls" sees her former selfish motives and is "embarrassed." The elder explains that she need not be embarrassed but that she needs to change her understanding. The leader makes the argument and changed behavior follows. Hence, consciousness transforms action that stimulates political change.

The second level of transformation takes place through actors connecting their inner powers, which embody a commitment to the good, with their external commitment to members of the community. In this process such actors seek just action. As in "Search Your Own Heart," it is not a private contemplative process but an awareness that comes through honest

Kumu Aina: Barriers Unite Citizens

discussions with others and depends upon an inner strength acquired through a commitment to others. The protagonists in these narratives transform the social system by developing this inner power. The Hawaiian tradition calls this <u>mana</u> and the Euro-American tradition calls it integrity. Integrity includes a sense of one's relationship to others as well as one's relationship to the transcendent purposes of life in the universe. The political significance of this inner power is that it becomes the center from which one can know the public good and go beyond his or her selfish narrow interests. <u>Mana</u> is a mixture of courage, conviction, and strength. From this spiritual center, one can act in a just way. Kumu Aina citizens talk about <u>mana</u> as an awareness of the proper order of things, which enables one to save and protect others. One such example is the way citizens speak about those who know how to be with sharks in the water. Unlike other parts of Oahu, the shoreline of Kumu Aina is not protected by a reef and sharks swim within a few miles of shore, where people dive for fish. Those who consider themselves shark people do not show fear when sharks appear close to them in the water. On the other hand, neither do they display aggressive behavior. They either firmly and quietly hold their position or slowly withdraw, so that the shark will see that the <u>mana</u> (personal spirit) of the swimmer is strong. These people consider sharks their brothers and respect them. It is not so much that they have special techniques for dealing with sharks; instead, they have a special kinship relationship with sharks. This special relationship gives them ways of acting that combine knowledge, experience, and commitment. It is the relationship, not the technique, that makes them able to do the things they do.

In a similar way, Kumu Aina leaders count on relationships and their personal spirit to enable them to deal with those who differ from them or even may pose threats. They can give way to others without fear and without letting go of their own being. The students learn about this on Kauai. The teacher tells them that if they feel something push against them they should move. This shows respect without fear. In a similar manner Kimo deals with the aggressive behavior of the Seattle students; he does not withdraw from them but maintains a quiet presence until he can find a way to enter their realm. Transformation takes place through the protagonist's relationships, not through some particular action. The emphasis on transformed consciousness as a precondition for new action fits with the emphasis upon religious or spiritual commitments as a part of social change. Religion itself involves tying things together, making sense out of them, and it entails an understanding of the cosmic connections between God, human beings, and nature; and from this cosmic vision flows a social political vision.

Kumu Aina citizens begin to address problems by exploring their roots in their consciousness, so that they can clarify their own ideas about the good in the context of their cosmic vision and proceed to solve political problems from this center. Solving social problems depends upon respect for the spiritual connections among phenomena. Hence, the protest against the bombing of Kaho'olawe is more than simply a rallying point for a political movement or a turf war between the U.S. Navy and native Hawaiians. It is an assertion of a philosophical stance that teaches that the land serves as a wise elder--a member of the community-- not simply as a resource, at the disposal of human purposes. This does not mean that land is not a resource for it is, serving the life of the community, as do its human members. Making use of its services, however, does not mean disregarding its own life. The continued life of the land is as vital to the community as the continued life of its human members. The land has life of its own, which should itself be served by those who inhabit it. As the Hawaiians put it, "the life of the land is fulfilled in righteousness."[5] Just actions require that this understanding be fully integrated into the community's consciousness.

Transformation begins with the development of consciousness through commitments to others. Leaders who have this insight then, like Margarette, acquire the strength to surrender themselves to the common good, even to sacrifice their lives for others. Action involves a willingness to surrender to the common need and humble oneself before others. Once the young woman, in the story of the trial meeting, publicly admits her error she experiences humility and readies herself for leadership. Right action is not prideful, for it recognizes its power, not as an attribute of the ego, but as deriving from one's membership in a community and from one's ability to see the connections between one's commitments to others in the community and the natural and spiritual forces of the universe--all those forces that hope for the good and just.

Contradictions

The tension between outstanding leadership and humility manifests itself throughout these narratives. The young woman who wants to be sure that those on trial do not think themselves better than the demonstrators experiences the pain of this tension. She knows the necessity of humility but misdirects it. She wants to ensure that others possess it but does not embody it in her own actions. By humbling her, the elder woman helps her to experience her own humility and, thereby, prepares her for leadership. Her expression of embarrassment denotes precisely the correct experience, if leadership is to be a genuine possibility. As it did for Lawrence, such an experience can lead to insight and renewed energy. Leaders are those who fully experience powerlessness. Margarette manifests a contradiction between power and humiliation for she is not only humiliated by her agonizing death but her status as a child in a powerful household places her in most humble circumstances. Her power, however, reaches to the grandmother and beyond her brutal death to the priest, whose faith she helps restore. Her spiritual power brings social promise to the household. The students--especially Fred, who staunchly declares his scorn for "superstitious" beliefs--undergo a humbling experience in confronting their own fears, their own interdependence, made manifest in the circle that they draw around their leader on the second night and in their final recognition of the limits of their own understanding. "I won't say nothing," Fred declares, using the double negative to amplify the fact that he has limitations and has come to know himself as having by no means a monopoly of all important knowledge. For these students, freedom from fear requires recognition of the importance of their interdependence and collective existence.

In the light of this contradiction then, the error the Interagency Council makes is that it lacks humility. It proceeds as if it is in possession of all relevant knowledge. The homesteaders outraged at this pretension and humble the council members. There is a problem, however, inasmuch as those who are not Hawaiian lack the ability to deal with this humbling experience and so they withdraw. The Hawaiian on the council recognizes their painful experience but remains with the project despite its momentarily devastating effects on her. She goes through the humiliating experience and emerges as a leader. For the most part, her colleagues may explain this as an expression of her loyalty to the Hawaiian people, which in part it is; but this explanation falls short because it fails to see her action as a process by which leaders dedicate themselves to a people. Such experiences, however, cannot be brought upon oneself. One cannot volunteer for them. But, once such an experience presents itself, the true leader recognizes the situation, confronts his or her own failings and, instead of withdrawing, begins to participate more fully. Such a situation is an opportunity to be more fully integrated with a community. The night marchers give the students their opportunity, and the elder woman gives the young woman activist in the trial her opportunity. Leaders cannot appoint themselves to the humbling experience.

One image of such humility is represented by Margarette, who says that no matter how far she falls, she will always fall into the hands of God. This suggests that the humiliating experience can lead to rescue by the good and, in turn, become a power for bringing good into the human political community. In that case, her own humiliating death plays a role in the conversion of the priest, which itself may represent the conversion of the entire community, since the priest is in charge of its well-being. Once they have the experience necessary to make humility a central part of what they are, potential leaders can find their own story in it and in the context of that story develop an identity with others. The narratives argue, therefore, that leadership requires waiting passively for an experience while actively confronting the problems one sees. This quiet anticipation and willingness to act decisively enables leaders, political actors, to embody both power and humility, which then makes it possible for them to transcend their own wills to power by opening them to the common good. Their commitment can then be directed toward community members and can inspire them to reach for the just order of things.

Climbing over Barriers: The Power of Laughter

The following story explains more fully the way in which citizens acquire freedom by creating relationships with others. The woman who tells this story is a native Hawaiian who is active in the political life of Kumu Aina, as well as in the state of Hawaii. She and her husband live a simple life, working hard to raise their children and to offer the kind of friendship to their neighbors that these narratives describe.

> I find freedom comes to me through other people. I don't acquire it alone. I find that circumstances come about where I have to respond to another person and, in doing so, there are all sorts of barriers to overcome--they might be family barriers, or things that I have to get done--so that I am not free to get to that person to help them.
> I climb over all of these barriers no matter what they are, and finally I reach my friend. We sit down, and we talk, and we talk and we talk and she is really troubled. But, talking with her, I realize that I, too, experience similar problems. The things that are bothering her bother me. I say, "Hey, I came here to help you, and you are helping me."
> Then we are both laughing about the situation, because we find out that we are similar. Because we both experience the same kind of dilemmas and problems in our lives we can become very sensitive to one another. And we are able to find an answer that gives us hope that the action we take will make it right.
> When I come out of that experience, I feel that I have been freed. I went to help my friend and then, by giving myself to her, I am liberated and so is she. We grow together. It happens all the time because the more you are aware of other people and sensitive to them, the more you become what you hope for others.

The story explains that freedom is not the absence of restraint or authority, and it cannot be found it isolation. Whether the problem is a personal one or, as is more likely the case here, a political one, the solution lies in struggling to connect with others, to overcome the barriers, and to delight in friendships. Freedom comes through other people, through relationships; it can only be found in community.

TABLE 6. KUMU AINA — Private

	Establishing Kinship Ties (1)	A Threat to Kinship Ties (2)	Assertion of Family Unity & Authority (3)	Moment of Release (4)	Humiliation (5)
Pilikia and Friendship	Family lives in Kumu Aina	Boy lost from family because of his love for music	With help of friends mother finds him; Grandmother then says he is a good boy	Boy is sent to mainland school	Students there humiliate him
Margarette	Margarette lives with her uncle	Evil threatens this family	Granny has the keys to all the doors	Margarette gets her to give up the keys, which enslave her	The servant humiliates Margarette
Pulling Together	Teacher takes ninteen students on a trip to Kauai	The first night, they all sleep in different places	Teacher tells them to be careful not to offend Kauai residents	Fred says he is a Christian and doesn't believe in that "kind of stuff"	Night marchers frighten students; they are humiliated
A Community Grant	Interagency council meets and talks about grant	This grant threatens the Homestead Association Board, which represents one family	The board asserts its right to administer the grant		Board humiliates interagency council members
Search Your Own Heart	'Ohana asks narrator to sit in meeting	External forces— university and Marxism threaten unity of 'Ohana	By sharing mana'o, they assert their Hawaiian tradition and authority of family	Mana'o represents a release because it integrates thoughts and feelings	Young girl is embarrassed by her actions
Barriers to Freedom	"I find freedom comes to me through other people"	Friend threatens family and obligations		She climbs over these barriers	

220

		Public		
Issue of Challenge (6)	Mediation and Unification: Pulling Together (7)	Action Directed Toward Social Transformation (8)	Liberating Action (9)	Returning Home (10)
He challenges them and explains he is Hawaiian	A friend helps him and he becomes their leader	They unite and he manages successful campaign for school president	He leaves this school after he has been accepted	He returns home to Hawaii to study
She challenges the servant and explains that she does not perform miracles	She mediates for the family by praying and by showing courage and trust in God	The servant kills her	At the moment of her death, the priest whom she prayed for, is converted	She goes home to be with her father
This experience challenges their own explanation; they ask what happened	Kai helps them understand this experience	They all sleep in a circle after a word of prayer	They have their own story and a new understanding of spiritual life and social existence	They go home to tell their story
Narrator continues to work with board and challenge their ideas even though other council people withdraw	Narrator endeavors to mediate between homestead and social agencies	They find an advocate who will transform communication network between homeowners and government	Homesteaders board takes over grant	Same family rules board
'Ohana challenges Navy use of Kaho'olawe as bombing target	They will all unite and demonstrate at the trial	They assert there is justice with their cause, no matter what the court decides; they will demonstrate in a Hawaiian way	They experience liberation from external authorities; they don't need "atta boys" or "atta girls"	Leader and young woman at peace
She challenges these barriers that keep her from helping her friend	She and her friend talk and mediate for each other	Through discussion and laughter, they come to a decision	They liberate each other and so grow	The freedom comes

10
Politics in Reflection

>   Ever drifting down the stream--
>   Lingering in the golden gleam--
>   Life, what is it but a dream?
>
>   Lewis Carroll
>   <u>Through</u> <u>the</u> <u>Looking-Glass</u>

Carroll's words sound like a reflection of the idle summer day that he refers to in earlier stanzas--a day for floating in a boat and telling a tale--but his meaning is deeper, for he wants his reader to consider the real power of the imagination. Our images, our visions, guide our actions; and in this sense, image is more fundamental to changing the world than action. Or, instead, one could say that making images and insinuating them into the public world is itself an action. Images lead; other actions follow. This has an important implication for understanding politics in America. Because many Americans think that storytelling, symbol making, talking, and dreaming do not play central roles in shaping political life, they are unable to participate in the most vital aspect of political action. But, this is a most unrealistic and impractical view, because it leaves out the crucial political work of envisioning, forming the vision, making the dream that will direct other actions. Of course, many feel that the story has already been written, the dream already formed by the founders who wrote the Constitution and set it all in motion. This only means, however, that they are satisfied with the story as it has been told, and the problem is that they keep repeating the same story over and over. But, because it was made in a different time, they are unable to live it. The story has an empty ring, not because it is untrue or impossible but because it isn't really theirs. What I have argued in this book is that to tell a story is to make it a part of one's life, to make it one's own. I have also argued that America's story is still in the making. A central aspect of American politics is in continuing to make the story and in becoming more aware of one's role in political life by telling it.

The narrators in this book have told their stories to show how politics works in their communities. Through these stories, they impart some of the political wisdom they have gained through living those stories. In telling them, they offer a political theory about how community works. The narrative analysis is an attempt to make that theory explicit, and like all political theories, it is complex, for politics is complex. Even so, I want to try to give an overview of the wisdom these leaders offer us. To do this, I first show how these two communities represent contrasting visions of politics, each of which has a place in a long-standing tradition of political theory. Put most simply, the Essex narratives mirror the tradition of liberal political theory, while the Kumu Aina narratives reflect an understanding of politics not unlike that which we associate with classical Greece. Second, I shall show how each community challenges the tradition it represents by asking questions and offering solutions that go beyond it. Because both communities exist in the context of the American political culture, their questions, challenges, and solutions have some important common aspects, despite their diversity. These challenges, questions, and solutions offer hope for moving politics in America closer to justice, as we continue to develop and reflect on the political story that, at this moment, we are writing, telling, and living.

LIBERALISM IN ESSEX AND THE POLIS IN KUMU AINA

Essex citizens understand themselves to be a part of liberal political theory, in the sense that America itself takes the foundations of its political theory from the liberal tradition. Speaking this way, of course, does not mean that conservatives have no standing in America. Quite the contrary, for both those who, in the everyday American sense, call themselves liberals and those who call themselves conservative come out of the tradition of liberal political theory. This tradition has itself taken shape in continuing dialogue and confrontation with other equally distinct and opposing traditions: the principle of rule by divine right, which has been the primary basis of monarchy; socialism, which argues for a world in which democratically controlled governments take over all of the most important elements of economic life; and Marxist communism, which also argues for government control of the economic sphere, but would put government in the hands of a single-party dictatorship of the proletariat directed toward the final disappearance of the state. To be sure, in the everyday American sense of the word, Essex citizens would be classified as conservatives, but in this wider sense, in their very conservatism, they exemplify the values of liberal political theory. They believe unquestioningly in constitutionally limited government predicated on the consent of the governed, in an extensive array of individual rights against government intrusion into their lives, and in the governing of the sphere of economic enterprise primarily by the forces of the marketplace, with government "stepping in" only when minimal concerns for social welfare seem to demand it. This essentially liberal perspective lies at the very center of their pride in their understanding of themselves as a "typical" American community. They do represent America, and in so doing, they self-consciously attempt to follow the vision that the liberal tradition has held out to them and that they have embraced.

Kumu Aina citizens, on the other hand, see themselves as being different from Everytown, U.S.A., taking pride in the uniqueness of their community, whose cultural values differ from the mainstream. Their understanding of politics is more like that of the classical Greek tradition. In their autonomous cultural perspective, they are in some ways like a Greek city-state, but more important they see politics as both a vital activity and a source of delight. For them, politics is an end in itself. Public political life, far from being feared as a threat to private interests, as is so typical of the liberal perspective, is cherished as a guardian, not only of private interests but of community vitality as well.

Classical Greek political theory was based on a public/private distinction that located economics in the sphere of the family. In their public lives, Kumu Aina citizens are relatively disinterested in economics and, like the Greeks, tend to consider it a private or personal matter—necessary but not all that interesting. In their narratives, Kumu Aina leaders express little concern over money or other manifestations of wealth, and wealth is not taken as a sign of social worth. Even though many citizens have a hard time financially, this does not preoccupy them. The two protagonists who explicitly talk about financial assets (in "My Home" and "One Dollar Down") discuss them in terms of the security of residence that they make possible, so that they can continue to live in the community--and, therefore, continue to live their public lives. Personal economics is not unimportant; but it is simply not as important as being a participating member of a healthy community. It is not their economic roles that shape their public identities but their personal ties, their kinships and friendships with others.

In contrast, Essex citizens view their public identities largely in terms of their economic roles. As capitalism and liberal political theory have evolved, economics has become a public political concern, and the Essex narratives reflect this concern. Finding a career, an occupation, is important because it enables citizens to find a place in the community. Through it, they build a web of relationships shaped by their ability to participate and contribute to the business world. It is assumed that, within that web, many citizens can play different parts. Striving for equality in the public realm, they stress the similarities among them--their interchangeability--down-playing ethnic and other differences, which are understood as inimical to public life. In this context they must then work hard to establish their individuality which is developed and expressed in the private realm of the family not in the public world. In the public world all are equal before the law; each vote counts the same as another. Persons are interchangeable and capitalism depends upon a depersonalized mechanized approach to public interaction. In the private world, every home is a castle with its own rules and rulers. The home becomes the place where personal feelings and individual expression can reign.

To be sure, Kumu Aina citizens see themselves as a cohesive community, but at the same time, they emphasize and cherish cultural and personal differences, seeing no contradiction in doing so. Plato adopts a similar perspective in his discussion of the Republic and the various contributions that rulers, warriors, and artisans make to its well-being. As the narrator of "Learning About Injustice" explains, every person, every culture, has some special talents that he or she can develop and bring into the public world as a contribution to the community. Every person and, for that matter, every natural living being has a value and a purpose. In this sense, Kumu Aina citizens begin with the assumption that they are different, then work to establish common bonds. In doing this, they find themselves fulfilled by political activity. Politics is a process that enriches their lives. As the narrator of "Barriers to Freedom" explains, only in community can one can experience freedom.

Essex citizens, on the other hand, embrace the liberal idea of politics as an instrumental activity necessary to achieve order, but that requires citizens to trade some of their freedom for peace and safety. The social contract, the underlying shared understanding that they must somehow live peaceably together, restrains them to that end. It does not liberate them. Because entering into politics is thought of as hard work, citizens conceive of themselves as engaging in political action on an irregular basis, when a crisis calls them into action. They prefer to seek fulfillment in their private lives, which promise the joy of a supportive family community and a needed respite from the competition and struggle that must be waged in the political economic realm. Politics in this political economic worldview can best be understood as a game that spews out winners and losers, and the best strategy is to fight to win and, failing that, to minimize one's losses. A way of dealing with loss is to see the game as a learning experience and use it to prepare for the next round.

Kumu Aina citizens, in contrast, stress that politics does not involve only "getting things" from the system but also helps citizens to satisfy their recognized need for participation in community with others. This may involve struggle--climbing over barriers--but rewards with stronger friendships and heightened self-understanding. In "Search Your Own Heart," the narrator shows how politics--even strategy sessions--can lead to insight into one's own life. Politics opens up a new way of seeing the world for those who participate.

Essex citizens, too, learn from their political experience but their knowledge is more like an improved set of tools than a new way of thinking--a new consciousness. They learn the rules of the game, including something about the conditions under which these rules can be bent. Since politics is essentially a negotiated contract, the more they are able to use the rules, the more powerful they can become. Competition is taken for granted, but the rules keep the competition orderly. Most of them are embodied in the law, which itself is grounded in the Constitution. Justice comes from following the rules, obeying the law, and cherishing the Constitution. Issues of morality or ethics are private matters, which can only be decided in the privacy of one's bathroom (as "Looking in the Mirror" suggests), even though the public realm depends upon such private commitments.

The primary business of politics is to impose minimal necessary controls on citizens in the interest of public order, which means that those who are "out of order" can expect some physical restraint. The threat of punishment keeps citizens from allowing their competitive passions to make them forget that they are parties to the contract for maximum public order and minimum interference with private life. "Alleys and Anger" illustrates the point: The man never actually gets his gun, even though the council approves the alleys; restraint prevails and all turns out well. The politics is best that controls the passions and excesses of citizens.

For Kumu Aina citizens, justice is a more complex issue. Institutions and courts cannot be counted upon to dispense justice, because justice is not the application of the law or even the fulfillment of the intentions underlying it. Justice requires harmony in the community, and genuine harmony requires sensitivity to the particulars of a situation. Justice is an art, and just people are as aware of their shortcomings as they are of their strengths. Kumu Aina citizens consider humility a virtue. They do not keep up appearances in order to show their worth but place a high value on moderation and openness to varied positions. As the Caribou narrative suggests, justice comes only after everyone's story has been genuinely heard. Otherwise, the law, however "equally" applied, will almost certainly work an injustice. Nor is it good to be too greedy, warns the narrator of "Ways of Leaders." Evil, greed, and purposeful wrong action are a part of social existence. Death, pain, and injustice are their results. But these blights on the community are not permanent conditions; through social action, injustice can be exposed and eradicated. The Goliaths who would dominate citizens without regard for their special natures and circumstances can be conquered or, better yet, come to find their satisfactions in community rather than in domination. In this model, courage and authenticity, not "civic spirit," is required of political actors who challenge these authority structures, and the primary goal of political activity is simultaneously to <u>undo</u> injustice and <u>do</u> justice.

A central value difference between the cultures of Essex and Kumu Aina lies in Essex's emphasis on independence, including the independence of society from nature, and Kumu Aina's emphasis on interdependence, including the intimate connections between nature and society. The story of the senior citizens shows the importance of "doing it yourself," and the Independence Day celebration dramatizes both the independence of the nation and the belief that it is a nation of "independent" people. The Beaver Valley story illustrates how Kumu Aina differs. While the beaver's error is in his "earnest" individualism and his illusory gift to his fellow creatures of freedom from work, the real struggle in the story is between the tranquil animal existence of the pond, whose inhabitants thrive on their mutual dependence and their balanced connectedness to nature (even though they lose sight of it for a time) and the "advanced" technological society (which emerges when the goal of the easy life takes over). The leader with the large teeth (born a beaver but maturing into a bulldozer) had the potential for enriching the community but instead he "ate" it up because, being able to "do it all himself," he lacked humility. Thus deprived, for all that he was able to build, he was utterly incapable of building community; he could only destroy it. Because he could do it all, the others became idle and withdrawn. Instead of struggling to define and realize together their own visions of the good life, they merely gave in to his. When they lost their pond life, the last tree, they lost their own life. Neglecting to revere the connection between the life of the environment and that of the community, they lost both. This tension between modern technology and more simple means of life appears in the Lawrence and David stories as well as in the story of Ernest. In each of these Kumu Aina stories, advanced technology and the drive for wealth distorts relationships and threatens to undo communities.

In the cosmology of Essex, citizens are valued for conforming to and fitting into the structure of institutions; social institutions are valued because they fit into the political institutions that legitimate them. The system is a neat series of concentric circles, which begins with the individual in the center and moves outward to the limits of deliberate human action. From beyond these limits, chance occasionally intervenes to affect the social order of things. At the innermost private center of things religion and spiritual matters give occasion for individual reflection and shape as they will the orientations that these private individuals bring to the public world.

In contrast to these static concentric circles, Kumu Aina's cosmology is dynamic, like the changing spirals of the curling waves in the surf. They rise and fall, breeding life and death while constantly changing. Citizens acquire worth by having the courage to challenge these forces and transform them into occasions for art. For the art of politics, with its focus on taking the measure of institutions and finding ways to make them serve their visions of justice, citizens find the required energy in the commitments they make to one another. The struggles they engage in bring new life, just as Lawrence's struggle created a new nation. Laws and rules do not maintain this community but, rather, the commitments that citizens have to each other. As the ocean metaphor suggests, harmony and balance encompass and integrate political, social, natural, and even spiritual phenomena.

The hero or heroine of the Kumu Aina story liberates citizens by challenging social structures and institutions that, because they derive from an alien cultural perspective, are seen as primary sources of injustice. The Essex hero or heroine brings about social change by creating new organizations and structures, designed to foster civic spirit or provide amenities for specific constituencies, and by inserting them into an established institutional structure, which is generally assumed to be operating in the interests of the community. The Essex pioneer lives through discipline, self-reliance, and judicious innovation. The Kumu Aina liberator lives by having the courage to create new relationships and to make old ones stronger while continuing to try to "make it right."

ESSEX AND KUMU AINA: NEW DIRECTIONS IN POLITICS

The Essex stories display a yearning for more public life. These citizens work very hard at creating more public activity. It is leisure activity, to be sure, but it also has potential for serious political reflection, in part because it represents leisure activity. But, more important, such activity can bring people out of their private enclaves and into the public world where they can experience community on a more inclusive basis than is afforded by their families. The narratives hold out promise that these excessively private citizens of suburbia acknowledge their own deprivation and are acting to change their circumstances.[1] They also clearly point out the problems that are endemic to an intensely competitive society in which "climbing the ladder" is so highly valued and, in that context, counsel that, in the interests of community, "niche finding" also merits respect and praise. The Essex narratives also emphasize the importance of mixing fun with politics. The community deteriorates if political life is no more than obeying the rules and minding one's own business in a bureaucratic world, where everyone is treated as a number. It is hard take pride in a community held together by such stern, mechanical, and impersonal bonds. Communities in America need more dancing in the streets, more parties in which to explore their pasts, more senior travel clubs, and more pools where citizens can play together. Politics needs to be plentiful--and fun.

Kumu Aina citizens also delight in the public life they share. They are less worried about "climbing up ladders," however, than about "climbing over barriers" so that they can be together. But the togetherness or community that they so explicitly value must be one in which differences among them, both cultural and personal, are acknowledged and cherished for what they contribute to community, rather than repressed as a condition for it. It should not merely tolerate those differences but respect them, for through such differences the community can grow. Nature itself should be cherished for its autonomous contributions to the life of society and not treated as an alien matter, grist for the mill of human ambition. Nature and the human community each has its own spirit, and each spirit contributes to the whole. Therefore, the people and their leaders must be humble. Political work is the responsibility of the entire community, not only "big beaver." Friendship, at once is the end of politics and the necessary condition for it. To be sure, politics can be painful, but it can also be fun, even an occasion for laughter--like the laughter in Caribou's courtroom and the laughter between the two friends in "Climbing over Barriers: The Power of Laughter." In the prospect and reality of such laughter, we can find ourselves willing to tell our own stories and able to delight in the stories of others.

Stories can give us new ways of understanding the world by opening us up to new perspectives, because to understand a story requires us to become engaged in it, as partisans who cannot resist committing themselves to its perspective, if only for a moment. In that commitment, we can understand the lives of others and begin to see how to seek justice for and with them. By <u>looking</u> very carefully at our stories, we can understand more about our shared political life, which itself is an unfolding public story. In the light of that <u>reflection</u>, we can work to make our public life more just, guided by visions shaped from the materials not of nightmares but of promising dreams.

The Dormouse slowly opened his eyes. "I wasn't asleep," it said in a hoarse, feeble voice, "I heard every word you fellows were saying."

"Tell us a story!" said the March Hare.

"Yes, please do!" pleaded Alice.

"And be quick about it," added the Hatter, "or you'll be asleep again before it's done."

Lewis Carroll
<u>Alice</u> <u>in</u> <u>Wonderland</u>

Notes

CHAPTER 1

1. William Flint Thrall and Addison Hibbard revised by C. Hugh Holman, A Handbook to Literature (New York: The Odyssey Press, 1960), pp. 33, 135, 194, 300-301.
2. Joseph Campbell, Myths to Live by (New York: Bantam Books, 1972).
3. Joseph Campbell, The Hero with a Thousand Faces, Bollingen Series XVII (Princeton: Princeton University Press, 1949).
4. Mircea Eliade, Myth and Reality (New York: Harper and Row, 1963), p. 2.
5. Claude Levi-Strauss, "From 'The Science of the Concrete'" in The Discontinuous Universe, eds. Sallie Sears and Georgianna W. Lord (New York: Basic Books, 1972), p. 361.
6. Claude Levi-Strauss, The Raw and the Cooked (New York: Harper and Row, 1969), p. 12.
7. Bruno Bettelheim, The Uses of Enchantment (New York: Alfred A. Knopf, 1976), pp. 66-73.
8. For examples of feminist consciousness raising, see Joan Cassell, A Group Called Women (New York: David McKay Company, 1977) and for religous scholarship, see Carol Christ, Diving Deep and Surfacing (Boston: Beacan Press, 1980).
9. See Joan Cassell, A Group Called Women.
10. Adrienne Rich, The Dream of a Common Language (New York: Norton Press, 1978) and see Dale Spender, Man Made Language (Boston: Routledge and Kegan Paul, 1980).
11. Anne Sexton, Transformations (Boston: Houghton Mifflin Company, 1971), pp. 53-57.
12. Eric Voegelin, The New Science of Politics (Chicago: The University of Chicago Press, 1952), pp. 74-75.
13. Semiotic analysts speak about pattern in a society as the grammar of the society, hence moving from linguistic grammar to social grammar, from rules that govern speech to rules that more generally govern social action.
14. Alan Bloom, trans. and ed. The Republic of Plato (New York: Basic Books, 1968), p. 290.

15. The Republic, p. 291.
16. For an argument on narratives as articulations of cultural contradictions, see Claude Levi-Strauss, Structural Anthropology (New York: Basic Books, 1963), and The Raw and the Cooked.
17. Because it blends tradition and transformation, the narrative captures the attention of such diverse theoretical interests as philosophical hermeneutics, Marxist aesthetics, and feminist analyses and such theorists as Lucian Goldmann, Jurgen Habermas, Eric Voegelin, Elisabeth Schussler Fiorenza, and Paul Ricoeur.
18. The Republic, p. 284.
19. Ibid., p. 281.
20. Paul Ricoeur develops the term productive reference in "The Function of Fiction in Shaping Reality," Man and World, Vol. 12 (1979): pp. 123-141.
21. For semiotics, see Jonathan Culler, Structuralist Poetics: Structuralism, Linguistics, and the Study of Literature (Ithaca, New York: Cornell University Press, 1975) and Fredric Jameson, The Prison-House of Language (Princeton: Princeton University Press, 1972).
22. Michel Foucault. The Order of Things (New York: Random House, 1970).
23. Ricoeur, "The Function of Fiction in Shaping Reality."
24. Ibid., p. 139.
25. Ibid., p. 135.
26. Ricoeur, "The Function of Fiction in Shaping Reality," and The Rule of Metaphor (Toronto: University of Toronto Press, 1977).
27. For "power of metaphor" Robert Cahill, Lecture, University of Hawaii, 1976.
28. Walter Benjamin, Reflections (New York: Harcourt Brace Jovanovich, 1978,) pp. 220-229.
29. Ricoeur, "The Function of Fiction in Shaping Reality."
30. Herbert Marcuse. The Aesthetic Dimension (Boston: Beacon Press, 1978).
31. For discussion of organic unity of art see T. S. Eliot, The Sacred Wood (London: Methuen and Co., 1950).
32. Robert E. Lane. Political Thinking and Consciousness (Chicago: Markham Publishing Company, 1969).
33. For linear logic and plot development, see Seymour Chatman, Story and Discourse (Ithaca, New York: Cornell University Press, 1978).
34. This phenomenon is even recognized by empirical social scientists, who use a scenario to

Notes

focus on the possible outcomes of an action.

35. The Republic, p. 290.

36. Paul Ricoeur, in Time and Narrative (Chicago: The University of Chiacago Press, 1984), refers to this as followability, building on W. B. Gallie's, Philosophy and Historical Understanding (New York: Schoken Books, 1968).

37. See Seymour Chatman, Story and Discourse, for his argument about plot and explanation.

38. This distinction between madness and imagination is from Alkis Kontos of the University of Toronto in his lecture in Spokane, Washington, Spring 1986.

39. Robert E. Spiller et al., Literary History of the United States (New York: MacMillan, 1974), claim it "the most influential novel in all history," p. 505.

40. Richard Rorty, Philosophy and the Mirror of Nature (Princeton: Princeton University Press), 1979.

41. See, particularly the work of Michael J. Shapiro, William Connolly, and Fred Dallmayr.

42. Aristotle, The Basic Works of Aristotle, ed. Richard McKeon (New York: Random House, 1941), p. 1129.

43. Aristotle, p. 1127.

44. See Michael J. Shapiro Language and Political Understanding. (New Haven, Connecticut: Yale University Press, 1981).

CHAPTER 2

1. Martin Gardner, ed., The Annotated Alice (New York: Bramhall House, 1960) p. 191.

2. Arguments supporting this "practical" telos of social science are found in Hans-Georg Gadamer, Reason in the Age of Science (Cambridge, Massachusetts: MIT Press, 1983), and Richard Bernstein, The Restructuring of Social and Political Theory (Philadelphia: Univeristy of Pennsylvania Press, 1978).

3. For overview from literary perspective see Jonathan Culler, Structuralist Poetics (Ithaca, New York: Cornell University Press, 1975).

4. Claude Levi-Strauss, "The Structural Study of Myth" in Structural Anthropology pp. 206-231.

5. Michel Foucault, Archeology of Knowledge (New York: Random House, 1972) and Claude Levi-Strauss, The Raw and the Cooked.

6. For explanation of his method see "The Structural Study of Myth," pp. 206-231 and "Overture" in The Raw and the Cooked, pp. 1-32.

7. Levi-Strauss, "The Structural Study of Myth," pp. 206-231.

8. They develop from a semiotic language theory, which emphasizes that speech and, hence, storytelling involves a circuit of communication.

9. I have taught this method to undergraduates and had them develop their own analysis of television dramas and literary works.

10. Performing the anlaysis requires beginning with individual narratives and then establishing the general pattern.

11. The list is not exhaustive and so the reader is limited by the story itself.

12. Colin Murray Turbayne, The Myth of Metaphor (Columbia, South Carolina: University of South Carolina Press, 1970).

13. Turbayne explains that cross-sorting "vision" metaphors with scientific thought produces new scientific explanations. It produces new ways of thinking about science. This results in such expressions as "I see" for "I understand."

14. Michel Foucault, Madness and Civilization (New York: Random House, 1965).

15. Turbayne, p. 27.

16. Seymour Chatman, Story and Discourse (Ithaca: Cornell University Press, 1978), pp. 31-36.

17. Edmund Leach, "The Legitimacy of Solomon," in Introduction to Structrualism, Michael Lane, ed. (New York: Basic Books, 1970), pp. 248-292.

18. For this argument see Gadamer, Reason in the Age of Science.

19. Clifford Geertz, The Interpretation of Cultures (New York: Basic Books, 1973).

20. Ibid., p. 54.

21. Claude Levi-Strauss, The Raw and the Cooked, p. 13.

22. This orientation depends upon a semiotic language theory.

23. Paul Ricoeur, The Conflict of Interpretations (Evanston, Illinois: Northwestern University Press, 1974), p. 48.

24. Claude Levi-Strauss, "Overture" in The Raw and the Cooked, pp. 1-32.

25. Hans-Georg Gadamer, Truth and Method (New York: The Seabury Press, 1975), pp. 91-92.

26. Ibid., p. 93.

27. Paul Ricoeur, The Conflict of Interpretations, pp. 27-61.

28. Ibid., p. 55.

29. Paul Ricoeur, The Philosophy of Paul Ricoeur (Boston: Beacon Press, 1978), p. 155.

30. Jurgen Habermas, Knowledge and Human Interest (Boston: Beacon Press, 1971).

31. Gadamer, Reason in the Age of Science, pp. 113-138.

32. Hans-Georg Gadamer, Philosophical Hermeneutics (Berkeley: University of California Press, 1977), p. 29.

CHAPTER 3

1. See Owen Barfield, Saving the Appearances (New York: Harcourt, Brace & World, 1965), for analysis of liberalism and "keeping up appearances."

2. This is taken from a high school publication prepared by students to explore the historical background of Kumu Aina.

3. These figures represent data from 1976, which is the time the interviews were completed.

4. Anthropologists who study myth select their stories on the basis of their religious status and content. If the story describes a genesis, it represents a sacred myth.

5. This did not give me a random sample of the community, but gave me a list of persons seen as community leaders.

6. In Kumu Aina, three citizens declined the interview, and so I selected one additional person from my list in order to have an even number of women and men.

7. I measured each narrative in terms of the time it took to tell the story, which assumes that the pauses and silences are a part of the narrative.

CHAPTER 4

1. One leader explicitly used the term "Americana" to describe Essex.

2. Aristotle, p. 1143.

3. This private/public distinction that accords more public significance to nonfamily activities constitutes a liberal political perspective that has experienced considerable critical scrutiny by feminist scholars. Nevertheless, it is the minister's political perspective.

4. Dan Nimmo and James E. Combs, Mediated Political Realities (New York: Longman, 1981), pp. 124-140.

5. Woody Hayes, You Win with People (Columbus, Ohio: Typographic Printing Press, 1973).

6. See Nancy C. M. Hartsock, Money, Sex, and Power (Boston: Northeastern University Press, 1985), pp. 186-209.

7. For explanation of this term, see Murray Edelman, The Symbolic Uses of Politics (Urbana: University of Illinois Press, 1967).

8. Within the anthropological literature that analyzes myth this figure would be seen as a trickster.

9. A large multinational corporation for which Chrome constitutes a pseudonym.

10. Christopher Lasch argues that this has been the family's role in modern liberal America, in Haven in a Heartless World (New York: Basic Books, 1977).

11. I use the term liberal to designate the liberal political ideology of American communities, which contrasts with facism and socialism.

CHAPTER 5

1. This etymology presented by Kumu Aina citizens is the second meaning given by Mary Kawena Pukui and Samuel Elbert, Hawaiian Dictionary (Honolulu: The University Press of Hawaii, 1971).

2. While this detail varies from the book and film, what the marrator wishes to explain about politics requires restructuring Lawrence's role turning him into a working class figure.

3. The desires of Kumu Aina citizens are often ignored by the "larger" interests of urban Honolulu. The application of this narrative to the immediate circumstances in Kumu Aina and the hope it offers to citizens is clear.

4. While this tale in some aspects is an archetypical military tale, in this particular version it has some important points to make about politics in Kumu Aina.

5. This is documented in my field notes and also in Mary Kawena Pukui et al., Nana I Ke Kumu (Honolulu: Hui Hanai of Queen Liliuokalani Children's Center, 1972), pp. 166-167.

6. While, the end is known from the biblical account, it is important that the narrator does not conclude the tale because his emphasis is upon this still present struggle in Kumu Aina.

7. For an explanation of the differences between these positions see Clinton Rossiter, Conservatism in America (Cambridge, Massachusetts: Harvard University Press, 1982).

8. Daniel Inouye, quoted in Honolulu Star

Notes   239

Bulletin, November 19, 1980.

CHAPTER 6 NOTES

    1. Mark Roelofs, *Ideology and Myth in American Politics* (Boston: Little, Brown and Company, 1976).

CHAPTER 7 NOTES

    1. Noel Kent, *Hawaii: Islands Under the Influuence* (New York: Monthly Review Press, 1983), pp. 83-91.

CHAPTER 8 NOTES

    1. E. F. Schumaucher *Small Is Beautiful* (New York: Harper & Row, 1973).

CHAPTER 9 NOTES

    1. Mai means "come" in Hawaiian.
    2. For ho'noponopono, I am drawing from *Nana I Ke Kumu*, pp 70-70, as well as the teachings of the persons I interviewed.
    3. *Nana I Ke Kumu*, p. 149-150.
    4. Ibid., p. 150.
    5. The state motto is "The life of the land is fulfilled in righteousness."

CHAPTER 10 NOTES

    1. Robert Bellah et al, *Habits of the Heart* (New York: Harper and Row, 1985), point out the problems with such privatized enclaves, and I borrow the "enclave" image from them.

Bibliography

Andersen, Johannes C. *Myths and Legends of the Polynesians.* Rutland, Vermont: Charles E. Tuttle Co., 1969.
Arendt, Hannah. *The Human Condition.* Chicago: The University of Chicago Press, 1958.
Aristotle. *The Basic Works of Aristotle,* Richard McKeon, ed. New York: Random House, 1941.
Artaud, Antonin. *The Theatre and Its Double.* New York: Grove Press, 1958.
Austin, J. L. *How to Do Things with Words.* New York: Oxford University Press, 1962.
Barbour, Ian G. *Myths, Models and Paradigms: A Comparative Study in Science and Religion.* San Francisco: Harper and Row, 1974.
Barfield, Owen. *Saving the Appearances: A Study in Idolatry.* New York: Harcourt, Brace & World, 1965.
Bateson, Gregory. *Steps to an Ecology of Mind.* New York: Ballantine Books, 1972.
Barthes, Roland. *Critical Esssays.* Evanston, Illinois: Northwestern University Press, 1972.
--- *Mythologies.* New York: Hill and Wang, 1972.
--- *The Pleasure of the Text.* London: Cape, 1976.
--- *Elements of Semiology.* New York: Hill and Wang, 1977.
Bauman, Zygmunt. *Hermeneutics and Social Science.* New York: Columbia University Press, 1978.
Beckwith, Martha. *Hawaiian Mythology.* Honolulu: The University Press of Hawaii, 1971.
Bellah, Robert N., Richard Madsen, William M. Sullivan, Ann Swidler, and Steven M. Tipton. *Habits of the Heart.* New York: Harper and Row, 1985.
Benjamin, Walter. *Reflections.* New York: Harcourt Brace Jovanovich, 1978.
Berger, John. *Ways of Seeing.* England: British Broadcasting Corp. and Penguin Books, 1972.
Berger, Peter L., and Thomas Luckmann. *The Social Construction of Reality.* New York: Doubleday & Co., 1966.
Bernstein, Richard J. *The Restructuring of Social and Political Theory.* Philadelphia: University of Pennsylvania Press, 1978.

--- Beyond Objectivism and Relativism. Philadelphia: University of Pennyslvania Press, 1983.
Bettelheim, Bruno. The Uses of Enchantment. New York: Alfred A. Knopf, 1976.
Boorstin, Daniel J. The Americans: The Democratic Experience. New York: Vintage Books, 1973.
Campbell, Joseph. Masks of God. New York: Penquin Books, 1970.
--- The Hero with a Thousand Faces. Bollingen Series, XVII. Princeton: Princeton University Press, 1949.
--- Myths to Live By. New York: Bantam Books, 1972.
Carr, Elizabeth Ball. Da Kine Talk. Honolulu: The University Press of Hawaii, 1972.
Carroll, Lewis. The Annotated Alice: Alice's Adventures in Wonderland and Through the Looking Glass. New York: Bramhall House, 1960.
Cassell, Joan. A Group Called Women. New York: David McKay Company, Inc., 1977.
Caudwell, Christopher. Illusion and Reality: A Study of the Sources of Poetry. New York: International Publishers, 1937.
Chatman, Seymour, ed. Approaches to Poetics. New York: Columbia University Press, 1973.
Chatman, Seymour. Story and Discourse: Narrative Structure in Fiction and Film. Ithaca, New York: Cornell University Press, 1978.
Christ, Carol. Diving Deep and Surfacing. Boston: Beacon Press, 1980.
Chomsky, Noam. Language and Responsibility. New York: Pantheon Books, 1977.
Crossan, John Dominic. The Dark Interval: Towards a Theology of Story. Niles, Illinois: Argus Communications, 1975.
Culler, Jonathan. Structuralist Poetics: Structuralism, Linguistics, and the Study of Literature. Ithaca, New York: Cornell University Press, 1975.
Dallmayr, Fred R. Language and Politics. South Bend, Indiana: University of Notre Dame Press, 1984.
Daws, Gavan. Shoal of Time: A History of the Hawaiian Islands. Honolulu: The University Press of Hawaii, 1976.
Derrida, Jacques. Speech and Phenomena. Evanston, Illinois: Northwestern University Press, 1973.
Detwieler, Robert. Story, Sign and Self: Phenomenology and Structuralism as Literary Critical Methods. Missoula, Montana: Scholars Press, 1978.
Dolbeare, Kenneth, and Patricia Dolbeare. American Ideologies. Chicago: Markham Publishing, 1971.
Douglas, Mary. Natural Symbols: Explorations in

Bibliography

        Cosmology. New York: Vintage Books, 1973.
Dundes, Alan. The Study of Folklore. Englewood Cliffs, New Jersey: Prentice-Hall, 1965.
Edelman, Murray. The Symbolic Uses of Politics. Urbana: University of Illinois Press, 1967.
Eliade, Mircea. Myth and Reality. New York: Harper and Row, 1963.
Fenton, John. Midwest Politics. New York: Holt, Rinehart and Winston, 1966.
Foucault, Michel. Madness and Civilization. New York: Random House, 1965.
--- The Archaeology of Knowledge. New York: Random House, 1972.
--- The Order of Things: An Archaeology of the Human Sciences. New York: Random House, 1970.
Freud, Sigmund. The Interpretation of Dreams. New York: Basic Books, 1965.
Frye, Northrop. The Stubborn Structure: Essays on Criticism and Society. Ithaca, New York: Cornell University Press, 1970.
Fuchs, Lawrence H. Hawaii Pono: A Social History. New York: Harcourt Brace Jovanovich, 1961.
Gadamer, Hans-Georg. Truth and Method. New York: The Seabury Press, 1975.
--- Philosophical Hermeneutics. David E. Linge, trans. and ed. Berkeley: University of California Press, 1976.
--- Reason in the Age of Science. Cambridge, Massachusetts: MIT Press, 1983.
Gallie, W. B. Philosophy and Historical Understanding. New York: Schocken Books, 1968.
Gallimore, Ronald, and Alan Howard. Studies in a Hawaiian Community. Honolulu: Pacific Anthropological Records, No. 1, 1969.
Geertz, Clifford. The Interpretation of Cultures. New York: Basic Books, 1973.
De George, Richard, and Fernande De George, eds. The Structuralists From Marx to Levi-Strauss. New York: Doubleday and Co., 1972.
Giddens, Anthony. New Rules of Sociological Method. New York: Basic Books, 1976.
--- Central Problems in Social Theory: Action, Structure, and Contradiction in Social Analysis. Berkeley: University of California Press, 1979.
Goffman, Erving. The Presentation of Self in Everyday Life. New York: Doubleday, 1959.
--- Frame Analysis: An Essay on the Organization of Experience. San Francisco: Harper and Row, 1974.
Gray, Francine du Plessix. Hawaii: The Sugar-Coated Fortress. New York: Random House, 1972.
Habermas, Jurgen. Knowledge and Human Interests.

Boston: Beacon Press, 1971.
--- *Communication and the Evolution of Society.* Boston: Beacon Press, 1979.
Heidegger, Martin. *On the Way to Language.* San Francisco: Harper and Row, 1971.
--- *Poetry, Language, Thought.* Albert Hofstadter, trans. San Francisco: Harper and Row, 1971.
Hawkes, Terence. *Structuralism and Semiotics.* Berkeley: University of California Press, 1977.
Hirsch, E. D. *The Aims of Interpretation.* Chicago: The University of Chicago Press, 1978.
--- *Validity in Interpretation.* New Haven, Connecticut: Yale University Press, 1979.
Horkheimer, Max, and Theodor W. Adorno. *Dialectic of Englightenment.* New York: Seabury Press, 1972.
Howard, Stuart Alan. *Ain't No Big Thing.* Honolulu: The University Press of Hawaii, 1974.
Jameson, Fredric. *The Prison-House of Language: A Critical Account of Structuralism and Russian Formalism.* Princeton, New Jersey: Princeton University Press, 1972.
Joesting, Edward. *Hawaii: An Uncommon History.* New York: W. W. Norton and Co., 1972.
Kalakaua, David, "King: His Hawaiian Majesty." *The Legends and Myths of Hawaii: The Fables and Folk-lore of a Strange People.* Rutland, Vermont: Charles E. Tuttle Co., 1972.
Kariel, Henry S. *Beyond Liberaliism, Where Relations Grow.* New York: Harper and Row, 1978.
--- *Saving Appearances: The Reestablishment of Political Science.* Belmont, California: Duxbury Press, 1972.
Kent, Noel J. *Hawaii: Islands Under the Influence.* New York: Monthly Review Press, 1983.
Lane, Michael, ed. *Introduction to Structuralism.* New York: Basic Books, 1970.
Lane, Robert E. *Political Thinking and Consciousness.* Chicago: Markham Publishing, 1969.
Lasch, Christopher. *Haven in a Heartless World: The Family Besieged.* New York: Basic Books, 1977.
Lasswell, Harold, and Abraham Kaplan. *Power and Society.* New Haven, Connecuticut: Yale University Press, 1950.
Leach, Edmund. *Culture and Communication: The Logic by Which Symbols Are Connected: An Introduction to the Use of Structuralist Analysis in Social Anthropology.* New York: Cambridge University Press, 1976
Lee, Dorothy. *Freedom and Culture.* New York: Prentice-Hall, 1959.
Levi-Strauss, Claude. *The Savage Mind.* Chicago: The

University of Chicago Press, 1962.
--- <u>Structural Anthropology.</u> New York: Basic Books, 1963.
--- <u>The Raw and the Cooked: Introduction to a Science of Mythology: 1.</u> New York: Harper and Row, 1969.
--- <u>From Honey to Ashes: Introduction to a Science of Mythology: 2.</u> San Francisco: Harper and Row, 1973.
--- <u>The Origin of Table Manners: Introduction to a Science of Mythology: 3.</u> San Francisco: Harper and Row, 1978.
Macksey, Richard, and Eugenio Donato, eds. <u>The Structuralist Controversy: The Languages of Criticism and the Sciences of Man.</u> Baltimore: The Johns Hopkins University Press, 1970.
Macpherson, C. B. <u>The Political Theory of Possessive Individualism: Hobbes to Locke.</u> New York: Oxford University Press, 1962.
Marcuse, Herbert. <u>The Aesthetic Dimension: Toward a Critique of Marxist Aesthetics.</u> Boston: Beacon Press, 1978.
Mead, George H. <u>Mind, Self, and Society.</u> Chicago: The University of Chicago Press, 1974.
Mills, C. Wright. <u>The Sociological Imagination.</u> New York: Oxford University Press, 1974.
Mitchell, W. J. T. ed. <u>On Narrative.</u> Chicago: The University of Chicago Press, 1981.
Perkins, Leialoha Apo. <u>Natural and Other Stories About Contemporary Hawaiians.</u> Honolulu: Kamalu'uluolele, 1979.
Plato. <u>The Republic of Plato,</u> Alan Bloom, ed. New York: Basic Books, 1968.
Pukui, Mary Kawena, and Samuel Elbert. <u>Hawaiian Dictionary.</u> Honolulu: The University Press of Hawaii, 1971.
Pukui, Mary Kawena, E. W. Haertig, and Catherine A. Lee. <u>Nana I Ke Kumu (Look at the Source).</u> Honolulu: Hui Hanai of Queen Liliuokalani Children's Center, 1972.
Rabinow, Paul, and William M. Sullivan, eds. <u>Interperative Social Science: A Reader.</u> Berkeley: University of California Press, 1979.
Rich, Adrienne. <u>The Dream of a Common Language.</u> New York: Norton Press, 1978.
Ricoeur, Paul. "The Model of the Text: Meaningful Action Considered as a Text." <u>Social Research,</u> Vol. 38, No. 3 (Autumn 1971), pp. 529-562.
---"Creativity in Language." <u>Philosophy Today,</u> Vol. 17, No. 2/4 (Summer 1973), pp. 97-128.
---<u>The Conflict of Interpretations.</u> Evanston, Illinois: Northwestern University Press, 1974.

---*Political and Social Essays*, David Stewart and Joseph Bien, eds. Athens: Ohio University Press, 1974.
---*The Rule of Methaphor.* Toronto: University of Toronto Press, 1975.
---*Interpretation Theory: Discourse and the Surplus of Meaning.* Forth Worth: The Texas Christian University Press, 1976.
---*The Philosophy of Paul Ricoeur: An Anthology of His Work,* Charles E. Reagan and David Stewart, eds. Boston: Beacon Press, 1978.
---"The Function of Fiction in Shaping Reality." *Man and World,* Vol. 12 (1979), pp. 123-141.
---*Time and Narrative.* Chicago: The University of Chicago Press, 1984.
Roelofs, Mark. *Ideology and Myth in American Politics.* Boston: Little, Brown and Company, 1976.
Saussure, Ferdinand de. *Course in General Linguistics.* New York: McGraw-Hill Books, 1966.
Scholes, Robert. *Structuralism in Literature: An Introduction.* New Haven, Connecticut: Yale University Press, 1974.
Schutz, Alfred. "Some Leading Concepts of Phenomenology." *Collected Papers,* Vol. I: *The Problem of Social Reality,* Maurice Natanson, ed. The Hague: Martinus Nijhoff, 1967.
Searle, John. *Speech Acts.* Cambridge: Cambridge University Press, 1977.
Sebeok, Thomas A., ed. *Myth: A Symposium.* Bloomington: Indiana University Press, 1955.
Sexton, Anne. *Transformations.* Boston: Houghton Mifflin Co., 1971.
Shapiro, Michael J. *Language and Political Understanding.* New Haven, Connecitcut: Yale University Press, 1981.
Siskind, Janet. *To Hunt in the Morning.* New York: Oxford University Press, 1973.
Slotkin, Richard. *Regeneration Through Violence.* Middleton, Connecticut: Wesleyan University Press, 1973.
Spender, Dale. *Man Made Language.* Boston: Routledge and Kegan Paul, 1985.
Thompson, Stith. *The Folktale.* Berkeley: University of California Press, 1977.
Thompson, William Irwin. *Evil and the World Order.* New York: Harper and Row, 1976.
Turbayne, Colin Murray. *The Myth of Metaphor.* Columbia: University of South Carolina Press, 1971.
Voegelin, Eric. *The New Science of Politics.* Chicago: The University of Chicago Press, 1952.

Whorf, Benjamin Lee. *Language, Thought and Reality.*
    Cambridge, Massachusetts: MIT Press, 1956.
Wolin, Sheldon. *Politics and Vision.* Boston: Little,
    Brown and Company, 1960.
Wolff, Janet. *Hermeneutic Philosophy and the Sociology
    of Art.* Boston: Routledge and Kegan Paul, 1975.
Wright, Will. *Six Guns and Society: A Structural Study
    of the Western.* Berkeley: University of
    California Press, 1975.

Index

Africa 25
Aristotle 17, 23, 24, 72

Benjamin, Walter 15
Bettelheim, Bruno 17

Campbell, Joseph 6
capitalism 35, 225
Carroll, Lewis 1, 26, 27, 28, 30, 52, 67, 98, 128, 148, 172, 196, 222, 231
Catholicism 53-54, 57, 59, 85
Chatman, Seymour 36-27
Christianity 8, 22, 39, 122, 203, 208, 214
Cinderella 8, 38
Civil War 22
Cook, James 103

deconstruction 29, 31

Eliade, Mircea 6
"Emperor's New Clothes" 22
empiricism 12, 21, 30-31, 47, 50
ethnicity 52, 65, 225
ethnocentricism 120
ethnomethodology 42

feminism 8, 38, 48
Foucault, Michel 23, 29, 35-36
Frankfurt School 15
Freud, Sigmund 7

Gadamer, Hans-Georg 44-49
    Truth and Method 45
Geertz, Clifford 43, 45

Habermas, Jurgen 49
Hamlet 17, 18, 34, 38
Hawaiian Renaissance 103-104, 199

Hayes, Woody 75
haole 100, 161, 197, 206
heiaus 57, 104
hermeneutics 29-31, 41-48
Hobbes, Thomas 172
Homer 10
ho'oponopono 104, 211
hula 59, 116

Inouye, Daniel 125

Jackson, Jessie 18
Judaism 53-54, 57, 86-87, 90, 182, 208

Kaho'olawe 'Ohana 102, 104, 123, 206, 210, 216
Kennedy, Robert 132
King Lear 18

Leach, Edmund 39
Levi-Strauss, Claude 6, 7, 29-32, 43-46
liberalism 11, 15, 20, 55, 91, 95, 100-101, 110, 123, 198-199, 202, 223-226
Lincoln, Abraham 22, 34
"Little Red Riding Hood" 7
Locke, John 172

Macbeth 9
mana 211-215
mana'o 104, 207, 213
Mao Tze-Tung 48
Marcos Ferdinand 13
Marcuse, Herbert 20
Marxism 20, 207, 223-224
Moby Dick 33
myth 3-8, 32, 38, 110, 144, 188, 191

Oedipus Rex 32
'ohana 122

Ohio State University 75
Orwell, George 20
Oshi, Side 117
Oshi, Toyotomo 117

phenomenology 42
Plato 2, 8-20, 114, 214, 225
pokane 204
positivism 6, 30, 42, 43
Pound, Ezra 22
Protestantism 53-57, 80,
 134, 173, 181

Reagan, Ronald 18
referential language
 theory 12-14, 25, 42
Rich, Adrienne 8
Ricoeur, Paul 13-16, 44-48
Roelofs, Mark 144

Saussure, Ferdinand 26
semiotics 12, 13, 23-26
Sexton, Anne 8

Schumacher, E. F. 192
Shakespeare, William 44
Siam 181
Simon, Neal 80
socialism 20, 223
Socrates 10, 114
Solomon 39
Stalin, Joseph 48
structuralism 29-31, 47-49,
 65, 68, 129

taro 58, 108, 122
"The King and I" 181, 185
The Republic 2, 9, 225
Turbayne, Colin Murray 35-36

Uncle Tom's Cabin 22, 39

Voegelin, Eric 8

wahine 161

Yeasu, Tokugawa 117

About the Author

ELOISE A. BUKER is an Assistant Professor in the Department of Political Science at Gonzaga University.